Table of Contents

DOROTHY M. HORNE

1908–2000

In Remembrance

Foreword

IT WAS ABOUT 25 years ago, upon returning from a trip to Ithaca, perhaps, or Brattleboro, or possibly Cambridge that I happened to remark to that notable Saratogian Miss Dorothea Brownell that it seemed as though Saratoga Springs had by comparison less civic life. "Don't you know *anything?*" she said in her inimitable way, which always contained verbal italics. "It's a town founded *entirely* for frivolous purposes."

Well, it is true Saratoga Springs came into existence to please visitors and, today, some 220 years later, that remains its focus. It is true it has never had much in the way of industry. But it had—and continues to have—shops and offices and schools and churches and government buildings and houses, all the fittings of an American "village," as Dorothea insisted on calling it, even though it received its city charter in her childhood. In these first years of the 21st century Saratoga is one of the most beautiful and lively and healthy cities in all of New York State. And it has another distinction—its history was exceptionally well-documented by visitors with an astonishingly broad range of perspectives. For Saratoga Springs was famous in its youth, far beyond its considerable renown today.

In the 1820s or 1830s, a European tourist, debarking from a sailing ship on the New York docks on a summer day, might well have been asked if he were going to Saratoga. And that, in short, resulted in a vast body of literature, greater than that of any other small American community. Nineteenth-century Saratoga Springs, despite its eccentricity, was a microcosm. "All the world is here," wrote former New York City Mayor Philip Hone in 1839. We can learn more about what people said, and did, and thought about Saratoga Springs than we can about any comparable place on the North American continent. And, unlike most communities, we can see this remarkable community as others saw it, rather than through the single point of view of the local elite, who frequently controlled the interpretation of history and the publishing industry.

Thirty years ago the United States was approaching its bicentennial, and interest in American history was rising. Some of us, being young, idealistic and unencumbered, set out to learn about life in the past. A number of techniques were essayed. I was then most involved in the use of first-person narratives and other primary documents to strip away the layers of misinformation and *attempt* (for we can do no more than that) to understand life in the 18th and 19th centuries.

After coming to Saratoga Springs in 1978, I became aware of the rich trove of diaries, letters and travel books that chronicle the city's past. In 1992, as a fellow at Yaddo, the Saratoga Springs artists' colony, I began the research for this anthology. Inspired initially by Roger Haydon's *Upstate Travels*, and later by Bayrd Still's *Mirror for Gotham*, I began in the files of local historical agencies. I used the bibliographies of William Matthews and others; I was given the great privilege of stack access at Harvard's incomparable Widener Library; I searched important manuscript collections and hired help to search others at a distance. Before long my files bulged with more than 225 different accounts by visitors and residents.

My bias toward first-person narratives is evident in the project itself. Much of what was written about Saratoga Springs, while indeed useful, is prescriptive literature: tourists' guidebooks, instructions on using the mineral waters, newspaper articles, magazine essays. My objective, however, is to present the reader with the unaffected words of ordinary people. Travel books recounting actual experiences, diaries or journals written on the spot, and personal correspondence between relatives or friends are the ideal sources for community history. In a few cases I couldn't resist an unusual autobiography or a memoir, perhaps because it was written by a member of an underrepresented group or by someone recalling childhood. The masterful essay on Saratoga by Henry James is another exception. It is the most formal writing in this anthology, as well as the longest by far; it stands on its own as an important literary work complementing the other documents.

The first few documents pertain to what is now Schuylerville. While seemingly a departure from the book's focus, this was a conscious decision. Saratoga Springs grew from old Saratoga, and they were one town until 1819. The city's earliest history—its discovery, initial economic growth, and the namesake battle—is inextricable from the river village.

This anthology ends around the year 1900. Few 20th century diaries or letters are in public collections, and far fewer travel narratives were published after the 1880s. The 20th century literature about Saratoga Springs is extensive, but it bears little relationship to the material in this collection.

I am grateful to many who have helped me along the way. Edward Doctoroff of the Widener Library extended privileges that made possible my discovery of a number of obscure books. The staffs of the Saratoga Room at the Saratoga Springs Public Library and of the Historical Society of Saratoga Springs, and our City Historian *emerita*, Martha Stonequist, all supported my effort. I benefited from the reading of the manuscript by Mary Caroline Powers and advice from Phyllis Aldrich. The illustrations were chosen with the assistance of Bob Joki of the Robert Joki Collection, Wendy Anthony of Skidmore College, Jamie Parillo and Erin Doane of the Historical Society of Saratoga Springs, and staff of the American Antiquarian Society and the Library of Virginia. Thanks also to the Corporation of Yaddo, which granted me a fellowship in the summer of 1992 during which this book was conceived. And I'm grateful for the extraordinary artistry of Martha Costello, cartographer, and Stinehour Wemyss Editions, book designers.

The writings in this anthology come from the pens of Saratogians, of other Americans, and of Europeans from no fewer than eight nations. They were written by rich and poor, women and men, children and the elderly, blacks and whites. They communicate to us the experiences of people encountering a particular place in the world. We cannot live what they lived; we cannot entirely comprehend what the village seemed like to them. But with this collection we can understand how Saratoga Springs became the wondrous place it was in the 19th century and that it remains in 2004.

FIELD HORNE
Saratoga Springs
1 April 2004

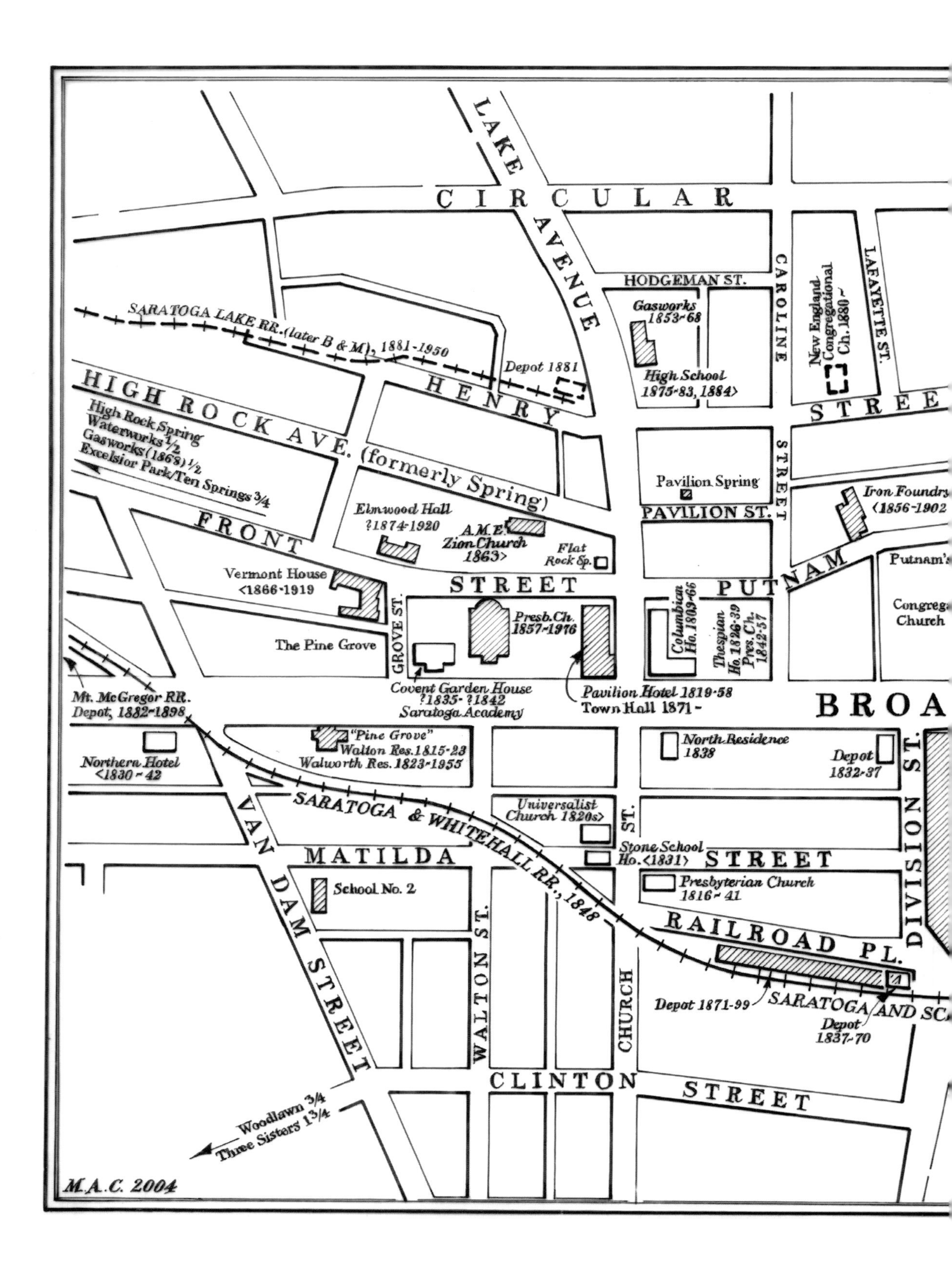

CIRCULAR
LAKE AVENUE
HODGEMAN ST.
CAROLINE
LAFAYETTE ST.
New England Congregational Ch. 1880~
Gasworks 1853-68
High School 1875-83, 1884>
SARATOGA LAKE RR. (later B & M), 1881-1950
Depot 1881
HENRY
STREET
HIGH ROCK AVE. (formerly Spring)
High Rock Spring
Waterworks 1/2
Gasworks (1868) 1/2
Excelsior Park/Ten Springs 3/4
Pavilion Spring
PAVILION ST.
Iron Foundry
<1856-1902
FRONT
STREET
Elmwood Hall ?1874-1920
A.M.E. Zion Church 1863>
Flat Rock Sp.
Vermont House <1866-1919
PUTNAM
Putnam's
Congrega
Church
GROVE ST.
The Pine Grove
Presb. Ch. 1857-1976
Columbian Ho. 1809-66
Thespian Ho. 1826-39 Pres. Ch. 1842-57
Covent Garden House ?1835-?1842 Saratoga Academy
Pavilion Hotel 1819-58 Town Hall 1871-
Mt. McGregor RR. Depot, 1882-1898
BROA
"Pine Grove" Walton Res. 1815-23 Walworth Res. 1823-1955
North Residence 1838
Depot 1832-37
Northern Hotel <1830-42
DIVISION ST.
SARATOGA & WHITEHALL RR., 1848
Universalist Church 1820s>
VAN DAM STREET
MATILDA
Stone School Ho. <1831>
STREET
School No. 2
Presbyterian Church 1816-41
RAILROAD PL.
WALTON ST.
CHURCH ST.
Depot 1871-99
SARATOGA AND SC
Depot 1837-70
CLINTON
STREET
Woodlawn 3/4
Three Sisters 1 3/4
M.A.C. 2004

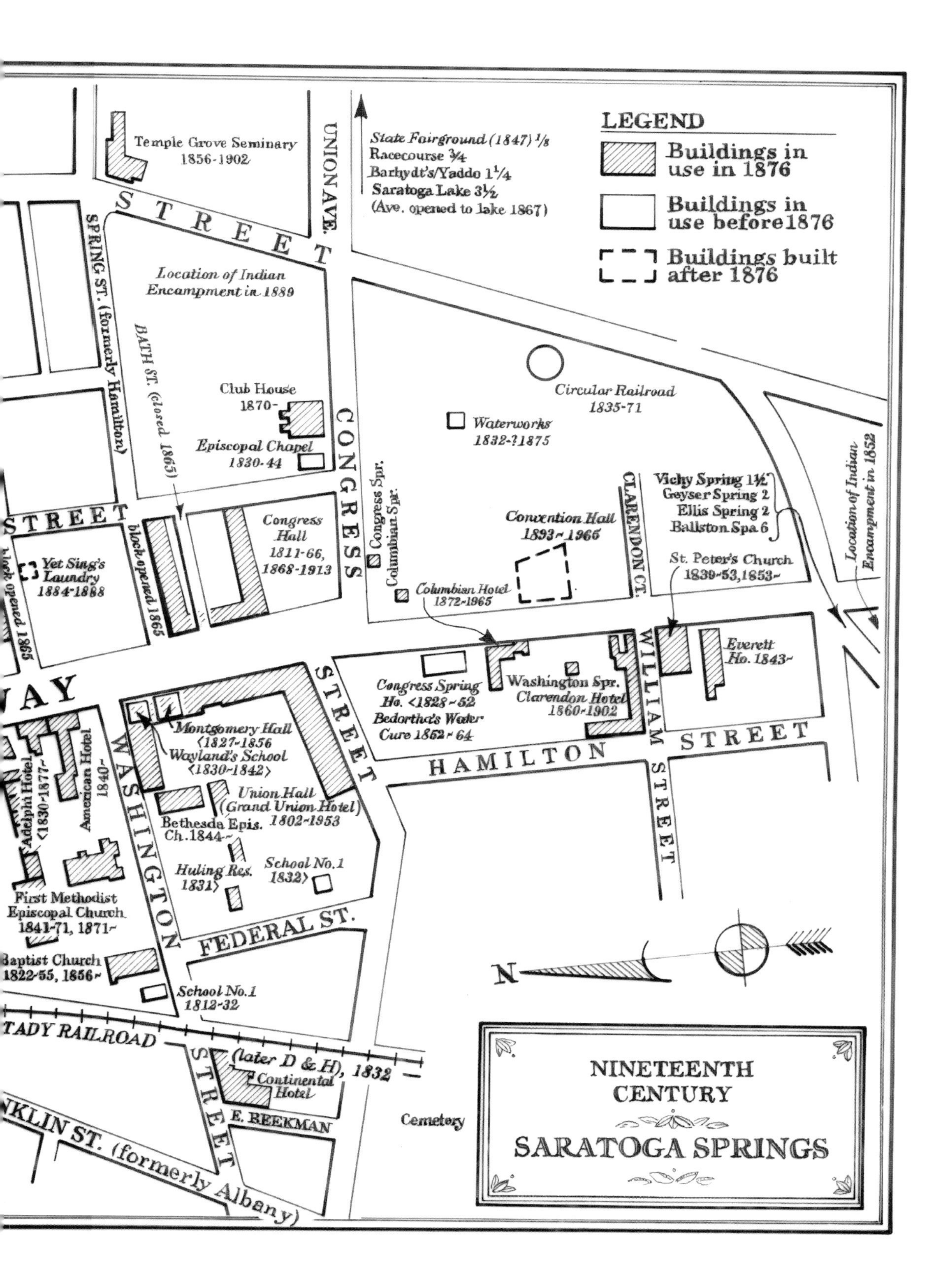
LEGEND
Buildings in use in 1876
Buildings in use before 1876
Buildings built after 1876
NINETEENTH CENTURY
SARATOGA SPRINGS
State Fairground (1847) 1/8
Racecourse 3/4
Barhydt's/Yaddo 1 1/4
Saratoga Lake 3 1/2
(Ave. opened to lake 1867)
UNION AVE.
Temple Grove Seminary 1856-1902
STREET
SPRING ST. (formerly Hamilton)
Location of Indian Encampment in 1889
BATH ST. (closed 1865)
Club House 1870-
Episcopal Chapel 1830-44
CONGRESS
Circular Railroad 1835-71
Waterworks 1832-?1875
Congress Spr.
Columbian Spr.
Convention Hall 1893-1966
CLARENDON CT.
Vichy Spring 1½
Geyser Spring 2
Ellis Spring 2
Ballston Spa 6
St. Peter's Church 1839-53, 1853-
Location of Indian Encampment in 1852
Congress Hall 1811-66, 1868-1913
block opened 1865
Yet Sing's Laundry 1884-1888
Columbian Hotel 1872-1965
WILLIAM STREET
Everett Ho. 1843-
Congress Spring Ho. <1828-52
Bedortha's Water Cure 1852-64
Washington Spr.
Clarendon Hotel 1860-1902
HAMILTON STREET
Montgomery Hall <1827-1856
Wayland's School <1830-1842>
Union Hall (Grand Union Hotel) 1802-1953
Bethesda Epis. Ch. 1844-
Huling Res. 1831>
School No. 1 1832>
Adelphi Hotel <1830-1877-
American Hotel 1840-
WASHINGTON
First Methodist Episcopal Church 1841-71, 1871-
FEDERAL ST.
Baptist Church 1822-55, 1856-
School No. 1 1812-32
TADY RAILROAD (later D & H), 1832
Continental Hotel
STREET
E. BEEKMAN
Cemetery
NKLIN ST. (formerly Albany)
N

Editorial Note

I BELIEVE documents should be read as they were written. In this anthology, excerpts are rendered as I found them. In a few cases, I inserted periods to aid the reader; where I added more than one or two in a document, I so indicated in the bibliographical statement. Otherwise, capitalization, punctuation and spelling are exactly as I found them. The term *sic* is used when necessary. While I have quoted some of the diaries, letters and travel narratives in their entirety, I have generally excerpted them, choosing specific passages that enlighten us about American community life. Because most of the selections are a part of a larger whole, I have done so without inserting ellipses. Book titles, names of ships, and foreign words have been set in italics to aid the reader, whether or not they were in the original. Otherwise, italics reproduce those in the source. Each document is preceded by a short comment and a bibliographical entry. I used standard multi-volume reference works (*American National Biography, Dictionary of American Biography, Dictionary of National Biography*) to identify the writers. Where other sources were consulted, they have been cited. Finally, there is a glossary of unfamiliar English and French words, which are preceded in the text by a dagger (†).

Sawmills, which were very profitable

Per Kalm, 1749

The earliest narrative about the territory called Saratoga comes from the pen of a Swedish naturalist, Per Kalm (1716–1779). Kalm studied under Carl von Linné [Linnaeus] at Sweden's Uppsala University at a time when interest in scientific agriculture was awakening in that nation. When the Swedish Academy of Science decided to send a scholar to North America to investigate useful plants and trees, Kalm was its choice. He sailed in August 1748 on a two and a half year journey. From his base at the old Swedish colony of Raccoon [Swedesboro], New Jersey, he explored Pennsylvania, New Jersey, New York and Québec. He reached New York City in June 1749, proceeded up the Hudson to Albany, and visited the Cohoes Falls and Crown Point on his way to Québec. In October, he returned by the same route, adding to his observations of both Albany and New York City. His journals, published as En Resa til Norra America *(3 vols., 1753–61), provide some of the earliest scientific observations of the New York environment and its native and European people.*

Kalm spent a night at Saratoga on the west bank of the Hudson on his northbound journey, lodging in "a little hut of boards," and two nights there while heading south. The settlement there had been destroyed two years earlier, and Kalm does not appear to have been entertained by the Schuyler family who had been its proprietors. He makes no mention of mineral springs in the forest to the west. He did observe remains of an English colonial fort, destroyed several years earlier, and the ruins of Schuyler's sawmills. The description that follows, written on 24 and 25 June 1749, is significant for being the earliest by thirty years of the Saratoga country.

Peter Kalm, *Travels into North America*, 3 vols., translated by John Reinhold Forster (London: The Editor, 1771), 2: 286–291. Another edition is in print: Adolph B. Benson, ed., *Peter Kalm's Travels in North America* (1937; reprint, New York: Dover, 1987).

June the 23rd. This night we lodged with a farmer, who had returned to his farm after the war was over. All his buildings, except the great barn, were burnt.

June the 24th. The farm where we passed the night was the last in the province of *New York*, towards *Canada*, which had been left standing, and which was now inhabited. Further on, we met still with inhabitants: but they had no houses, and lived in huts of boards; the houses being burnt during the war.

As we continued our journey, we observed the country on both sides of the river to be generally flat, but sometimes hilly; and large tracts of it are covered with woods of fir-trees. Now and then we found some parts turned into cornfields and meadows; however, the greater part was covered with woods.

SARATOGA has been a fort built of wood by the *English*, to stop the attacks of the *French Indians* upon the *English* inhabitants in these parts, and to serve as a †rampart to *Albany*. It is situated on a hill, on the east side of the river Hudson, and is built of thick posts driven in to the ground, close to each other, in the manner of palisades, forming a square, the length of whose sides was within the reach of a musket-shot. At each corner are the houses of the officers, and within the palisades are the barracks, all of timber. This fort has been kept in order and was garrisoned till the last war, when the *English* themselves in 1747 set fire to it, not being able to defend themselves in it against the attacks of the *French* and their *Indians*; for as soon as a party of them went out of the fort, some of these enemies lay concealed and either took them all prisoners, or shot them.

I SHALL only mention one, out of many artful tricks which were played here, and which both the *English* and *French* who were present here at that time, told me repeatedly. A party of *French*[1] with their *Indians*, concealed themselves one night in a thicket near the fort. In the morning some of their *Indians*, as they had previously resolved, went to have a nearer view of the fort. The *English* fired upon them, as soon as they saw them at a distance; the *Indians* pretended to be wounded, fell down, got up again, ran a little way, and dropped again. Above half the garrison rushed out to take them prisoners: but as soon as they were come up with them, the *French* and the remaining *Indians* came out of the bushes, betwixt the fortress and the *English*, surrounded them, and took them prisoners. Those who remained in the fort had hardly time to shut the gates, nor could they fire upon the enemy, because they equally exposed their countrymen to danger, and they were vexed to see their enemies take and carry them off in their sight and under their cannon. Such *French* artifices as these made the *English* weary of their ill-planned fort. We saw some of the palisades still in the ground. There was an island in the river, near *Saratoga*, much better situated for a fortification. The country is flat on both sides of the river near *Saratoga,* and its soil good. The wood round about was generally cut down. The shores of the river are high, steep, and consist of earth. We saw some hills in the north, beyond the distant forests. The inhabitants are Dutch, and bear an inveterate hatred to all *Englishmen.*

We lay over night in a little hut of boards erected by the people who were come to live here.

June the 25th. SEVERAL saw-mills[2] were built here before the war, which were very profitable to the inhabitants, on account of the abundance of wood which grows here.

The boards were easily brought to *Albany* and thence to *New York* in rafts every spring with the high water; but all the mills were burnt at present.

He saws up great quantities of plank at his mills

CHARLES CARROLL

Soon to become a signer of the Declaration of Independence, Charles Carroll (1737–1832) of Carrollton in Maryland was sent with three others as a commission to authorities at Montréal in the spring of 1776. It was not successful in its object of securing Canadian support for the Revolution, but he spent a week beginning 9 April as a guest of the Schuylers. Note that he made no mention of the Saratoga mineral springs, which we know had recently been put to use.

Brantz Mayer, ed., *Journal of Charles Carroll of Carrollton, During His Visit to Canada in 1776* (Baltimore: Maryland Historical Society, 1876), 55–57.

WE ARRIVED in the evening, a little before sunset, at Saratoga, the seat of General Schuyler, distant from Albany thirty-two miles. We spent the whole day in the journey, occasioned by the badness of the roads, and the delay the wagons met with in crossing two ferries. The roads at this season of the year are generally bad, but now worse than ever, owing to the great number of wagons employed in carrying the baggage of the regiments marching into Canada, and supplies to the army in that country. General Schuyler informed me that an uninterrupted water-carriage between New York and Quebec might be perfected at fifty thousand pounds sterling expense, by means of locks, and a small canal cut from a branch that runs into Wood creek, and the head of a branch which falls into Hudson's river; the distance is not more than three miles. The river Richelieu or Sorel is navigable for batteaux from Lake Champlain into the St. Lawrence. The rapids, below St. John's are not so considerable as to obstruct the navigation of such vessels.

The lands about Saratoga are very good, particularly the bottom lands. Hudson's river runs within a quarter of a mile of the house, and you have a pleasing view of it for two or three miles above and below. A stream called Fishkill, which rises out of Lake Saratoga, about six miles from the general's house, runs close by it, and turns several mills; one, a grist mill, two saw mills, (one of them carrying fourteen saws,) and a hemp and flax mill. This mill is a new construction, and answers equally well in breaking hemp or flax. I requested the general to get a model made for me by the person who built it. Descriptions of machines are seldom understood. I was informed by the general that it is customary for the great proprietaries of lands to lease them it for three lives, sometimes on fee-farm-rents, reserving, by way of rent, a fourth, or, more commonly, a tenth of all the produce; but the proprietaries content themselves with a tenth of the wheat. On every transmutation of property from one tenant to another, a quarter part of what the land sells for is sometimes paid to the original proprietary or lord of the manor. The general observed to me that this was much the most advantageous way of leasing lands;—that in the course of a few years, from the frequent transmutations of tenants, the alienation fines would exceed the purchase of the fee-simple, though sold at a high valuation. General Schuyler is a man of good understanding improved by reflection and study; he is of a very active turn, and fond of husbandry, and when the present distractions are composed, if his infirm state of health will permit him, will make Saratoga a most beautiful and most valuable estate. He saws up great quantities of plank at his mills, which, before this war, was disposed of in the neighborhood, but the greater part of it sent to Albany.

We had gained the ground on the enemy's right wing

Ebenezer Wild

Before there was a spa, there was a battle that changed the course of history. The journal of a nineteen-year-old soldier, Ebenezer Wild (1758–1794) from Braintree, Massachusetts, gives us a soldier's perspective on the second engagement of the Battle of Saratoga. One of many journals kept by soldiers during the Saratoga campaign, it is notable for its matter-of-fact voice: Wild shifts without comment from a bored recitation of the weather to a plain, unemotional description of a very bloody fight.

"The Journal of Ebenezer Wild," *Proceedings of the Massachusetts Historical Society*, Second Series (Boston: The Society), 1891, 6: 78–99. This document was recommended for inclusion by Eric Schnitzer of Saratoga National Historical Park.

2 October. We started at daylight and went about a mile, and came to a mill called Jones up Skylers Creek, where there [are] a number of houses pretty close round it. We set fire to the mill and several other buildings and a large quantity of grain, and took 7 prisoners here. We were discovered by a party of the enemy on the other side of the river, which caused us to leave the place quicker than we should otherwise have done. Notwithstanding, we took a considerable booty, and proceeded on our way home as fast as we could conveniently. We arrived at headquarters between 8 & nine o'clk in the evening with 10 prisoners, 3 of which were commissioned officers, and 12 horses and 18 horned cattle. After we delivered our [prisoners] to the guard, and our cattle were [taken] care of, we marched to the commissary's store, where there was a gill of rum and one hard biscuit delivered to each man. After we had refreshed ourselves we marched very silent to our camps & were dismissed. What was very remarkable we never exchanged a shot the whole scout.

6 October. Very warm but something rainy. Last night about 2 o'clk went out a scout of 500 men with one days provision, commanded by Col°. Vose. The scout Col° Vose commanded returned this evening just at dark. 16 deserters from [the] enemy came in to us to-day.

7 October. A very pleasant morning. This afternoon about 3 o'clk we were alarmed. We marched out as far as our advance picket;

stayed there till about sunset. About 5 o'clk an engagement began on our left wing which lasted till after sunset,—very brisk on both sides. About sunset our B^{d} Major brought us news that we had gained the ground on the enemys right wing and made a great sloter [slaughter] of them,—taken a great number of prisoners with a considerable booty. Our bridge marched off from our lines in order to attack their lines upon their left; but it being pretty dark, and not to our advantage to attack them at that time of night, we returned to our camps again.

8 October. This morning something foggy, but very warm. About 8 o'clk we marched from our camp in pursuit of the enemy. We marched as far as their lines, and made a halt there a little while. The enemy had retreated to some works they had in their rear, where they fired from and did us some damage. As we were marching along inside their lines, they fired a number of cannon at us. Col^{o} Voses had his horse shot from under him. We marched through their lines to the left, and so up through the woods, up opposite Saratoga, and halted there some time. The Genl discovered that [it] would not be for our advantage to proceed on our expedition; so we returned to our camps again without any loss. We heard when we returned to our camp that Genl Vinkearne [Benjamin Lincoln] was wounded.

9 October. This morning very cloudy and cold. 10 or 12 deserters came to us from the enemy's army this morning. About 9 o'clk Genl Gates sent in a flag of truce to see where the enemy were, which, when he returned, brought news that the enemy had retreated from their encampment, leaving great part of their provision and stores. About 10 o'clk this morning it began to rain, and held on very steady all day and till about 9 o'clk, and then cleared away—cold and very windy.

10 October. This morning clear and very cold. We had orders to pack all our things up and be ready to march at the shortest notice. About 10 o'clk we started in pursuit of the enemy. After we had passed their encampment we found great destruction of [the] enemy's emnishon [ammunition] and stores, particularly one amushon [ammunition] wagon with 300 weight of gunpowder in it and many other valuable articles. And we likewise saw a number of dead horses which appeared to be hured [hurried] to death. We marched within a half mile of the enemy, and encamped in the woods. There was a considerable firing on both sides.

11 October. This morning very foggy. We drew a gill of rum a man,

& about 8 o'clk we marched from our encampment in the woods to a small eminence above the meeting houses. After staying there awhile we marched into the woods nearly where [we] lodged last night. After making a small halt there we marched back again into woods near the mills up Skylers creek, where [we] lay all day and at night encamped here in the woods. This morning our people took the enemy's advance picket, consisting of an officer and 36 men, all British troops. The enemy have been fortifying and defending themselves as well as they could; but our people almost [? elbowed] them, and fired on them and did them much harm.

12 October. This morning clear and pleasant. We remained here in the woods all day. A considerable smart cannonading the biggest part of the day on both sides, and we fortified against the enemy considerable on the hills all round us. There was some rain in the first of the evening.

13 October. This morning dark and cloudy. There was no firing on nare [nary] a side till about 8 o'clk, when we fired some cannon from our side. After that there was considerable firing on both sides all day. We continue still here in the woods.

14 October. This morning very foggy. The enemy lay very still yet. There has been a cessation of arms all day. Very pleasant weather.

15 October. Very pleasant weather all day. Gen[l] Burgine [Burgoyne] and Gen[l] Gates have this day agreed on terms of capitulation.

A fog of seven drafts

COUNT FRANCESCO DAL VERME

On 2 July 1783 the New York Royal Gazette *reported the arrival on the city's wharfs of an Italian count: Francesco dal Verme (1758–1832), a member of one of Milan's oldest and most distinguished families. When he set off on the customary Grand Tour of the Continent in February 1782, dal Verme harbored the notion of going to America to see the country and meet some of its great men. Repeated letters to his father at home in Milan finally brought the desired permission, and he sailed from Falmouth in England on 14 May 1783.*

Armed with letters of introduction to General Washington, members of

Congress, and others, the young nobleman quickly found his way in the new nation. Within weeks of his arrival, he was riding northward on the New York frontier with Washington, sharing the hardships of travel as well as the hospitality that was lavished upon the hero of the Revolution. It was on this journey, while they were guests of General Schuyler at Saratoga [Schuylerville], that he visited the mineral springs, writing the earliest detailed description of them that has come to light.

Accepting hospitality carried obligations. After returning home by way of the West Indies in July 1784, the young count soon had an opportunity to reciprocate the kindnesses shown to him. Thomas Jefferson visited him in 1787, spending a day in an Italian dairy observing the process of making parmesan cheese. In the following year Jefferson sent two young men of his acquaintance with letters to dal Verme, who introduced them to the glittering social life of the Lombard capital.

Dal Verme's journal was never intended for publication and, in fact, remained in the family archives until it was translated and published in 1969.

Elizabeth Cometti, ed., *Seeing America and its Great Men: The Journal and Letters of Count Francesco dal Verme 1783–1784* (Charlottesville: University Press of Virginia, 1969), 12–15. Reprinted with permission of the University of Virginia Press. Biography is found in the introduction, pages i–xxvi. See also *The Writings of George Washington* (Washington: GPO, 1931–44), 27: 99, 501.

JULY 26. After breakfast left for Fort Edward (14 miles), where we watered the horses. At four o'clock in the afternoon we had dinner in Saratoga (15 miles) at the home of General Schuyler. Visited a sawmill in which fifteen saws simultaneously cut a log into sixteen boards. All the buildings at this place except the church were burned by the enemy.[3] Sky overcast.

July 27. Fog so thick that it was impossible to see beyond ten steps. (The local custom is to take antidotes against the ill effects of fog in dosages determined by the density of the fog, which may be of seven grades. Distinction is made between a fog of one, two, and up to seven drafts, by which is meant drafts of whiskey, rum, brandy, etc. Almost everyone in America conforms to this practice with happy results.) After lunch (and proper antidote which upon due consideration we unanimously decided should be of the fifth grade) we arrived at the mineral springs (12 miles). These are three springs whose water is very cold and constantly bubbling. At intervals the water from one of them overflows through a round hole, a palm in diameter, onto a rock three feet high shaped like a cone resting on its base.

They told us that ten years ago the rock was not more than two feet high and that its height had been increased by the †calcareous substance deposited when the water, which is usually six inches below the opening, overflows. The water has a salty taste and smells of sulphur. Many use it for treating gout, dropsy, and asthma, usually with full recovery when taken locally. It makes excellent bread without yeast and salt. The experiment made for us was entirely successful. The dough rose in less than two minutes—to be exact in 1 minute, 40 seconds, and 52 thirds [52/60 of a second] according to a man who had the watch which marked the seconds (he calculated these last in his head). Although we had a guide we lost our way in the forest and rode twenty instead of twelve miles to get to Colonel [James] Gordon's[4], where we found a good dinner.

Description of the chalybeate springs, near Saratoga

G. TURNER

The first published account of one of the Saratoga mineral springs was a short article in the Columbian Magazine *in 1787, based on a visit in 1783. The author, responding to a request by the publisher, wrote straightforward observations about the phenomenon, which had become known by word-of-mouth.*

G. Turner, "Description of the Chalybeate Springs, near Saratoga, with a Perspective View of the Main Spring, taken on the Spot," *Columbian Magazine* 1 (March 1787): 306–307.

THE FOLLOWING observations on the †Chalybeate Springs, near Saratoga, I have the pleasure to communicate in compliance with your request. Having, as yet, found no leisure to possess myself analytically of the particular properties of the waters, I can only speak of them generally.

The springs are found about eleven miles west from Gen. Schuyler's house, at Saratoga. They are scattered along a vale or slip of low wet land, lying between two pine ridges, which run north and south parallel to each other, at the distance of sixty or eighty yards.

High Rock Spring. *Columbian Magazine*, March 1788.

The most remarkable spring in figure lies north of the rest, and is known by the name of the Main Spring: as such, I shall begin with it, confining my remarks, chiefly, to this and one more, as having a prior claim to our notice: From these may be gathered a tolerable idea of all the rest, which are eight or ten in number, apparently alike in their essential qualities.

The Main Spring, then, is a well of clear water, contained in a stony crust, or rock, of a conic figure, being at the base twenty-six feet six inches in circumference; in height, on the west side, thirty-seven inches, perpendicular; and on the east side fifty-eight. On the summit there is a circular aperture, or bason, ten inches in diameter, which discovers the water bubbling up within a few inches of the top. This rock, or crust, is evidently a †petrifaction, composed of several strata, which have been formed under repeated overflowings of the water;—but at what times those overflowings took place—whether they yet continue at certain periods—or whether they have totally ceased, and when,—are matters of speculation among the curious. From the prevailing opinion of the country, I was once inclined to believe that this well had periodical discharges; and, as the report of the place pronounced them to happen every full moon (an opinion which few persons have ventured to contradict) I was prompted to very particular observations and enquiries on this head.—I visited the Springs in person in the month of July, 1783, when, it may be presumed, the weather was dry and sultry—and *then*, to the best of my recollection, I found the water within three or four inches of the brim of the bason. It was not then full moon; but I enquired of a gentleman, who had his daughter at the waters for the cure of the †king's evil, and had passed his time there the preceding full moon—if he had perceived any discharge from the bason:—To this he answered in the negative. This information, as it agrees with other evidence no less questionable, goes very far to prove that this spring is not at present influenced by the moon.

I next proceeded to examine how far it might be affected by the annual melting of the snow, which, communicating with the source of the spring, might so swell the water as to procure a periodical, but annual discharge from the aperture of the rock: and I was encouraged to believe this might be the case, by some of the country people, who roundly asserted, in opposition to the supposed lunar influence (but without assigning a cause) that the water did annually boil over.

Having occasion to visit Saratoga the following autumn, I was fortunately favoured with a season the most proper for terminating my doubts. It was the month of October. The season was singularly wet, it having rained, almost incessantly, for two months before: but how great my surprise ! when, instead of an expected redundancy of water in the bason, I found it retired six inches, or more, below the mark where I left it in July—yet the strength and pungency of the water was, as I thought, considerably weakened, as if occasioned by the falling of the rain.

This discovery has given a new turn to my speculations. From the nature and formation of the rock, which, as I have observed before, is a petrifaction, it is hardly to be doubted that the water it encloses used to overflow its limits; and that probably at stated periods: for how can we otherwise account for the existence and magnitude of the rock, or the different strata composing it? It will appear, I think, no less probable, that those periodical discharges have long since ceased, when I observe here, that the rock shews evident signs of decay. Admit this, and it follows that a considerable time must have elapsed between the last flux of water, and the first appearance of decay in the stone—from whence I would infer, that the exterior surface of the rock, being no longer drenched and fed by the water, but always exposed to the air, yielded to the corrosion of the latter, and fell into decay.

It is about fifteen years since those springs were first shewn by the savages to the settlers, who possibly received from them at the same time, a traditional account of the periodical overflowings of the water,—an effect which must have ceased, according to appearances, many years before.

12

The accommodations were very wretched
GEN. OTHO HOLLAND WILLIAMS

Maryland merchant Otho Williams (1749–1794) was the earliest health-seeker to keep a detailed record of his experience at the Saratoga mineral springs. He had served brilliantly as an officer in the war and became acquainted with Washington, who told him about the Saratoga waters. As a major at the defense of Fort Washington on Manhattan Island on 16 November 1776, he was seriously wounded in the groin and was thrown into a military prison. There, sharing a cell with Ethan Allen, he was subjected to harsh treatment, poor sanitation and short rations. Though released in a prisoner exchange in January 1778, his health was never the same. It seems likely that he was seeking relief from symptoms when he made the arduous journey to the site of the present city of Saratoga Springs in the summer of 1784. Saratoga's aristocratic era had not begun. Williams noted that most of the visitors were backcountry residents, since the accommodations were so poor. He conducted a number of simple experiments to determine the nature of the waters. The first adequate lodgings and the first published report on the springs were to follow in 1787.

Otho H. Williams, letter to George Washington, 12 July 1784. George Washington Papers, series 4, reel 94, Library of Congress, Manuscript Division. Transcribed by Field Horne.

Baltimore 12th July 1784

Dear Sir

AFTER I had the pleasure of seeing you in Philadelphia I made an excursion to New York and from thence up the North River[5] as far as Saratoga. One motive for extending my tour so far that [?cause] was to visit the springs in the vicinity of Saratoga which I recollect you once recommended to me as a remedy for the Rheumatism. They are now much frequented by the uncivilised people of the back country, but very few others resort to them, as there is but one small hutt within several miles of the place. Col. Armstrong and myself spent one week there which was equal to a little campaign, for the accomodations were very wretched and provisions exceedingly scarce. The Country about the springs being uncultivated we were forced to send to the borders of the Hudson for what was necessary for our subsistence.

During our stay we made a few little experiments upon the waters—Bark of a †restringent quality turned them to a purple color very suddenly, and we thought that Iron was discoverable even to the taste.

They have certainly a very great quantity of salt. A quart of the water, boiled down, produced a spoonful which being diluted in common water there remained on the surface a quantity of insipid, tasteless, matter like chalk, which we collected; then pouring off the water into a clean vessel we found remaining at the bottom some thing like †slaked lime. The water in which the first production was diluted being boiled down produced half a spoonful of very acute salt; But that which distinguishes the waters, in a very conspicuous degree from all others, is the great quantity of fixed air which they contain. They are exceedingly pungent to the taste, and after being drank a short time will often affect the nose like brisk bottled ale. The water will raise flour sooner than any other thing and cannot be confined so that the air will not some how or other escape—Several persons told us that they had corked it tight in bottles and that the bottles broke. We tried it with the only bottle we had which did not break but the air found its way through a wooden stopper and the wax with which it was sealed. A trout died in the water in less than a minute, or seemed dead, but recovered in common water—This experiment was repeated with the same effect. We observed, in digging that the rocks which are about the springs, and which in one or two places project themselves above the earth in a conic form, go not deep into the ground, but are formed by the waters which, the man who lives at the place informed us, overflow once a month when not disturbed, and the earthy parts being exposed to the air and sun petrefy, & increase. This opinion is strengthened by the shells and bodies of insects which we found in broken parts of the rock.

I have given you my observations because, I think you told me what you knew of these extraordinary springs was from information.[6]

At Clermont Mrs. Livingston charged me with a letter for Mrs. Washington and with her most respectful compliments to you Sir. All that amiable family joined in affectionate compliments to you and to Mrs. Washington: and I beg you will permit me to add my own,

I am Dr. Sir, most respectfully
Your most obedient
Humble Servant
O. H. Williams

General Washington

Swiming in a pigs trough
ELKANAH WATSON

A merchant and consummate promoter, Elkanah Watson (1758–1842) grew up in Plymouth, Massachusetts, the son of a cooper, but at 15 he apprenticed with Providence merchant John Brown. While traveling through the colonies on Brown's business, Watson began his lifelong custom of journalizing. When his apprenticeship ended in 1779 he went to France. He settled in Nantes and spent five years engaging in trade. After other adventures in the new American nation, he moved to Albany in 1789. The following year he visited the Saratoga mineral springs, recording his observations, as always, in his journal.

He already was envisioning a canal to the Great Lakes and publishing articles about the idea in the newspapers. He later claimed to have been the first to conceive the Erie Canal. While living near Pittsfield, Massachusetts, from 1807 to 1817, he promoted the newly-imported Merino sheep, and organized the Berkshire Cattle Show, an event that made a significant contribution to the development of American county and state fairs. He returned to Albany but, in 1825, moved to Port Kent on Lake Champlain where he died.

His unpublished journals, full of rich observations of early America, are in the New York State Library. His son published extracts in 1856 under the title Men and Times of the Revolution, or Memoirs of Elkanah Watson, *from which the following comments on Saratoga in 1790, somewhat misquoted, first reached the public.*

Elkanah Watson, Journal B, pages 373–374, and Journal E, page 63. Elkanah Watson Papers, New York State Library, Manuscripts and Special Collections. Transcribed by Field Horne. An inexact transcription of the relevant passage was

Elkanah Watson. *A Biographical Sketch of Elkanah Watson* (1864). Courtesy of the New York State Historical Association, Cooperstown.

published by Winslow E. Watson, ed., *Men and Times of the Revolution: Memoirs of Elkanah Watson* (New York: Dana and Company, 1856), 290–291 and 350–351.

SEPT 15th 1790 I arriv'd this Morng at the Saratoga Mineral Springs from Genl. Schuylers place at Saratoga on fish Creek; where I had been treated with hospitality by his son. There I remaind the day swiming in a pigs trough. I drink these exhilirating waters from the center of a rock. I found 10 or 12 decent people at a wretched tavern. The wildness of the Country & bad accommodations reminding me of the state of Bath in Eng'd in the barbarous days of King Blabud.[7]

The Saratoga waters were discovered about 20 years ago by the Rev'd Mr. Ball of Ballstown[8] by following a deer trail. From its natural position & the great virtues of these waters, it must in some future day become the Bath of America. At present all is rudeness, and barbarism—the accommodations are only fit for Indians, the rock thro' which the water Issue by a narrow passage is probably the work of petrefaction. Vessels are let down thro' this apperture or natural well to obtain water to drink. The miserable contrivance for bathing is nothing more than an open log hutt with a large piggs trough, which receives water from a spring; in this you rool from off a bench. These waters appear to be strongly impregnated with a saline substance highly charg'd with fixt air—as animating as champaign wine. Its taste grateful, leaving an unpleasant twang upon the palate: but those who are accustom'd to it, esteem it equal to Cyder. They are in high estimation for all †scorbutic complaints, gouts rheumatisms &c.—These rocks are situated in a marsh surrounded by a demi-circle of small romantic hills: upon the margin of which the road bends round. A little off from the road on the east I visited a new spring much salter amidst rocks and trees—they call it Congress water a very awkward name for water. I pass'd thro the new settlement of New Englanders, called Milton[9]—I stay at Tryons one story house upon the top of a hill in Ballston.[10]

There was a prospect of my gitting help
JAMES TUFTS

When the Saratoga mineral springs first became widely known, they attracted people for whom the medical treatment of the era had failed. One such visitor was James Tufts (1764–1841). A native of New Braintree, Massachusetts, Tufts graduated at Brown University in 1789 and studied for the ministry. In 1791 he was ill. With a pious attitude, he decided to try the Saratoga waters. In a small paperbound diary, he carefully recorded his journey, his spiritual outlook, his health problems, and his hopes during the four weeks he was away.

Like many of Saratoga's early visitors, he made the journey on horseback; the railroad was far in the future. And like many others, he believed he received some benefit from the waters. Perhaps he did, for he lived a long life. He was ordained in 1794 and accepted a call as the first minister of the church in Wardsboro, Vermont, where he preached and served the people for 46 years until his death at the age of 77.

James Tufts, diary, 1789–1791. American Antiquarian Society, Worcester. Transcribed by Field Horne with punctuation added. Biography is found in John P. Warren, *History of Wardsboro, Vermont* (Chicago: n.p., 1886), 6–8.

May the 7th 1791

Sat out from home to go to Saratoga Springs for my health. felt feeble & dubious whether I should be able to perform the journey. thought I was in the way of my duty desirous to be resigned to the will of God.

Rode the first day to Hadly. The second day sat out early in the morning crosed the river at Northhoamton [*sic*] rode threw the Town began to cross the mountain at Chesterfield rode that day to Pattridgfield lodged at Trust Browning. next morning felt weary and more then usually unwell. tarried there that day & night & was very kindly treated. next morning felt better sat out on my journey rode threw dolton Pitsfield & Lainsborough into Williams Town where I put up. tarried all night. in the morning felt very unwell so that I was affraid I should not be able to go any further but after gowing to bed and taking a short nap I felt better. sat out on my Journey about nine O. clock rode about Twelve miles. it came on a heavy rain. I put up in husac tarried there the remainder of the day and that night. The nixt morning I sat out on my Journey. rode threw Husac and camberidge. had a good rode the greatest part of the way. went as far as the North river. tarried there all night and the nixt morning crossed the river into Saratoga. rode about Twelve miles being a new Country and not much cleared thoug I had a good rode most of the way. I arived at the springs about Two o'clock. put ut [*sic*] at Esqr. Risleys[11] a respectable and cleaver family.

That day I used some of the water. from the intelligence I got was encouraged that it might help me. I used of the water sparingly for two days. the third day I drank Three quarts before before [*sic*] breckfast. It opperated in my favour proved a very gentle physiac. Feelt some melting of heart towards God that he had threw his blessing brought me hither and that there was a prospect of my gitting help. O, that I could feel more thankfull and sensible of the mercies of the Lord.

I found some agreeable people here. with some of them formd a considerable of an acquaintaince though the time was short. there seemed to be a benevolent & sympathetic spirit prevailing threw the most of the people that were here, there are some of almost all denominations and disorders, never was I at a place where there was such a number of disordered persons many of them in greate distress which was very malencholy and could not help raising disagreeable feelings and I cannot feel thankfull enough that my disorder is no worse and that there is a prospect of my receiving help.

May 30th. This day I had determined to set out for home but the day being very warm thinking it might be an advantage for my health to tarry some longer I did not set out.

June the 2d. I sat out from the springs to come home. bid the People farewel. I left the place with reluctance though that part of the country is not agreable and by reason of the numbers of People who resort thither many of them in distress would often caus a disagreeable maleacholy yet there were some whose company were very agreeable [illegible] Particularly the familey in which I boarded were much more so then I expected to find in that country.

June the [?12] Feel my self better as to my health then before I went my journey. I think there is a prospect of my having my health again though the pain in my brest remains yet but not so constant as before. If it should be the will of God that I should have my health I desire of the Lord grace and wisdom that I may be enabled & disposed to employ my time in that way which shall be most for his glory which end I desire to be resigned and prepared and not forget the mercies of the lord.

A shower bath of a very sorry fashion
HARRIOTT PINCKNEY HORRY

In the years before the Civil War, the planters of the South Carolina Low Country were frequent summer visitors to the springs. One of the earliest was Harriott Horry (1749–1830) of Hampton Plantation in South Carolina. Her journey in the summer of 1793 reveals what a small and rather intimate community the new nation was for those of wealth and culture. Mrs. Horry mentioned calls received from Mrs. Van Rensselaer and Miss Schuyler while she was at Albany, and an invitation from Henry Walton to stay at his home in Ballston town.

Mrs. Horry was traveling with her mother, Eliza Lucas Pinckney, her daughter, Harriott Horry, and two neices. Such a journey was possible for those with wealth who could purchase "a pair of strong old dutch horses" and then "hire a waggon and driver" to carry them many miles from the nearest boat or scheduled coach line. They were extraordinary women, though: Mrs. Pinckney had been left in charge of a plantation as a 16-year-old and had successfully experimented with indigo culture, while Mrs. Horry, whose father was a special agent for the colony, had been educated in England and had met the royal family.

Harriott Horry, diary. Pinckney Family Papers, South Carolina Historical Society, Charleston, S.C. Transcribed by Field Horne.

WE HERE crossed the Mohawk to the appearance of the meadows and the edge of the river very much resembles our rice fields. Skenectady is a large neat town but very thinly inhabited and appears to be much on the decline owing to the loss of the fur trade. We went on to Ballstown where we had a polite invitation from Mr. Henry Walton[12] to stay a day or two at his house but want of time obliged me to decline it and we went on and dined at Roger's Tavern, passed Milton and arrived at the Springs at Saratoga, put up at Risleys Tavern and examined the rock from which the medicinal water is taken. It is of the form of a hay cock with a hole in the top from which you dip up the water. The rock is about 4½ feet high and the water about two feet from the top tho' they told me it sometimes arose to within six inches of the top. It boils up which is both seen and heard and is of the most disagreeable tast, something like the imported †Chylibeate waters but much stronger. They have so much fixed air as to raise bread without leaven a loaf of which I had made my self to be convinced of it. There are several other springs near, from one of which they extract (by boiling) a quantity of salts of the nature of †Glaube salts of which I purchased a pound for 3/2. There are no convenient bathing houses yet erected but a shower bath of a very sorry fashion and the water is extremely cold.—From the Springs we passed fish creek upon which Genl. Schuyler has several Mills, particularly for sawing, each mill saws in 24 hours 500 boards 14 feet each. This creek falls into the Hutson near Genl Schuylers house 12 Miles from the springs.

1791
ABIGAIL
ALSOP

The road lay through a forest and was formed of logs

ABIGAIL ALSOP

20

One of the most vivid accounts of travel to Saratoga in its formative period is that of Abigail Alsop of Hartford, Connecticut. First published in 1834, it was widely read by Victorians after it was reprinted in William L. Stone's Reminiscences of Saratoga and Ballston *(1875). Timothy Dwight credited the tale to "a friend of mine, who possesses a most accurate memory," but Stone's book attributed the tale to "Mrs. Dwight." From internal and external evidence, the narrator appears to be Abigail Alsop, who married Theodore Dwight, author and editor, in September of 1792. The details of this journey from Hartford to Hudson show that young people, both male and female, were free to go off on an adventure together, and do so without much preparation. En route they experienced true frontier conditions, unfamiliar to well-to-do people from prosperous and long-established New England.*

Timothy Dwight, *Things as They Are; or, Notes of a Traveler Through Some of the Middle and Northern States* (New York: Harper and Brothers, 1834), 104–111.

OUR PARTY originally consisted of five, three gentlemen and two ladies, who travelled with two †gigs (then called chairs) and a saddle-horse. From Hartford, where I resided, and where the party was made up, our party proceeded westward, and some idea of the fashions may be formed from the dress of one of the ladies, who wore a black beaver with a sugar-loaf crown eight or nine inches high, called a steeple crown, wound round with black and red tassels, being less showy than the gold cord sometimes worn. Habits having gone out of fashion, the dress was of London smoke broadcloth, buttoned down in front, and at the side with twenty-four gilt buttons, about the size of a half-dollar. Large †waists and stays were in fashion, and the shoes were extremely sharp-toed and high-heeled, ornamented with large paste buckles on the instep. At the tavern where we spent the first night, we ladies were obliged to surround ourselves with a barrier of bean-leaves to keep off the bugs which infested the place; but this afforded only temporary benefit, as the vermin soon crept to the ceiling and fell upon us from above.

After three days we reached Hudson, where a gentleman who had come to attend a ball joined our party, sending a message home for clothes; and, although he did not receive them, and had only his dancing dress, persisted in proceeding with us. He mounted his horse, therefore, in a suit of white broadcloth, with powdered hair, small-clothes, and white silk stockings. While at Hudson it was determined to go directly to Saratoga, the efficacy of the water being much celebrated, as well as the curious round and hollow rock from which it flowed.

On leaving the battle-ground for Saratoga Lake, our party was reduced to four by the loss of four gentlemen, two of whom, however, intended to overtake us, if possible, before night. The country we had to pass over, after leaving the Hudson, was very uninviting, and almost uninhabited. The road lay through a forest, and was formed of logs. We travelled till late in the afternoon before we reached a house, to which we had been directed for our lodging. It stood in a solitary place in an opening of the dark forest, and had so comfortless an appearance that, without approaching to take a near view, or alighting, we determined to proceed farther.

The day was now at its close, and the forest seemed thicker and darker than before. When the last light at length had disappeared, and we found ourselves in the deepest gloom, our guide confessed that he had encouraged us to keep us from despair, and as to any knowledge of the road, he had never been there before in his life. He, however, dismounted, tied his horse behind our †chair, and taking the bridle of our own began to lead him on, groping his way as well as he was able, stepping into one mud-hole after another without regard to his silk stockings, sometimes up to his beauish knee-buckles. It seemed as if we were going for a long time down a steep hill into some bottomless pit, and every few minutes one wheel would pass over a log or stump so high as almost to overset us. At length we insisted on stopping, and spent a quarter of an hour in anxiety and doubt, being unable to determine what we had better do. We had heard the voices of animals in the woods, which some of us feared might attack us. At length, one of the gentlemen declared that a sound which we had heard for some time at a distance could not be the howl of a wolf, for which we had taken it, but must be the barking of a wolf-dog, and indicated that the habitation of his master was not very far off, proposing, at the same time, to go in search of it. The gentlemen were unwilling to leave us alone, but we insisted that they might need each other's assistance, and made them go together. But it was a long time before we heard from them again. How long they were gone I do not know, for we soon became impatient and alarmed, but at length we discovered a light among the trees, which, shining upon the trunks and boughs, made a beautiful vista, like an endless Gothic arch, and showed a thousand tall columns on both sides. We then discovered them returning accompanied by two men, who led us off the road, and stuck up lighted pine-knots to guide our friends. Under their guidance we found our way to a log-house, containing but one room, and destitute of everything except hospitable inhabitants, so that, although we were admitted, we found we should be obliged to make such arrangements as we could for sleeping. There was no lamp or candle—light being supplied by pine-knots stuck in the crevices of the walls. The conversation of the family proved that wild beasts were very numerous and bold in the surrounding forest, and that they sometimes, when hungry, approached the house; and there was a large aperture left at the bottom of the door to admit the dogs when in danger from the wolves. The floor extended on one side only to within the distance of several feet of the wall—a space being left to kindle the fire upon the bare ground; and when we wanted tea made, the mistress of the house could produce only one kettle, in which water was boiled for washing and every other purpose. She had heard of tea-kettles, but had never seen one, and was impressed with an idea of the usefulness of such an utensil. When we had spread the table out of our own stores, and divided teacups and saucers, a †porringer, etc., among us, we seated ourselves partly on the bedstead and partly on a kind of arm-chair which was formed by an old round table when raised perpendicularly[13], and thus partook of our meal.

We were, however, suddenly alarmed by cries or screams at a little distance in the forest, which some of us supposed to be those of wolves or bears. Our host, after listening a while, declared that they were the cries of some travellers who had lost their way, and proceeded with the gentlemen to search for them. They found, sure enough, our two expected friends, who had followed the path lighted by the torches, but unfortunately had wandered from it a little, and soon found before them a wall too high to reach from their stirrups. They attempted to retreat, but found it also behind them; and though they rode round and round, feeling for a place of exit, could find none, and then began to call for assistance, hoping that some dwelling might be within the reach of their voices. Being happily relieved and restored to us, the adventures of the evening served as a subject of pleasantry. They had unconsciously entered a pound or pen for bears, by a very narrow entrance, which in the darkness they could not find again, and thus their embarrassment and predicament were fully explained. We slept that night on our luggage and saddles; but our hospitable host refused all reward in the morning.

On reaching the Springs at Saratoga, we found but three habitations, and those but poor log-houses on the high bank of the meadow, where is now the eastern side of the street on the ridge near the Round Rock.[14] This was the only Spring then visited. The log-cabins were almost full of strangers, among whom were several ladies and gentlemen from Albany; and we found it almost impossible to obtain accommodations even for two nights. We found the Round Rock at that time entire; the large tree, which two or three years after fell and cracked a fissure in it, being then standing near, and the water, which occasionally overflowed and increased the rock by its deposits, keeping the general level five or six inches below the top. The neighborhood of the Spring, like all the country we had seen for many miles, was a perfect forest; and there were no habitations to be seen in all the vicinity, except the three log-houses which afforded us little more than a shelter. We arrived on Saturday, and left there on Monday morning for Ball's Town, which we reached after a short ride. But there the accommodations for visitors were still less inviting. The springs, of which there were several, were entirely unprotected, on the borders of a woody swamp and near a brook in which we saw bubbles rising in several places, which indicated other springs. There was a small hovel into which some of the water was conducted for bathing, but, as there was nothing like comfort to be found, we proceeded homeward, after spending a short time at the place.

Fire and the axe are rapidly levelling the woods

WILLIAM STRICKLAND

The late 18th century was an era of scientific advancement in agriculture. In England and in America, wealthy and educated gentlemen farmers practiced irrigation, fertilization and crop rotation. These progressive farmers exchanged their knowledge freely through books, journals, and agricultural societies. A clear interest in such matters was enough to gain a European visitor access to the "best men" of the new country.

William Strickland (1753–1834) of Welburn, Yorkshire, later sixth Baronet of Boynton, was such a progressive farmer. His travels in the United States from September 1794 through July 1795 were directed towards observation of both natural history and agriculture; in fact, he scarcely mentioned personal characteristics of or his opinions about the people he encountered, including Gen. Philip Schuyler.

Like any well-informed traveler of the period, Strickland knew about the springs "lately discovered" at Saratoga and, on an October tour of the upper Hudson Valley, visited them. He made the usual observations about the water and the High Rock, not quoted here. More illuminating for us are his observations on the pioneer farmers of Saratoga County. With a distinctly anti-democratic perspective, Strickland laments that farming in the new nation was largely in the hands of ignorant backwoodsmen. His thoughts on this matter, woven into the account of his visit to the springs, anticipate the ecological and political debates of the early 21st century, for he bemoans the careless destruction of the forest, its animals and, eventually, its soil by the unenlightened farmers, and the driving out of the "more humanized Savage the rightful proprietor of the soil."

The journal was written long after his return to England, although he intended it to sound like a daily record and it was clearly based upon careful notes taken on the spot.

William Strickland, *Journal of a Tour in the United States of America in the Years 1794 and 1795* (New York: The New-York Historical Society, 1971), 143–146. Used by permission. Biography and commentary are found in the introduction at pages xi–xix. The manuscript is owned by The New-York Historical Society.

THESE SPRINGS were not known, except to the Mohawks, in whose late country they are situated, till within about twenty years. At that time the ground about them was coverd with a thick and tall wood, but since their discovery, many acres of land lying above them have been cleared of the wood, with which they were shaded, which may have had a considerable effect upon the springs and greatly lessened the quantity of water flowing from them.

[T]hey are resorted to by people chiefly of the lower order, afflicted with sores and humours in the blood, but no tolerable accommodations are yet to be met with at the place, and there is nothing about it to tempt the visits of any one, being situated in a steril country, surrounded by pine barrens.

From Ballstown springs to Schuylers Mills[15] is a continued pine plain here and there broken by new Settlements. In a few places original woods of small extent remain producing trees of wonderful magnitude, and standing so thick on the ground that though there is no underwood and they have no branches for many feet in height, they admit not of view in any direction above a few hundred yards, frequently not one hundred; sound is equally destroyed, the report of a gun cannot be heard farther. The gloom and silence of these woods, whose branches forming a vaulted canopy, deprive the traveller of a view of the Skies, and admit not the rays of the Sun to strike the ground, but leave him only a faint and dubious light by which in a narrow path to pick out his way, but soon the whole will disappear, not to leave its like behind. The barbarous backwoodsman has got possession of the soil, and fire and the axe are rapidly levelling the woods. The backwoodsman has an utter abhorrence for the works of the creation, that exist on the place where he unfortunately settles himself. In the first place he drives away or destroys the more humanized Savage the rightful proprietor of the soil; in the next place he thoughtlessly, and rapaciously exterminates all living animals, that can afford profit, or maintenance to man, he then extirpates the woods that cloath and ornament the country, and that to any one but himself would be of the greatest value, and finally he exhausts and wears out the soil, and with the devastation he has thus committed usually meets with his own ruin; for by this time he is reduced to his original poverty; and it is then left to him only to sally forth and seek on the frontiers, a new country which he may again devour.

The man with an instrument

BENJAMIN WATERHOUSE

All of Saratoga's visitors in the late 18th century emphasized the uncivilized nature of the countryside, even if they marveled at touches of civilization at the springs, or the presence there of well-bred people. In some documents, though, we catch a glimpse of people who created an urbane, if not urban, environment in the midst of the frontier.

Benjamin Waterhouse (1754–1846) skirted Saratoga Springs when he traveled from Ballstown Springs to the Saratoga Battlefield in the summer of 1794. Asking for directions, he and his companions were directed to "go by the way of the Lake of Saratoga" until they came to "the man with an instrument." It seems likely they followed East High Street to the south end of the lake. There they found a German who had left New York City 18 years earlier to live in the wilderness—but brought his prized harpsichord with him.

Waterhouse, a native of Newport, studied medicine there and in London, Edinburgh and Leyden, where he received his medical degree in 1780. Three years later, he became Harvard's first professor of medicine. He is remembered for having introduced Jenner's practice of smallpox vaccination to the United States.

"Dr. Benjamin Waterhouse's Journey to Saratoga Springs in the Summer of 1794," *Yale University Library Bulletin* 40 (1965): 19–23. The manuscript is owned by the Yale University Library.

AFTER WE came out of the woods, we enquired of some people we met the way to Still-water. They directed us to go by the way of the Lake of Saratoga 'till we came to the old German's, or the man with an *instrument*. What this designation was, we could not tell. The second man we applied to said the same, and so said the woman, at whose house we called with the same enquiry. We amused ourselves with guessing what this man could be in the possession of, over & above his neighbours, which could designate him to the exclusive distinction of the man with an instrument; and in the midst of our conjectures, we came unexpectedly in open view of the beautiful little *lake of Saratoga*, and directly after upon the cottage of the old German. We were met at the door by an old man of about 70, who in the German accent & with city manners invited us to alight & walk in. We no sooner entered his neat little habitation, not much bigger than some of our Indian wigwams, but we discovered why he was called the man with an instrument, for in one corner of his Cottage stood a harpsichord, the only one perhaps ever seen by his wondering neighbours. There was the old man, his wife, & son; the latter appeared to be about 25. He sat down immediately to playing, & appeared by his countenance to have been in the habit of exciting astonishment. We therefore listened sufficiently to repay his civility. The old man however soon found that we had rather hear him talk than his son play. He told us that he and his wife were born at Frankfort; that music was his trade, and that he had been organist of a Church in New York[16] for a number of years; that when the great fire happened soon after the British took possession of it, and destroyed a great part of the City, together with the Church in which he was employed, he retired to this very lonely spot without the least wish ever to see a town again. We talked of Germany & Holland, and he seemed highly delighted when he found I had been in the same Cities, in those countries, and in the same Churches, and heard the great organ at *Harlem* as well as he. Every thing his cottage could afford to eat or to drink were soon on the table, and he seemed almost enraptured to find a person able and willing to talk of towns, Churches and organs which he himself had seen in the early part of his days.

Not shade enough to shelter a dog

ABIGAIL MAY

Although Abigail May (1775–1800) spent the summer of 1800 in Ballston Spa, she made two short visits to Saratoga Springs, "a delightful ride, of little more than an hour." She was also among the genteel visitors who began to set the style in the early years, for she was the daughter of John May, participant in the Boston Tea Party, Boston selectman, wharf owner, and Ohio speculator and, with his wife Abigail, one of the founders of the Boston Asylum for Female Orphans.

The younger Abigail May was one of the serious health-seekers; she was suffering from a crippling condition in one hand and from occasional seizures. After a long stay in Ballston Spa she left for her home in Boston which she reached on 30 August, but died nine days later.

1800
ABIGAIL MAY

Her journal took the form of letters to her adopted sister, Lucretia Dana (1773–1866). Ironically, her name is well-known in American history for having been given, just after her death, to her newborn cousin. Abigail May (1800–1877) married the Transcendentalist Bronson Alcott and became the mother of Louisa May Alcott.

28

Abigail May, diary. May-Goddard Family Papers, Schlesinger Library, Radcliffe Institute, Harvard University. Transcribed by Field Horne. An early or fair copy is in the New York State Historical Association, Cooperstown; a few losses in the original were filled from this copy without notation.

FRYDAY—JUNE 20th This day a party of 24 went to Saratoga—we started at eight oclock—9 Gentleman in a hack with four horses went first six ladies with Mr Dobson and the two boys Judah and George follow'd in another. Mr Baldwin, Miss Dunlap and four Gentlemen from Mac's[17] went on horseback—quite a cavalcade—the people run to the window as we passed to see what was the matter—after a delightful ride of little more than an hour we arrived at Saratoga—rested ourselves and then proceeded to the rock spring—we all of us disliked the water, and give a decided preferance to those at Ballstown—'tis flat dead and thick—we even conceited it did not smell well—after viewing all worth observation the ladies with two or 3 gents—to take care of them set of for the Congress spring—the remainder staid to amuse themselves with eggs and ham, while we took large draughts (I hope) of health—at the congress spring I was really pleased beyond my expectations with the *liquor* I mean—for there was not shade enough to shelter a dog—and a charming fire with a kettle boilling close to the spring which temper'd the air more than we wish'd however it might be made a charming place tho' now the scene is rude and wild beyond description. I was so well satisfied with the flavour of the waters—I drank four large half pints—that makes a quart does it not—concive for a moment how you would feel to swig a quart of any liquor by way of amusement in the morning—when we leave here I know not what we shall do for a substitute and have not made up my mind whether †toddy or †gin sling—will do best being used to water of so high a flavour—†Adams Ale is so insipid I can scarcely wash my mouth with it—to return to our company whom I left broilling in the sun while I drank my quart and descanted upon it you would have laugh'd at and pitied us—one bathed their head for head ache—another wash'd their Face for †St Anthonys fire—some wash'd their hands for salt rheum—others their knee, or ancle, for Rheumatism, and gout—eyes, ears, noses, in short each had an ail and apply'd accordingly—the springs I shall not particulary describe but again refer you to Aunt Goddard—who visited them when here—but we return'd to our carriages very well satisfied with our own quarters—and not a wish to change them—we got home in very good season for dinner—at which meal 3 students from the college in Williamstown joind us—Eleanora was so much fatigued with her equestrian excursion—she went to bed as soon as she had dined

How he got my bill up to 12/– I do not know

Alexander Coventry

The diary of Alexander Coventry (1766–1831), a Utica physician, is a document rich with the social and economic history of early New York. We are fortunate that Coventry visited Saratoga Springs twice, in 1802 and 1822. On the first occasion, he described in detail an octagonal domed structure covering the High Rock Spring and he stayed in Gideon Putnam's newly-completed hotel— indeed, a fire was kindled for Coventry using some boards which were probably scraps from its construction. He became one of the first Saratoga visitors to complain about high rates.

Coventry was born at Hamilton, Scotland, studied medicine at Glasgow and Edinburgh, and immigrated in 1785. He lived at Hudson in Columbia County, Romulus in Seneca County, and Utica. There he was a merchant and a physician, before he settled on a farm in Deerfield, just north of Utica, to devote himself to agriculture and fruit-growing. He was twice president of the State Medical Society.

The passages that follow are taken from a 1978 typescript in the collection of the New York State Library, Manuscripts and Special Collections, at pages 996–1005 and 1876–1886. Biography is found in Samuel W. Durant, *The History of Oneida County, N.Y.* (New York: Everts and Fariss, 1878), 444–445. The diary, covering the years 1783 to 1831 in 2,830 typewritten pages, was transcribed early in the 20th century, at which time it was on deposit at the New York State Library. Its present whereabouts are unknown.

FRIDAY, 23 SEPT. 1802. Saratoga. Proceeding you ascend a hill where you perceive a bluish stone, somewhat like limestone, and here the houses of entertainment are planted thick. Below this are the main Springs: descending under some buildings that have the appearance of being fixed for bathing, you see some springs at a wet, miry place with appearance of deposited limes: here you see little or nothing to attract your attention, but proceeding some †rods farther, you perceive a round topped building which is erected over the rock spring in the form of an octagon with sides of about 7 or 8 feet: posts, about 7 or 8 feet high, and open from the eaves, except one board which is on 6 sides and serves as a back to the seats which also occupy their 6 sides. The entrance which is on the North side being open, and only a board on the South, this place floored, but in the middle rises a circular rock, from 24 to 30 inches in diameter, and elevated in the middle about 8 or 10 inches above the floor which is simply fitted to it all around. In the middle or apex of this rock is a hole 10 or 12 inches in diameter, from which the water once flowed, and you hear a gurgling noise, as the flowing of water. Within it, about 2½ or 3 feet from the top, the hole enlarges, or rather the rock seems to be excavated and it is about 3½ feet to the water, on drawing which does not exhibit a very clear appearance, nor can it be said to be turbid, but the taste is the most distinguishing property: it has the pungency of water saturated with fixd air.

On the North and North East a sand bank comes within 2 rods of the spring rock. On the North West is a ledge of limestone rock at the distance of 3 or 4 rods from the rock, on the S.W. and to N.E. is a swamp which comes from about N.E. and goes S.W. the sand bank layer to the South East about 15 rods distant, the water oozes out in a marshy condition about 2 rods from the spring to the South from the bottom of a sandy part. The depth of the spring from the top of the rock, to the bottom of it is at least 6 feet.

Paid Holine 1/– and set out for the Congress spring. You pass along a flatt and come in sight of a large white house, where Putnam lives who owns the house. This house[18] is 70 feet long, and 44 feet wide: 3 stories high, has 17 fire places, 30 rooms, etc. Spoke to the landlord and asked for a room. He hesitated some time, at last showed me into a small bed room: finding my cloathes were wet, I asked for a fire, and he had one made with some pieces of boards, and I dried my cloathes, walked down to the spring which issues from

Union Hall. *Saratoga Sentinel*, 7 June 1825.

the East side of a pile or ledge of detached lime rocks, the highest part of which are 6 feet above the spring, but descends gradually to where the water bubbles out of a small hole, which seems to be in a solid block of limestone rock. This water is perfectly †pellucid, but the taste is more pungent than the Rock Spring, and it evidently contains more mineral. It flows slowly down the rock, and you put the tumbler against the rock to get the water, and you perceive the air bubbling out from it every time moment, and then a small gush of water. There is a swamp East of this place, and the adjoining country is a pine plain. Supped with 9 or 10 other boarders, some of whom appeared to be invalids. Had a pint of wine.

Saratoga Springs, Saturday, Sept. 24, 1802. Considerable frost last night. Clear and very pleasant this morning and through the day. Slept last night at Putnam's, breakfasted this morning, and a stage coming for a Mr. Gregory and his lady, and a Mr. Peake, gentlemen from Carolina, I took a seat with them. Paid Putnam a bill of 12/– Foolishly I did not inquire the items. He charges only 3$ a week for board, and how he got my bill up to 12/– I do not know.

A fishing party on the lake
Mary Grey Bidwell

Some visitors to the frontier springs were women traveling together. Among them was Mary Grey Bidwell (1764–1808) of Monterey, Berkshire County, Massachusetts. In July of 1803 she made the journey, certainly for health reasons, with her aunt and a cousin, also named Mary. Her husband, a prominent lawyer and state senator, and their two small children, Sarah, 7, and Marshall, 4, remained at home. During her stay at the newly-completed Putnam's Inn, she exchanged letters with her husband; three of hers and two of his survive.

Despite the complaint that brought her to the springs, Mary Grey Bidwell lived to be 94. But her comfortable life in Monterey was disturbed by political troubles. Mary's husband Barnabas, a Yale graduate and Federalist, modified his views in the late 1790s to become a Jeffersonian Republican. For 19 years until 1810 he was Berkshire County treasurer, although much of the actual work was performed by his law clerks while he was in Boston or in Washington, where he served in the House of Representatives in 1805–07. In preparing accounts for transfer of the county treasurer's office, a substantial discrepancy was identified, which Bidwell's political enemies blamed on him. He went into exile in Upper Canada [now Ontario], paid back the funds he denied he had taken, and lived to see his son, Marshall, elected to Canada's upper legislature.

Mary Grey Bidwell, letters to Barnabas Bidwell, 20 and 24 July 1803. Yale University Library. Transcribed by Field Horne. Biography is found in Joan T. Bidwell, *The Bidwell Family History 1587–1982* (Baltimore: Gateway Press, 1983), 43, and in the catalogue record of the collection.

Putnams Inn, Springs at Saratoga
Wednesday July 20th 1803

I doubt not, my dear friend, that you and mama will both feel gratified to know we accomplished our intentions, and arrived here to breakfast on Monday, where we find ourselves very agreably accommodated, both as to situation, apartments, & fare—three springs, of different qualities, are very near us. That denominated the Congress, or Salt Spring—recommended by Doctr Sergeant, as preparatory to the Bath, is very near us. I have just returned from taking a large, I hope *salubrious* draught, fresh from the rock, through which it oozes. At a small distance from this, is another, called the

"Putnam's Tavern & Boarding House," tavern sign, 1802. Collection of the Historical Society of Saratoga Springs.

Barrel Spring[19], from the cask, sunk to receive it. this last mentioned seems of a sulphureous nature, & strongly impregnated with fixed air. Further to the north, perhaps, towards half a mile, rise two other. the first, I think, the greatest natural curiosity I ever beheld. It is called the Round-Rock-Spring. The rock is a †petrefaction, & conical with an aperture at top resembling a well in miniature, which admits a small tin bucket prepared for the purpose. the waters, I imagin similar to those at Ballstown. The other called the Flat-Rock-Spring,[20] seems if possible more pungent than any I have tasted, but of the same nature with the Round Rock.

From the natural advantages of this spot, I imagin it will in two or three years more, become the grand resort—The prospects are extensive. it has a variety of waters, possessing various qualities. Congress Spring is the one described by Mr. Dresser, where, from a seat on the intervening Rock you may on the right hand, dip up fresh water, & the left Salt—This water, last mentioned, is as a good old lady observed "more sickisher" than any of the Springs, yet I swallow down 2 or 3 tumblers at a time.

As to the effect of the waters, I as yet perceive no special benefit to either of our little party. we ought not perhaps expect any so soon For we have not yet received the shower bath. Doct.[r] Sergeant advised I should drink the Salt Spring, three or four days to prepare me for the bath.

Repeating love—affectionate to all—with a kiss for my dear Sally & another for my equally dear Marshall I am truly & only your M.B.

Saratoga Springs July 24th, 1803

Yesterday, the gentlemen proposed a fishing party on the lake, & invited us to accompany them, we accordingly fitted out four gentlemen with us in Putnam's hack, & the two others in Mr. Johnson's chaise. The lake lies about four miles eastward from this spot. it is nine miles in length & three in breadth—We did not think of venturing upon it, but remained at an Inn on the bank, while the gentlemen went off in a boat, & caught a fine string of fish with which the lake seems crowded. Our ride was pleasant, the prospect at the lake delightful—the opposite banks of Stillwater, & the distant hills, in a charming state of cultivation, beyond which we could discover the green mountains of Vermont, losing their verdant summits in the clouds—altogether formed a prospect beautifully picturesque, of land & water—towering forests & cultivated farms.

Send the size of Sally's foot when you write—The bearer waits your Mary

Balltown for the dashers carries the bell

ROBERT GOULD SHAW

Robert G. Shaw (1776–1853), Boston merchant, visited Saratoga Springs in 1802, returned the following year and, based on random surviving letters, came many times more. His earliest known letter from Saratoga, addressed to his mother and dated 31 August 1813, contrasts the seriousness of its visitors with the frivolity of Ballston Spa (he calls it Balltown), then at its zenith as a resort. Shaw's grandson and namesake was commander of the first African American regiment raised for the Civil War, the subject of the film Glory *(1989).*

Robert Gould Shaw, letter to his mother, 31 August 1813. Robert Gould Shaw Letters, Massachusetts Historical Society. Transcribed by Field Horne. The collection also includes four Saratoga Springs letters by Shaw to Jacob Townley, Steuben, Maine, dated 1836, 1838, 1844 and 1845. Biography is found in Francis S. Drake, *Dictionary of American Biography* (Boston: James R. Osgood and Co., 1872), 819.

I AM NOW at the most celebrated springs in our Country tho' not in the Place most frequented by the gay and fashionable. Balltown for the †dashers carries the bell & while we have a humble collection of about thirty who really come to the Springs for the benefit of the waters, at Ballston they have more than five hundred of the giddy throng that are sporting in their †Gigs, †Curicles & Coaches with [?servants] in livery, in all the stile & gaudy show for which our Southern nabobs are so famous. Perhaps there never has been a year in America to equal the dissipation of the present. The miseries of this horrid and unjust war, as some term it, does not seem to be felt in fact it is felt only by the poorer classes & some few who live in remote parts of the Union where the cutting off of the intercourse with the more affluent parts of our Country deprives them of some of the necessaries & all the luxuries of life.

I have been in this place but two days therefore cannot say what effect the waters will have on me, if they opperate as they used to, I have no doubt of experiencing much benefit from my journey & the use of the Springs.

In the morning everyone drinks the water; at night they make fun of it

JACQUES GÉRARD MILBERT

Paris-born Jacques Milbert (1767–1840) studied art and became a professor of design at the Ecole des Mines. Having served as a geographer on a voyage to Antarctica in 1800, he seized the opportunity created by peace to travel to the United States in 1815. At first he worked on canal engineering. Soon, however, the Minister of France asked him to collect natural history specimens for the King's Garden, to which task Milbert devoted himself for eight years.

Early in his stay, Milbert discovered the Hudson River. He explored it with delight, noting natural beauty, everyday customs, and accommodations, and he drew excellent pictures of what he saw. In many cases they are the earliest views of the respective communities. By the time he came to Saratoga, which was probably in the summer of 1816, the town's hotels were becoming established as outposts of formal society. He noted, in particular, that without a previous acquaintance, he would have been left entirely alone.

Five years after his return to France, Milbert published Itinéraire Pittoresque du Fleuve Hudson et des Parties Letérales de l'Amérique du Nord, *recounting his travel up the Hudson to its Adirondack source, visits to New England, Philadelphia and Virginia's Natural Bridge. It remained untranslated until 1968, and is one of the more important accounts by a European of Federal-era America.*

Constance Sherman, trans., *Picturesque Itinerary of the Hudson River and the Peripheral Parts of North America* (Ridgewood, N.J.: Gregg Press, 1968), 48–51. Biography is found in the translator's preface, pages vi–ix.

THAT MORNING I promised myself to reach the village of Saratoga while it was still early, but it was eight in the evening when I arrived. I feared I should find neither food nor lodging, for at this season the village is overrun by a multitude of visitors from all parts of the Union. Finally, however, I was taken to a private home, rented as an annex by one of the baths. It was rather annoying to learn I was to share a room with three strangers, but I decided to accept the situation as Americans do. They get up, dress, and go to bed without appearing to notice that they are surrounded by people they don't know, and they almost never speak. I had time to freshen up before the supper bell rang about nine o'clock to summon those guests who had retired to their rooms or gone for a walk. Soon afterwards I went to the dining room, where about 150 people were assembled. Very well dressed, they did not appear ill. Fortunately I recognized a New York family at once and was invited to sit with them. But for this happy meeting I should have been left completely to my own devices, for it is the custom to speak only to acquaintances or to those to whom one has been introduced.

After supper we went to the salon, a room nearly as large as the dining room, where groups that were temporarily separated reassemble, and everyone passes the evening according to his tastes. Some of the guests gather to converse, and people staying at other establishments come to call, a courtesy to be returned the next day if not that same evening. Several ladies take turns at the piano and, despite a noisy obligato of arrivals, departures, and animated discussions, they pursue their sonatas unperturbed and receive the applause of the whole gathering. The evening is usually concluded by a walk in the woods.

Occasionally a certain number of guests issue invitations for a dance to which the public is not admitted. Those who attend give another party, and so the time passes with a series of gay affairs; in the morning everyone drinks the water religiously; at night they make fun of it.

The largest establishments in Saratoga are the Pavilion, Union Hall, and Congress Hall.[21] The latter is divided into a great many rooms, which, despite their small dimensions, usually house entire families, that are always large in this country. The façade is decorated with a colonnade, and the space beneath forms a covered walk. These houses are generally well run, with an excellent table but rather high prices, so proprietors derive an excellent profit during the season and hotels have increased in number during recent years. The newest ones are brick but the majority, including Congress Hall, are wood, and the latter could be reduced to ashes in less than three hours. I have often thought of this with the realization that the exits would not be adequate to let all the occupants escape.

Outside the main house are cabinets for the baths, which consist of small board cabins equipped with a wooden tub. An upper reservoir, filled from the outside, supplies water that is poured on the head or limbs of the patient. Our method is far superior.

Congress Hall has no garden, for you can't give that title to a very small area used for growing vegetables. Guests are thus obliged to walk in the dark forest or to go to Saratoga Lake, a distance of two miles. Every day the path is losing more of its lovely border and, if this forest destruction continues, we must expect to see all the resinous trees, these leafy giants of the North, perish in the wake of almost all the native tribes whom they used to shelter. The patients enjoy excellent fishing in Saratoga Lake or they may sail in little boats set aside for their use. The water is very cold and coated with ice during the winter. On the lower flank of the mountain a shady pool, called Owl Pond, is near a little village consisting of a cluster of farmhouses.[22]

The water in Saratoga mineral springs contains carbonic acid, carbonate of soda, muriate of soda, carbonized lime and carbonate of iron. As the number of patients that visit this muddy valley increases with every season, the village is growing proportionately.

I had become so heartily tired of Saratoga

James Skelton Gilliam

James Skelton Gilliam (ca 1794–1820), a lawyer and planter from Petersburg, Virginia, kept a lengthy and gossipy diary of his visit to Saratoga Springs in the summer of 1816. The journey was made by a "hard-going hack" on rough roads. Gilliam was of patrician breeding and ever conscious of the background of his fellow guests. Note, however, that there is not a trace of anti-Semitism in Gilliam's comment on his meeting with Moses Myers and family of Norfolk, Virginia: nothing more, or less, than "they are very pleasant people."

Gilliam visited Barhyte's Pond for fishing, now part of Yaddo, and Saratoga Lake, where he ate and fished at Riley's. In the end, though, he moved on to Ballston Spa, having become "so heartily tired of Saratoga."

James Skelton Gilliam, Diary. Personal Papers Collection, Library of Virginia. Transcribed by Field Horne. Very poor abstracts were published as "A Trip to the North," *Tyler's Quarterly Historical and Genealogical Magazine* 2 (1920): 294–309.

Saratoga July 8th 1816. Monday. I arrived here this evening about ½ 6 O'clock after having a agreeable ride from Albany,—disagreeable however on account of our hard-going hack, rough roads, indifferent horses & uninteresting country. We left Albany about 11 Oclock with five passengers exclusive of the driver in a two horse hack. The distance is about 38 miles. Our company was agreeable enough, notwithstanding its being composed of an unhealthy old man from New Jersey, a religious bigot from Bristol in Rhode Island, an inhabitant of Albany, & the driver. We stopped about every seven miles to rest our horses & to allow the Albany man & the old fellow from New Jersey to get a drink of Gin. About ¼ after twelve, we arrived at the River Mohawk, where a bridge is thrown across, a toll gate kept & a tavern established. Here the hack driver insisted on stopping to †*bate* his horses as he expressed it; & two from Rhode Island & Albany determined on having a dinner. This I was obliged to assent to altho I wished very much to get to Ballstown to drink some of the waters there before eating. We left this tavern about 2 O'clock. Our dinner would have disgraced the poorest house in the poorest county of Virginia. We paid 50 cts[23] for it. About 4 O'clock we reached Ballstown where we stopped to drink some of the mineral waters. The settlement appears to be completely in a valley. Whilst we were drinking our driver took his horses to a tavern to give them a slight *bating* of oats. In about a half hour we left Ballstown & reached Saratoga at ½ 6 O'clock. I do not like the appearance of any of the company that I have seen. I got out at Lewis tavern sufficiently contiguous to the famous Congress Spring—my companions went to what is called the upper village, to private lodgings. In a few minutes after arriving here I went to the Congress Spring & drank 4 or 5 tumblers of the water. It is stronger than the Ballstown, of course not so agreeable to the taste. Being quite unacquainted & not observing any disposition in the people to be sociable I have come to my private apartments at a very early hour.

Sara. Thursday 10th 1816 July. I do not as yet perceive any benefit from the use of the waters. I have just commenced using them twice a day—freely both in the morning & evening. Last evening I went to hear a preacher in the large room attached to the "Congress Hall" tavern. We walked over with rather a singular character in the form of a woman. She had travelled with us from New York to Albany in the steam-boat[24] & that she considered a sufficient acquaintance to speak to us. She observed she had been treated most rudely in the tavern, that she was from Charleston, expected her daughter & son in law every day, was quite uneasy at not finding them here, she had been gazed at by the people in the porch as she came up to the tavern as if she were some thief, upon uttering which she burst into tears. Mr. Gladden appeared to sympathize with her, & being a most excessively religious man offered her religious comfort &c. After shedding tears in abundance, she agreed to go with us to hear the sermon.

Saratoga July 20th Saturday 1816. Last [*sic*] we had a ball at the "Congress Hall tavern"—There were but few people present & most apparently averse to dancing. We danced I believe two sett dances & one †cotillion, in all of which Miss Borland was my partner.

Saratoga July 26th Friday 1816. Nearly another week has elapsed without writing last in this journal book. I shall endeavor in future to be more particular. Time runs off as rapidly as possible. I have become well acquainted with Mr & Mrs Stott. They are both most excellent persons. We have balls now very frequent. On Tuesday evening last, I went with a Miss Morriss from Halifax to our [*sic*]. She is about 30 years of age, very large & homely tho' quite jovial & conversible. As soon as she came into our house, I made myself acquainted with her anticipating from her quizzical appearance, a good deal of fun. When I went over to the ball room I did not know her name far less her standing in society, & that she & her sister came up to the tavern together without the protection of a gentleman or even a servant. I was surprised to learn that she was the sister of Judge Morriss of Halifax a man of great learning & respectability. I found also that she was acquainted with the first company from Boston & New York; my politeness to her appeared to excite her partiality for me, & she introduced me to all of her acquaintances & friends. She was of great service in this respect. We have become well acquainted. My acquaintance also at the large house[25] as we term it is now very extensive. I regret very much I did not take up my abode there when I first came here, as all the young & gay people go there. Miss Morriss & Mrs. Stott however have remedied most of the inconvenience, resulting from my putting up at Lewis tavern by introducing me to all their acquaintances. Our company has increased very much. There cannot be less than 350 at these springs. They are going & coming however every day; & on that account, it is difficult now to become well acquainted with many.

Saturday August 3d 1816. This morning I became acquainted with Mr Moses Myers[26] & his family from Norfolk in Virginia. They are very pleasant people. I spend my time quite agreeably in the company of the ladies at "Congress Hall." Every morning, about 11 O'clock, in the evening immediately after dinner, & after supper I see them. I walk with my acquaintances Mr Newbold from New Jersey, Mr Henry Hartford from Savannah, & Col. Lindsay from Virginia, at other periods of the day. Whenever we have balls I frequent them. Miss Livingstone is the belle of the day. She is really very interesting. I went with her & Miss Wilkins to Judge Waltons[27] this evening.

Saturday August 10th 1816. I have spent this day most disagreeably. Nothing but lounging & [?uninspiring] conversation appears to occupy the attention of people. I regret very much that the laws of our state prevent Billiards. It must be an amusing game. I have never yet attempted to play it. This evening I took my last evening walk with Miss Livingstone & Miss Wilkins. The thought of their departure distresses me excessively. Miss Livingstone gave me a most pressing invitation to call & see her at New York as I pass thro' which I promised to do.

Thursday August 15th 1816. Saratoga. About 10 Oclock, this morning, myself & Col. Lindsay walked down to see Messr Pugh & Harwood. After being there a few minutes a walk was proposed to the Flat-rock spring & agreed to. We all went down. Shortly afterwards we were joined by Judge Prevost & his daughter, Miss Yates & other young ladies. Being acquainted with all, we held a conversation together for some time. A few minutes after their departure, we returned to the rooms of Mr Pugh where we played 2 or 3 games of †whist. In the evening about 3 O'clock, myself, Col. Lindsay, Mr Pugh & Capt Pierce from Boston set out on a walk to a place about 2 miles below, much resorted to on account of the fine trout which are almost always to be obtained there. It is called *"Barite's"* from the name of the man who owns it, a Mr Barite.[28] Gentlemen go down very often for the purpose of dining there on fish. The owner has made a dam for the purpose of collecting water enough to turn a saw-mill; & in this pond he has been putting trout for the space of 15 or 20 years for the purpose of procreation & increase. He can catch them at almost any time & has a small pond about 7 feet by 3 made for the express purpose of keeping as many in as the call of individuals in one day might require. The trout is a most beautiful fish & affords a most agreeable repast. After staying there a half hour we departed & reached Saratoga about 5 O'clock.

Monday 19th Aug. 1816. Saratoga. This morning immediately after breakfast, I set out with a parcel of gentlemen, Col. Lindsay, Mr Eaton Pugh, Mr Tho. Neilson, Mr Bernard from the Rappahannock, Mr Williamson, from N. Caro, & Mr Coles from Wmsburg Va, on an excursion of pleasure to a Mr Riley's tavern on Saratoga-Lake. After passing over a good deal of very bad road, we reached the place of destination in about an hour & a half. Some of the party wished to fish & other [*sic*] to sail about the lake in a boat prepared with sails &c for the purpose. We of course separated. The party for fishing was carried to a platform with a cover, which Riley had fixed for the purpose about the middle of the lake, & the balance of the com-

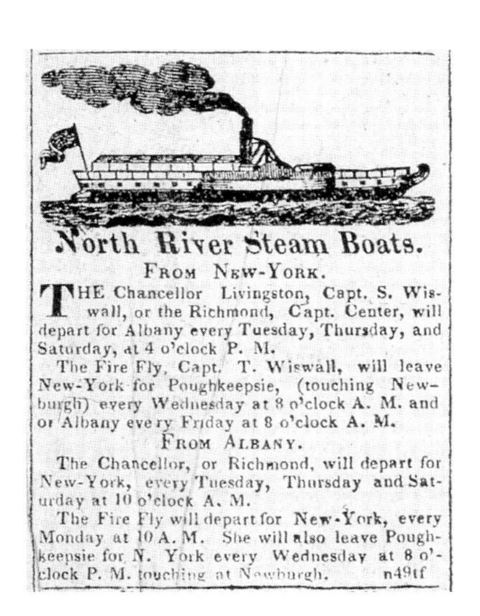

Steam Boat. *Saratoga Sentinel*, 15 May 1822.

pany to which I was attached sailed about a mile or so up the lake. The sail boat however had been badly rigged for any purpose of pleasure, & we soon grew tired of it. We returned & joined our companions in fishing—which we found as poor an amusement as sailing. I caught but one fish & none of the company more than two. We soon left our platform & returned to the tavern.

August 23d Friday—Ballstown Spa—1816. This day about eleven O'clock, I reached this place & have taken up my abode at the *Sans Souci.*[29] I had become so heartily tired of Saratoga.

There is great jealousy between these watering places

SOLOMON MORDECAI

One might not imagine a patrician Jewish Southerner as one of our early summer visitors, but Solomon Mordecai (1792–1869) was all that. The son of Jacob and Judith (Myers) Mordecai, Solomon was born in Petersburg, Virginia, the fifth of six children; five more were born to his father's second wife. In 1794, the family settled at Warrenton, North Carolina, where Jacob was a merchant and where, from 1809 to 1818, the family operated the Mordecai Female Academy.

In 1817, Mordecai traveled to Philadelphia, New York City, Saratoga Springs, Ballston Spa, and White Sulphur Springs, Virginia, apparently visiting the springs for his health, although he had not complained of any serious illness in his correspondence. In the Mordecai family the regular exchange of letters was a duty and definite rules or traditions governed the compositions. Solomon wrote frequently; the letters that survive are addressed to his sisters Rachel (1789–1838), Ellen (1790–1884) and Caroline (1794–1862). Solomon studied medicine in Philadelphia and, in 1823, settled in Mobile, Alabama. In the following year he married Caroline Waller, a Gentile, with whom he had nine children. He practiced medicine in Mobile until his death.

Solomon Mordecai, letter to Ellen Mordecai, 3 August 1817. Mordecai Family Papers, Southern Historical Collection, Wilson Library, University of North Carolina at Chapel Hill. Transcribed by Field Horne. Biography is found in the catalogue record, and in Malcolm H. Stern, *First American Jewish Families* (Cincinnati: American Jewish Archives, 1978), 141–142.

Saratoga Springs August 3. 1817

HERE AM I at length my dear Ellen at the very fountain of †Hygeia where I have already made two liberal potations—when I left New York it was with the intention of remaining for some time at Ballston, but a conversation with some gentlemen who had been in the habit of visiting these springs induced me to give the preference to those of Saratoga: they are a more powerful mineral and for that reason thought best to begin with—the general routine I find is to remain here for a week or ten days and then resort to Ballston, probably as being the first stage homeward—from the analysis[30] I have read, I discern that the principal ingredients are Soda, Iron, Magnesia & Salt: with the latter it is most powerfully impregnated, while drinking, the taste is not disagreeable. the water being remarkably cool and the fixed air occasions a sensation of sharpness not unlike that produced by the draught of Soda—it is only after you have drank that you are sensible of its extreme saltness—I speak of what is called the "Congress Water" there are several other springs of which I have not yet tasted—the properties of all are nearly similar but some being less highly charged with Salts are resorted to occasionally as †Tonicks—You will feel anxious to know how I am situated but you may lay aside all your anxiety on that score my dear when I assure you that I have been quite fortunate in getting a quiet room in a house not connected with the main building in which I take my meals. the houses are all so full already (for it is deemed early in the season) that I was almost deterred from coming on, indeed the accounts I received at Ballston induced a doubt whether I should be able to find a Bed even for the night. but you must know that there is great jealousy between these watering places which are but six or seven miles apart—I feel particularly pleased with my quarters because they afford me a retreat when I am tired of the bustle of the great world at our Inn—because I have an agreeable acquaintance in the room adjoining—and thirdly because at the head of the family to whom the house belongs is a very civil old woman on whom I can call in the case of a loose button &c^{a}—and lastly because the old lady has a †*tres jolie fille*, who officiates in the double capacity of my †*Blancheuse* and †*Fille de chambre*—the gentleman with whom you are next to be made acquainted is Mr. Toomer—a lawyer of Wilmington—an ~~elderly~~ middle aged man—not in very good health—agreeable in conversation and in manner quite a gentleman. Julius Walker whom I accidentally met in New York, and who afterwards called at my room mentioned to me Mr. T's intention of going up the Hudson, soon after getting in the boat I found him out and made myself known to him—his circle of acquaintance was even more limited than my own, and similarity of situation has since kept us together—my "English reserve," (you see I have not forgotten our elder [?d'ters] gentle hint) must be wearing off. I believe—in the course of the next week I shall probably go to one of the Balls and be able in my next to give you an account of the beauty and elegance of the Saratoga Belles—all that I have yet seen have had their pretty faces quite distorted either by the anticipation or the reality of the briny draught. Mr. Mann, whom I left in Balt° has not reached the Springs. I did not see them in either Phil[a] or N York. Mr. Heron & his Ladies whom I had parted with in N. York. I found on board the *Chancellor Livingston*, the steam boat which conveyed us to Albany[31]—from that place Mr Toomer a Mr. Morton & myself took a hack to the Springs. Uncle Ben[32] who was very attentive promises to forward my letters to this place, as I received none in New York. I think it probably [*sic*] I shall do so to the first mail from thence. you must be particular in directing to Saratoga Springs as there is a mail direct to them, furthermore they could go to Saratoga[33] which is eight miles distant. there is daily communication between these springs & those of Saratoga [intended: Ballston[34]] and a gentleman who is at the latter promises to forward any letters that may be received there for me. this is one disadvantage we labour under here having a mail but three days in the week, while at B: they have one every day—but I shall be satisfied if I have good tidings, though they be slow in their progress—as for any that I have to communicate, I may as well spare you the repetition. my appetite seems to be perfectly restored, tho I do not yet in the Saratoga phrase and deed, "eat like a Wolf"—my strength is returning with the restoration of my faculties †*pour manger*—and I hope yet to cheer you all with a pair of rosy cheeks. but am not very sanguine—my only cause for complaint & that a trivial one, is a cold in my head which I took in the Steam Boat & which bids fair to be quite removed before these lines can meet your eye. so you need not send me any wine whey or Bitter Herbs; tho' if you should dispatch mine Uncle Hal, I will return the compliment by a Bottle of our Spa. I find that they put it up not only for many of our Southern cities, but even for the W.I. islands. on reference to your letter of the 24th I find that my last, to Julia, replied to all & every of your kind enquiries now listen to a few of mine. has papa rec^{d}. any account or any thing more substantive from the gentleman of Georgetown—have Freeman and Hawkins given George occasion to turn to the C^{r} side[35]—is the number entirely completed?—did the lady from Richmond send out her daughter—how far have the Geog. Problem & myth^{o} classes progressed? Will you credit me, when I assure you that variety of incident change of [ ] and this endless series of novelty, have so bewildered me that I ha[ ] sometimes at a loss to recollect whether I left Alfred reading [ ] Homer? Jack you say was giving a finishing stroke to the Baling. I hope he behaves well and did not forget the Lampblack. I directed him to mix with the paint for the lower plank—this & much like information would be gratifying to your wanderer—I have brought with me D. Moore's travels, *Mordaunt, Fleetwood* & *Lalla Rookh*[36]—so you see I have fine amusent [*sic*] for leisure hours—when I mentioned Mr. Walker I should have told you that he is quite well. and is now in a counting room at New York that he may require some mercantile information previous to embarking in that precarious line this winter in Wilmington—his wife Mr T. tells me he left, convalescent—I never before experienced the misery of Cotton Ink which is certainly a most excellent contrivance for spoiling pens & soiling fingers if there were any Deity that presided over the Epistolary Department I would invoke her aid at this moment, for I fear that this letter and others from here will have a long & dangerous passage—you may if you please send yours to Uncle B. to forward from N.York my love to all—do you hear from me every week or oftener for I seem to be very often †*plume à la main* [ ]de often & take care of yourself.

farewell—ever yours—SM E.Ea.

In order to aid the operation, the ladies go directly to the house

WILLIAM C. LORD

Amplifying our understanding of the medical purpose for taking the waters is a wonderful letter by William Lord to his wife Elizabeth at home in Wilmington, N.C., during his long stay at the spa.

William C. Lord, letter to Mrs. William C. Lord, 18 August 1817. Lord Family Papers, Southern Historical Collection, Wilson Library, University of North Carolina at Chapel Hill. Transcribed by Field Horne.

YOU WOULD be amused & disgusted to see the vast crowd at the Spring in the morning, among whom are the first Ladies of company drinking the Water, when the object is known by all the men. But even this is not the Worse, for after drinking the necessary quantity of Water, in order to aid the operation, the Ladies go directly to the House & Walk the piazza (which is 200 feet long) among 20 or 30 Men & when they feel the affects, they pop out of sight for a short time, return, walk, be off, & return again. So on untill all that is required is over—

One of the finest places to see human nature

ELIZA WILLIAMS BRIDGHAM

Eliza Bridgham (1799–1882) visited the springs with her father, Samuel Bridgham, the attorney general of Rhode Island, in the summer of 1818. Much like Abigail May, she kept a journal of her travels addressed to a favorite sister. On the first page Eliza inscribed: "To Her Royal Highness / the Lady Abigail of Providence / this Journal / Is most respectfully dedicated, / By her affectionate Sister, / ELIZA." The convention of writing a journal as if it were a series of letters seems to have been very effective. Unlike simple memoranda of travel, letter-journals are full of vivid observation, intimate comment and, often, wry wit. As many inland New Englanders did, Eliza and her father traveled entirely by road, reaching Saratoga Springs via Bennington, Cambridge and Union Village [Greenwich]. Her journal is the earliest discovered that discusses the Ten Springs, just undergoing initial, limited development. Nine years after her journey, Eliza Bridgham married William Samuel Patten, and lived to be nearly 83.

Eliza Williams Bridgham, "A Journey through New England and New York in 1818," *Magazine of History* 2 (1905): 14–27, 90–95. Biography is found on 14.

Wednesday 29th. Saratoga Springs.—We arrived here safely this morning, dear sister, & have found in one house quite a little world. Much do I wish you & a few other choice spirits were here, then I should enjoy it; this house, which is called "Congress Hall," accommodates 150, at this present time. It is 197 feet in length & three stories in height, & is kept by S.P. Schoonhoven[37], a Dutchman, don't you think it quite an establishment? Among the great number here, I have seen but one I knew, & that was Mr. William Richmond. He has been very kind & attentive to us. Oh! I have wished a dozen times that some man of talents & observation would spend the summer, & study characters—& then let me see the result; I am sure he could not have a better opportunity to view human nature. Here are rich & poor, old & young, sick & well, learned & illiterate, all in the same dwelling, some whose manners are superior, for refinement & elegance, others who are really clownish. If the Author of *"Letters from the South"*[38] were here, he would have ample foundation for something amusing—the springs are finely described by *Salmagundi*[39]—there are about one thousand persons in the place, almost every house is a boarding-house; you can see the people flocking to take the water at all times of the day. The first springs are called "the Ten Springs,"[40] & by some are thought the best. They are situated half a mile from the centre, at the extremity of the village; next comes the "President Spring,"[41] then the Rock Spring; they are very similar in their tastes, some are more highly charged than others: the Rock Spring is very curious: it boils constantly & springs up from a solid rock many feet. It is perfectly round through which the water issues: many suppose this rock to have been formed entirely by the water, but that seems incredible. Next comes the "Congress spring" which is by far the most celebrated. The water of this, I think is pleasanter than the others it has more life & animation. It is really astonishing to see these springs boil so much, they are constantly in motion & now & then boil as hard as any water you ever saw. So much for the waters. As to the town, it is one of the most unpleasant you ever saw. It is all sand & surrounded entirely by pine woods, not one pleasant walk or ride round it. Old Seekonk[42] now, is delightful to it. There is one church[43] here, & the people are so very complaisant, as to leave all the body pews, for the reception of strangers, while they occupy the wall pews & gallery. This is one of the finest places, to see human nature, you can imagine. Here you see all sorts, from all parts. There are several gentlemen here, from Europe, & the West Indies, & four ladies from Spain. But, among so much style & fashion I am inclined to be homesick & hope Father will certainly leave here, tomorrow. I have seen all there is to be seen & so am anxious to turn my face homeward. I am more convinced than ever that "the sweetest spot delineated on the Map of Life is Home!" Adieu, for tonight!

I am so great a beau in spite of the gout
RALPH IZARD

Charlestonians, with great disposable wealth and an unhealthy environment in summer, were numerous at Saratoga until the Civil War. Ralph Izard (1785–1824) of Charleston was a dutiful son; while at the springs in 1819 he wrote frequently to his mother. She was Alice (DeLancey) Izard, a member of a wealthy Huguenot family from Westchester County. Ralph, of Beckley and Mount Hope plantations, had served with distinction in the U.S. Navy prior to the War of 1812. He was traveling with his wife, Elizabeth (Middleton) Izard, and their children, Anne, 10, and Alice, 8. Charlotte, 2, and six-month-old Ralph remained with his mother. Elizabeth died at Charleston in 1822 and Ralph soon remarried. In August of 1824, while traveling north on the Hudson, he was suddenly taken ill and died at a country seat in Columbia County.

Ralph Izard, letter to "Mother," 2 August 1819. Izard Family Papers, South Carolina Historical Society, Charleston, S. C. Transcribed by Field Horne. Biography is found in *The South Carolina Historical and Genealogical Magazine* 2 (1901): 216, 224–226; *The South Carolina Historical Magazine* 57 (1956): 224; and Richard N. Côté, ed., *Dictionary of South Carolina Biography* (Easley, S.C.: Southern Historical Press, 1985), 1: 177.

Saratoga Springs—2 Augt 1819.
Monday night.
Congress Hall.

MY dear Mother—

TOMORROW MORNING at five o'clock I hope to have my wife & children arranged comfortably in an excellent carriage that I have hired to take us to Whitehall. We shall breakfast at a place called Sandy hill[44], passing by Glenns falls—& we calculate on arriving at

The Pavilion. *Saratoga Sentinel*, 16 June 1819.

Whitehall in afternoon making our journey of 40 miles with ease. On Wednesday at 2 o'clock P.M. the Steam boat *Phoenix* leaves Whitehall & after touching at a variety of places on both shores of lake Champlain, will land us at St Johns in Canada the next day in time to proceed in carriages to La Prairie, 18 miles & from thence in batteaux to Montreal 9 miles—from whence I shall take care to communicate to you the result of this amphibious locomotive expedition. I am delighted to see the improvement in in [*sic*] Elizabeths appearance—everybody agrees with me that she looks decidedly better. She is fortunate in having such excellent companions as Mrs Rutledge & Mary, Mrs Ladson & Josephine, Mrs Cotesworth Pinckney & a host of others that it would be useless to name. We have this moment returned en masse from paying a visit at the Pavilion[45], another boarding house, to Major Butler & his daughters & grandsons. He has had a very unfortunately disagreeable journey of 6 days from New York. He has given up his prejudices respecting steam boats I believe. He has a horror of ladies riding in Stage coaches & I fear that my having confessed to him that my wife had actually been guilty of riding in one from Bordentown to Amboy has lowered us not a little in his opinion. His daughters have borne the journey perfectly well. Eliza is much better.—Elizabeth received a letter today from Patience dated at Utica mentioning that they had been detained by the illness of poor little Ann. She was better & they were about to proceed on their way to Niagara. Genl. Rutledge left this yesterday for Ballstown in company with his son in law John Parker—I rode over to Ballston this morning & found the former very much worse. I fear he will not be able to move from thence. I did not choose to mention to Major Rutledge how ill I thought his cousin, because I thought it would affect his wifes health & materially alter their arrangements for tomorrow; for they are to accompany us to Canada & as the Genl has Mr Parker with him & an excellent servant, the presence of the Major was not at all requisite. There is a ball tonight at the Pavilion, to which most of us in this house subscribe—*our* ladies having packed up their finery, do not go—I am so great a beau in spite of the gout that I cannot be excused. You will laugh at my making use of one of my wifes excuses for finishing a letter—Your accounts of our youngest darlings has comforted us very much & has given my wife additional strength & spirits to undertake her journey—We calculate on being back in 12 or 13 days at farthest & hope to be rejoiced at finding a letter or two from you *here* on our return.—Please to direct to Saratoga Springs

Your most affect[e] & dutiful son
Ra: Izard

For gentlemen to lounge and smoke and tell stories in
JEREMIAH FITCH

From Jeremiah Fitch (1778–1840) of Boston, who spent a three-night weekend in 1820 at Congress Hall, sleeping at a private house nearby, we have perhaps the earliest description of what might be called Saratoga porch-sitting, a custom that reached great heights after the Civil War. Fitch was a farmer's boy from Bedford, Massachusetts, who went to Charlestown in 1792 and learned the merchant's business. He moved to Boston, became an importer of drygoods, and was sufficiently prominent to serve as one of the last selectmen of the town, and as a common councilman of the city after it was chartered. His traveling party included his wife, Mary (Rand) Fitch, and their children, Caroline, 12, and George, 10. Little Mary, 7, was probably along but, because she is not mentioned she must have been spared the "powerful operation" of the mineral waters.

Jeremiah Fitch, "An Account and Memorandum of my Journey to Saratoga Springs," *Massachusetts Historical Society Proceedings* 50 (1916–17): 192–193. Biography is found in Abram E. Brown, *History of the Town of Bedford* (Bedford, Mass.: The Author, 1891), Part 2, 11–12.

1820
JEREMIAH FITCH

28 JULY, *Fri.* the next day at about noon we left for Saratoga and arriv'd their at half past 1 o Clock P M and put up at Congress Hall, kept by G V Schoonhoven took private lodgings at Mr. Clements[46] about 10 rods from the Hall. this Hall is 200 feet in length by about 30 in width, 3 stories high, 3 halls comprises the whole lower floor, one is for breakfast, dinner and supper, the middle hall is for Gentlemen and Ladies to walk and sit in, being elegantly furnish'd. the eastern hall is for balls, and other amusements. in front of the building is a piazza the whole length and height, 18 feet wide and another back of the building as high but not quite as wide. the former is for Gentlemen and Ladies to walk in, in the evening the latter is for Gentl to lounge and smoke and tell stories in: This place is a delightful village. there is four or five large Hotels besides a number of boarding Houses and taverns, the Pavillion is the next in respectability to the Congress Hall. while we were at the latter, there was 211 boarders besides from 40 to 50 servants the former at 10 the latter at 5 dollars[47] per week; drank freely of the waters which operated powerfully on Mrs. F. and Caroline; not quite so much on George or myself.

29 July, *Sat.* spent this day very agreeably in company with about 50 Bostonians, for a description of which, see the end of this Book. last evening was a ball at Congress Hall, there is generally one 5 night in 7 during July and August

30 July, *Sun.* This day went to meeting heard Rev Mr. Mathews from New York, the visitors at the springs generally attended: hold a fowl over the spring 20 seconds and it will kill it. hold it over 15 seconds and it will appear to die and will after come to life, the experiment I saw. while at Saratoga I drank the waters from 4 different springs.

They are rich and able to build and furnish it—so we go

Esek Cowen

In the first three decades of the young community of Saratoga Springs, lots were surveyed by the Putnam family and by Henry Walton along Broadway and several short side streets, gradually filling up with hotels, shops and private houses. Because the mineral springs first discovered (Congress and High Rock) were half a mile apart, the development tended to extend north from Congress Spring rather than south. The houses and businesses around High Rock Spring were called the Upper Village. There was little incentive to build south of Congress Spring.

By the early 1820s, the community was growing rapidly. John Livingston (1750–1822) of Oak Hill, Columbia County, was the proprietor of Congress Spring and lands adjacent to it. In the spring of the last year of his life, his on-site agent Esek Cowen (1784–1844) was busy with arrangements for the lease or sale of Livingston's lots on the south side of Congress Street and on the Malta road, which became South Broadway.

The letter from which the following excerpts are taken was sent by Cowen to Livingston to report on his success and ask Livingston's wishes. It is a rare document, illuminating the process of real estate development in a Federal-era village. From Cowen's report, it is clear that great optimism was in the air.

Cowen, a native of Rhode Island, came to Greenfield as a child in 1793, thence to Hartford, Washington County. He was largely self-educated, but studied law at Sandy Hill [now Hudson Falls] and practiced in Northumberland before moving to Saratoga Springs in 1812. At the time he was acting as Livingston's agent, he was serving as Saratoga Springs town supervisor. Later, in 1828, he was appointed circuit judge and then, in 1835, a judge in the state Supreme Court.

"Century-Old Letter Tells of Plans to Expand Saratoga," *Saratogian*, 17 August 1912, 8. Biography is found in Sylvester, 138–140.

Saratoga Springs, April 6, 1822.

Dr. Sir.

You were right in calling the rent of the corner lot $25, though it is very small as you will see by the map. Mrs. Ketchum complies with your conditions. Since the Lots have been laid out[48] there have been several applicants for lots, say 6 or 8 good ones either on purchase or lease. Most of them it is a pity to disappoint. You will see by the Map the size of the Small Corner Lot. As there is no chance either for cellar or gardens on the Three Small Lots South of this I have made them of the size laid down on the Map, and they will answer a good purpose either for mechanics shops or stores.

Elisha P. Langworthy[49], a good watch & Clock maker of Ballston Spa, and a man of property (and as it is a favorite character with you, I should add a clergyman), is anxious to buy and build a good house on Lot No. 29 which will immediately raise to a competent price the said three small lots, as they will then lay between two respectable houses, viz. Mrs. Ketchum's house which is about going up, and Langworthy's which will go up shortly, if he can have the Lot. Risley Taylor[50] (a respectable young man who contemplates going into trade) wishes another irregular Lot (No. 34) on lease. The lots bordering on Congress Street and the Malta Road have been actually Surveyed and Staked out, after running a line around the whole Lot as laid down upon the map and taking the general direction of the Malta Road. The different relative positions marked; as the Congress Spring, Congress Hall etc. are accurately taken on Survey. The other Lots with their Streets excepting Cold Spring Street are merely Suppositions, i.e., not surveyed, and may be modified as you please upon actual survey.

The lots will no doubt meet with a rapid disposal either by sale or lease. They will put down competition, because they are, in general 6 feet wider than Walton's or Putnams, though not quite so deep.

The posts and boards are drawn, and I am about building the general fence Contemplated by us around the lots.

Walton writes his agent, that he has bought the lots of you laying East of Congress Spring. Shall I say to him "Take possession."

I have given Congress Street the legal width, to which the commissioners would have power to extend it, merely, 4 †rods. This will save all possibility of botheration in that quarter. You will see by the Map that the continuation of Broadway along Malta road, which is now narrower than old Broadway may be continued as it is, or modified by you according to circumstances when you come to operate on the Eastern side.

The commissioners have not yet recorded the alteration of the Ballston Road, and in laying down lots I have disregarded it entirely.

If they will not accommodate us, by the proper alterations we can obviate the difficulty by the requisite cross streets; or by an arrangement for a Ballston road farther west as proposed by Mr. Beekman, or both. However, I think they will do right; and as the village progresses to the South, will alter so as to commode us.

There is another large boarding house going up immediately South of Martin Sweeny Stable;—200 feet long of brick.[51]

The undertakers are rich and able to build and furnish it.—So we go. We have cocked our eye upon the land around the Cold Spring.[52] Surrounded as you know by a little Amphi-theatric hill, as the future Vaux Hall[53] of this great city. Not less than 10 or a dozen dwelling houses are now building here.

$21. rent; or $300 price on sale would I think be considered a reasonable average value upon the lots actually surveyed. If we now go about disposing of lots, it will be necessary for you to send me the price and rent of each Lot. By fixing these, and carrying an even hand, we shall, in time (and no distant time neither) extend our village as far south of the Congress as it is now north.

The Map which you received is a duplicate of one in my possession; So that I can understand your letters referring to the Map which you have, the same as if it was in my possession.

It is important that I should hear from you immediately after you receive the Map, about the prices and rents, unless we postpone our present applicants, en masse, to another year.

I am sorry to hear of your ill health; but hope the return of Spring will restore your wonted energy of body. I have monopolized your room at Congress hall as requested in your last, so that if you can acquire sufficient elasticity of nerve to bring you here, you will lack neither accommodation nor congress water to complete the cure. With respect and esteem

Yours
Esek Cowen.

John Livingston, Esq.

Waiters of all countries, sorts and sizes: black and white

ALEXANDER COVENTRY

Alexander Coventry, whose 1802 journal entry was reproduced above, returned to Saratoga Springs in 1822 to find it transformed. His journal entries for that summer carry the first mention of black waiters, whose presence was remarked upon by many visitors in the 1850s and later. Coventry, who had moved in the intervening years from Utica to a farm in Deerfield, just north of that city, was impressed by the "considerable village" he found on his return, but disliked "the scramble at meals, the bustle and crowd, the want of common politeness." And, like many visitors, he was disconcerted to find that the other guests were "all strangers, mostly Southerners," because this limited his social interaction in a time and place in which introductions were essential to forming acquaintances. He left for Ballston Spa after three days.

WE ARRIVED in sight of the buildings at Saratoga Springs. These appear well through the pines. The Springs are situated in a valley of moderate depression: the buildings are on a plain, North of the valley where a wide street runs, on which are many superb buildings for boarding houses. We stopt at Congress Hall: this is near the Congress Spring. This is a most extensive building, 200 feet front, with 2 wings each 80 feet: each, the main part 3 stories high: it has attached a billiard room 2 stories high and 80 feet long. The house was so crowded that Mr. B. and I had to were obliged to lodge above the billiard room, these being the only two rooms unoccupied into which our baggage was taken, and we changed our linen: About ½ past 6 a bell called us to tea, and we sat down in the dining hall where at two tables, 150 people were seated.

Congress Hall, Saratoga Springs, 25 July, 1822. Cloudy and rain in A.M. cleared up about 1 P.M. Got up early this morning and walked to Congress Spring. The water rises in a square box and is dipped with tumblers by boys who serve you in expectation of pay. A railing surrounds an area about 10 feet diameter: people are constantly filling bottles and casks with the water and hundreds resort to the Spring in the morning. There are about 800 strangers at Saratoga, most of whom drink this water every morning. To me it seemed to have lost much of its carbonic acid, and had not the liveliness it possessed when I was here 15 years ago, when it made the nose tingle like champaign wine: it then oozed out of a limestone rock, and it took sometime to fill a tumbler. At the second bell sat down to breakfast where we had coffee, steak, fowl and fish. There are many waiters, and of all countries, sorts and sizes: black and white. Was amazed at the vivacity of a French waiter: he went on the run: his arms and legs in perpetual motion. After 2 P.M. sat down to dinner: when the bell rings there is a confused rush into the hall and everyone scrambles for a seat: those who have servants have one stationed by a chair which is said to be engaged: the chair is turned forward the top leaning against the table. There is no ceremony and little politeness observed, a modest man has a poor chance. The company at this house are all well dressed: they are chiefly from the South: the men of good size but swarthy: the old women yellow and ugly: the young women rather pretty, all delicately formed, but no bloom: the handsomest pale with lovely features. Many young men, but little or no dandyism: the amusements with the men are billiards and cards, with the ladies shuttle cock, and walking through the day, and at night †cotillions.

The two principal Houses are Congress Hall kept by Mr. Schoonhoven, and the Pavillion but by whom kept I did not learn: both extensive houses. establishments. charges $10 pr. week[54]—6/– dinner, 4/– tea: and you may have wine from 1$ to 4$ pr. week.

This is a considerable village, with mechanics of all kinds: a circulating library, with reading room[55] and almost every other convenience. I did not observe above 3 out of the 150, who sat down to the table, who appeared in delicate health.

There are a number of springs in this place: they all seem situated in a vale which seems a water course, and is perhaps 30 or more feet below the plain. This vale on the North side seems bounded by limeston rock, and the rocks scattered along the vale. Above Congress Spring it seems like pudding stone, cemented by †calcarious. The Springs seem to differ but little. All are saline; some more †chalybeate than others. The Congress Spring which is most resorted to, contains in one gallon (231 cubic inches) of water, 676 grains of solid matter, of which ½ is muriate of Soda, or common salt, ¼ carbonate of lime, the remainder carbonate of magnesia, carbon of iron; but what distinguishes this above the others, is the quantity of carbonic acid gas it contains, which is 1½ its bulk. Thus a ½ pint tumbler of the water, evolves three gills of carbonic acid gas. It is acidulous and pleasant to the taste: all the other springs contain more or less, but not in the same proportion, and most of them are more †chalybeate. Had an excellent dinner: a variety of meats and vegatables, with pies, tarts, almonds raisins etc. but the scramble among the guests, and bustle among the waiters, and all being strangers, many ugly, swarthy women, as if they had escaped from the grave yard, and men of similar cast, certainly did not add to the enjoyment of the meal, for me. There were in the 150 who sat down to dinner, but two persons that I knew. Enos Brown and David Childs. Mr. B. had a bottle of wine. *Il je vail le homme grande.*[56]

Friday, 26 July, Saratoga Springs. Ther. at Utica 43°–69. Cool last night: fine agreeable this morning. Last evening attended a vocal concert by Mrs. Holman. She accompanied the piano: her voice was the sweetest and most extensive that ever I heard: she sang 8 songs, among which were "Robin A Dair", "Charlie's My Darling" and "Dalec Doman". It was the finest specimen of singing that ever I heard: each word was very distinct. Mrs. Holman has agreeable features, is middle sized, is a native of England. She was on the theatre while a widow: she married a Classon's: he †rised her ill, they separated, and she took her first name. She is much respected. Tickets 8/– about 150 attended. A number of ladies there, but none very handsome. This morning drank 3 one half pint tumblers full of water before breakfast, but it had no cathartic effect. Mr. B. and I walked to the Pavillion, about 40 †rods, and here drank at the Flatt rock Spring: it has less fixed air, is more nauseous. The Pavillion is a superb House, nearly equal to Congress Hall: belongs to Mr. Henry Walton. It is mostly frequented by gentlemen from New York. It has a very fine garden, to the North of which is a very close grove of white pine, which forms a thick shade, under which is a nine-pin-ally. Met Mr. Sanford from New York here: he is a well looking, gentlemanly man: formerly U.S. Senator from N.Y. From the pavillion we walked to the High Rock Spring this a ½ mile from Congress Spring. in a N.W. direction you descend several flights of steps to this Spring: it may be 50 feet below the plain. The rock has the form of a flat hay cock. about 6 feet in diameter, and 3 feet in height: in the center of the top is a round hole 10 inches wide: from this the water is dipped with a rod 4 feet long. This rock is evidently formed from the deposition of lime from the water, which about 50 years ago flowed over the top of the rock; within the aperture, on the surface of the water, there is a collection of gas—carbonic acid—A boy who had a number of chickens exposed one of them putting it in the hole: in 15 seconds it was senseless, and in 20 seconds it would have been extinguished. The water of this Spring was discovered about 40 years ago: it is similar to Congress Spring, but less acidulous.

All these springs are situated at the foot of a limestone bank, on the West side of a narrow valley, which has a small stream, running N.E. No probable surmise has yet been offered for the extrication of the carbonic gas with which the water is impregnated. The vicinity seems a plain, with pine: some places limestone: mostly sand on the surface.

The village seems to consist from Congress Spring on the South, to High Rock N.E. The street is wide and level, and the houses, although not united are thick: many of them large and elegant particularly Congress Hall, The Pavillion, and Rutenon's [Putnam's] Hotel[57]. The population ordinarily about 300: strangers now increase it to 800. There are mechanics of all kinds, and a constantly rottling of carriages. There are 2 large churches Called on Dr. Steele[58], who seems a polite and gentlemanly person, well informed: has written an account of the county. Stopt at the Reading Room and Circulating Library. Here all the newspapers are kept, and a mineralogical museum began where the different species of rocks are labelled. This is a very useful and amusing study to those fond of Geology. Got an account of the "Battle of Waterloo"[59] from the Library.

Saturday. After breakfast paid my bill at Congress Hall, $4 for 2⅔ days' board. †Porter and brandy 2/–. The house was too crowded, my room inconvenient, had been promised another, but even after the bedding was removed was disappointed. The scramble at meals; the bustle and crowd, the want of common politeness, every one elbowing his neighbour: the guests all strangers, mostly Southerners; the men, tall, spare, dark complexions, the women sallow, old, and wrinkled, and even the young, when rather pretty, without bloom or colour; all was very disagreeable to us, and we preferred a change. Schoonhaven takes no care or concern: he seems to have good servants, and a nephew or son-in-law who is active.

Mr. Broadhead offering to go to Ballston, we started about 9 A.M.

Americans eat so fast

EDWARD ALLEN TALBOT

In 1818, young Edward Talbot (ca *1796–1839) immigrated with his parents from Ireland to London, Upper Canada. In 1820, he went to Montréal where he married, returning a year later to London to continue work on a manuscript on his immigration and his travels in Canada. In August 1823 he set off via Saratoga Springs for England where, in the following summer, his book was published, one of the earliest of the many travel books describing a visit to the spa. Along with many others, he commented on the distinctive customs of hotel meals.*

Talbot was something of a visionary. He projected a railroad line from London to the head of Lake Ontario, and a suspension bridge at Niagara; and he spent a great deal of time in an attempt to invent a perpetual motion machine. In 1834 he did, in fact, patent a steam engine for use in propelling vehicles on a road as well as on rails or water, but it was not practical. Caught up in the Canadian Patriot movement of 1837–38, he took a position as newspaper editor in Lewiston, New York, but, suffering from alcoholism, he soon died in the poorhouse in nearby Lockport.

Edward Allen Talbot, *Five Years' Residence in Canada Including a Tour of the United States of America in the Year 1823* (London: Longman, 1824), 348–351.

THE NEXT place which we visited, after we left Schuylersville was Saratoga, principally famous on account of its numerous springs and as a place of fashionable resort during the Summer months. When I arrived at Saratoga, many of the fashionables had returned to their respective homes, for the season was then pretty far advanced. But there was still a great number of visitors at all the hotels in the village. The inn at which I stopped was the Congress Hall, which is the largest in the place, being one hundred and ninety-six feet and a half long, two stories and a half high, with two wings, each extending backward sixty feet. In the front is a neat and commodious piazza, that opens upon a beautiful garden, and a small grove of pine-trees which appertain to the establishment. This hotel is said to be capable of accommodating two hundred persons, all of whom breakfast, dine and sup at the same table. A number of waiters, I dare say not less than twenty, are in attendance; and, as in this land of independence no gentleman ever deigns to carve a dish, the duty of a waiter is very arduous. The plan pursued at table, here as well as in every other part of the United States which I have visited, is this: When the company have taken their seats, each person casts his eye right and left along the whole range of the table, for the purpose of noting what is the nature of its contents. As soon as he has fixed upon a particular dish, he calls out for it to the waiter, who brings it from its station on the table, and, setting it before the person who asked for it, waits until he has carved whatever part of it he prefers, and then returns it to its former situation. This practice creates a great deal of confusion; for, during the whole of the repast, nothing can be heard but cries of "Waiter, bring me this!" and "Waiter, bring me the other!;" and nothing can be seen, but waiter bumping against waiter, and dish rattling against dish. There is no sort of ceremony observed at the most fashionable houses; for as soon as a gentleman has satisfied his appetite, he rises from his seat, and, walking out in the Piazza, begins to smoke his segar. The generality of Americans eat so fast, that one might suppose they were engaged in determining a wager; for by the time that a man of moderation, both as it respects the quantity which he eats and the time which he consumes in mastication, has nearly done his dinner, the whole table is deserted as well by the company as by the meats. I have hitherto spoken of the visitors to Saratoga as if they were all gentlemen; but I should not forget to say, that many ladies resort to the springs of this place, though few of them, I think, on account of any sickness they wish to get rid of. At Congress Hall, the house which I have just described, there were ladies whom I had frequently the pleasure of meeting in a morning at a neighbouring spring, called the Congress Spring. They used to make a regular practice of drinking a small portion of the waters; and I then thought, from the emaciated and sallow appearance of their countenances, they did so for the purpose of curing the jaundice or other similar complaint. But when I arrived in New York and observed the faces of the females in that city, I found that these were characteristic of the American females, and by no means betokened sickness or ill health.

Some sprigs of English nobility who are quite exquisite!
WILLIAM ELLIOTT

For Southern planters, a trip to Saratoga Springs was a means of escaping the diseases of the Low Country in summer, an opportunity to improve one's health, or a stop on the Grand Tour of the North, which also included the Hudson River, the Erie Canal, Niagara Falls, Montréal, Québec, Lakes Champlain and George, and even Boston.

William Elliott (1788–1863), a rice and cotton planter at Beaufort, South Carolina, made a number of visits to the spa between 1823 and 1858. In many cases, his wife Ann Hutchinson Smith Elliott (1802–1877), remained behind, and his affectionate and newsy letters were addressed to her. In the letter quoted here, he describes a ball hosted by the residents of a particular hotel to which those of other hotels were invited, a custom that appears in the Abigail May diary as early as 1800.

William Elliott was a progressive agriculturist who championed crop diversification, as well as the need for industrialization in the South. In public life he served at various times in both the House and Senate of South Carolina. He was a staunch unionist, believing that the South's economy would not stand on its own, but he defended slavery as "sanctioned by religion, conducive to good morals, and useful, nay indispensible." He and his wife, Ann, had nine children, three of whom were born before his 1823 journey: Thomas, 5, William, 3, and Ann, 1.

William Elliott, letter to Ann Elliott, 18 August 1823. Elliott and Gonzales Family Papers, Southern Historical Collection, Wilson Library, University of North Carolina at Chapel Hill. Transcribed by Field Horne with punctuation added. The collection also includes his diary kept during his visit. Biography is found in the SHC catalogue record.

Saratoga Springs 18th August 1823

My Dear Ann

I SENT you a little box from N York, to the care of Ladson & Dawson which I forgot to mention in my letter—It contained a fashionable worked handkerchief of the latest french fashion for your self—a doll dressed in the last fashion (so as to give you an idea of the present style) for little Ann, and a book a piece for the boys. I hope you have received these in safety.

I promised you an account of the people here, and of the customs & discussions—and I hardly know where to begin—we have such variety—and such fluctuation. We have most beaux at the Pavilion, and most belles at Congress Hall—We have had among the political characters Mr. Van Beuren[60]—Mr. Cambreling[61]—Mr. Poinsett—Mr. Tatnall Mr. Clinton Mr. Otis—Gen[l] Scott[62] & others—among the military and besides our own Southern representation among the fashionables (decidedly the most conspicuous) we have had beaux from all quarters, not excepting some sprigs of English nobility who are quite *exquisite!* We have Mr. Cornwall & Lady—which latter, is the daughter of Lord Charles Somersett—and niece to the Duke of Beaufort—We have Mr. Harvey—son of the Earl of Bristol and such a fop—I never could have imagined—he outrages Bond St.

Among the belles, besides Miss Pacard, whom I have already described, we have Miss Donnel of Baltimore, who was a light & airy figure, with a regular set of features, and delicate complexion—Miss Barnwell of New York, of a tall & commanding figure & dignified expression—Miss St. George of N. Orleans—dark eyes, & flexible handsome features—with many others (as the advertisement says) too numerous to mention—We have balls alternately at the two houses—and we of the Pavilion have completely triumphed over the other party in the splendour of our preparations—they adorned their ball room with wreaths, and hung up their complimentary mottoes—not in the best taste of poetry—With Poinsett to give the design of our decoration—and with Crafts and myself to answer their poets be assured we had our revenge. We threw open by means of folding doors—133 feet of dancing room—at the upper end we reared a pavilion sparkling with lamps & perfumed with flowers—festoons of wreaths fell from the windows & adorned our chandeliers—and at the head of the pavilion shone this motto in transparency—"The Stars that lightened many a sphere / In clustering radiance sparkle here!" a compliment which the belles, were not slow in apprehending, and which gained your husband an ovation of praise—but vanity is infectious, and you will know from this passage that I have been in company with Crafts—

I am now just setting out for Niagara. I go in company with Mr. Ralston of Philadelphia Mr. Smith Jr of Baltimore and some other gentlemen—In six days we shall be at the Great falls thence—we may descend Lake Ontario—proceed to Montreal & Quebeck and cross by way of Burlington on Lake Champlain to Boston. Mother &

Nancy do not go—they remain here a week and then to Boston—where I expect to find them at the end of my grand tour. I am likely to make this journey under pleasant auspices as my friends here are furnishing me with such letters as are likely to gain me access to every thing I may desire to see. Write on receiving this to Boston—and write often if you wish to give me the greatest gratification I can possibly enjoy in your absence—adieu my dear wife God bless you all aff[ectionately] yours W Elliott

The largest species of white wooden buildings

AN ANONYMOUS SCOT

We know almost nothing about the writer of this travel diary kept between 1821 and 1824 except that he was a Scot. His visit to Saratoga Springs took place in the summer of 1824, and his lively style, which suggests he intended it for publication, provides another perspective on British visitors, who were many after the end of the War of 1812.

"Diary of a Journey through the U.S., 1821–1824," BV Diary, 1821–1824. The New-York Historical Society. Transcribed by Field Horne.

AFTER A comfortable supper and sleep in a warm pleasant foggy morning I proceeded through pine forests interspersed with barren heaths and cultivated feilds. It had nothing of the look of promise the sterility of the soil and hovels on the flats with a female scratching the earth with a hoe on one part and another driving a "steed of bones and leather" attached to an old plow which her husband held, were scenery fit for Lapland or Kamschatska. And how much stranger still did the landscape become as fashionable pomp appeared in its centre when the beautiful village of Saratoga from the brow of a hill was seen lying in the centre of a moor. I entered its spacious street sufficiently broad for any metropolis and adorned on each side with the largest species of wooden white painted buildings. This is a village of boarding houses kept in superlative style. Their extended fronts furnished with piazzas all their length were filled with gay idlers and in the windows above smiling maidens and jolly matrons exhibited their fine forms. These buildings had so many adjoining houses behind that they seemed like soldiers barracks.

The street was full of bustle, coaches wheeled along, dandies on horseback drilled about. The hostlers slang mingled with the voices of merchants fashionables and planters from every part of the union. The mineral springs were in a ravine on the right side of the village. I walked down to their sites and found them surrounded by groups of every description. The pale emaciated and lame; pampered epicures and spare gentlemen with red pimpled noses; the healthy who wished to keep what they possessed and wags who laughed all the others to scorn.

It was Congress spring which I first approached which bubbles up in the center of a rivulet and is prevented from mingling its waters with the stream by a trough which is sunk up which it rises. The platform around it was filled with the squires and misses.

Little urchins drew the †medicable beverage from the springs which the gallants delicately handed round in tumblers to the [fair] sex. The ladies tasted and sputtered at every mouthful, their noses reddened, eyes watered, and lips compressed. This is considered the best spring in America and raises the reputation of Saratoga above Ballston Spa. The waters are bottled and sent to every state of the union as also to many other parts of the world. The second fountain I drank from is called Columbia[63] spring a few yards from that of Congress. Some lingerers only were participating of its bounties. The Flat rock spring appeared to have waters similar to these and was surrounded with baths of all descriptions dipping and showering warm and cold. The fourth fountain called High rock spring still farther north is a peculiar natural curiosity.

Everything seems superficial and temporary

An anonymous New Englander

Another anonymous travel diary was kept by a visitor from somewhere east of Hopkinton, New Hampshire, who arrived at the spa on 14 August 1825. He stayed only four nights before leaving on his "western tour" to Niagara Falls and other points, but he wrote a thoughtful and not excessively critical commentary on the conditions he found.

"Sketch of a tour to Saratoga." New York State Library, Manuscripts and Special Collections. It is accession number 10251, having been purchased from Robert W. Lull of Newburyport, Massachusetts. Transcribed by Field Horne.

14TH. The road from Sandy hill to Saratoga 21 miles is mostly over a sandy barren plain contrasted with which the village of Saratoga Springs appears to the best advantage. It was near evening when we arrived and the Pavillion which was lighted up for a ball. the numerous other boarding house and buildings ranged along the broad Street with the multitude of company gave the place quite a lively appearance. The company with whom we had travelled several days verry pleasantly went to the pavilion and we to the United States as there we found friends whom we previously expected to meet.

The Congress, Pavilion & United States are houses of the same class but in point of elegance and convenience would perhaps take precedence in the order named. They are extensive buildings with spacious piazzas on both sides their whole length. The lower floor is usually divided into but two or three parts by folding doors which may be thrown open, exhibiting a long and splendid area which may used [*sic*] for dining, balls &c. A few acres of ground are attached to these buildings laid out with some taste. But though there is much attention at splendour everything seems superficial and temporary and a lodger can not help feeling that the extravagant price he pays is not for what he receives but for what his host must have during the long and dreary intervals in which there is no company. The crowd of visitors with which every house was a few days since overwhelmed already begin to disappear. Indeed there are not many inducements besides the waters for a long tarry at this place. The morning is occupied till 8 in walking to and about the congress spring drinking from o to 8 glasses of its waters hailing old acquaintance making new and returning to breakfast after which an hour may be lounged away on the piazzas and the remainder of the forenoon spent in making calls drinking from the high rock flat rock Hamilton &c or at the Atheneum[64] till dinner at two. This performance is made the most of, and verry fairly disposes an hour or more of lingering time. How those who do not play at billiards, chess, ride or join the ladies get rid of the afternoon I know not. The evening either with balls musick or conversation go something better.

United States Hotel.
Saratoga Sentinel,
8 June 1824.

The mineral springs are situated along a slight ravine through which passes a small stream of fresh water. The Congress Spring originally came up in the bed of this brook. This water is distinguished from the rest by its cathartic power and is the grand morning resort of drinkers. It is fited up with a large platform for visitors with a lower one in the center around the large tube in which is heard the motion of the water. [?Small] boys each with a rod suspending 3 glasses which they thrust into the fountain wait on the company with water. Around the rail of this uper platform from 5 to 8 in the morning is collected a continually changing croud from all the various classes ages & conditions of men and women kind from almost every climate. The waters doubtless have a verry sudden effect for most of them look in good health. The eating at the hotels (which is also carefully attended to) may assist, though I have not yet learned the particular mineral properties it contains. The water of the collumbian a few †rods from the Congress is similar to it but less powerful. The High rock Flat rock and Hamilton are said to be †tonic. The High rock ¼ of a mile from this is of a sugar loaf shape about 4 feet high with a natural apperture in the centre up which the water boils about ⅓ of the way and is said to pass off by a crack. The constant accretion to that stone from the slops of water is verry apparent. All these waters I believe to be powerful and ought to be drank with caution. Chemists pretend to analise them verry accurately and confidently tell us their component parts but unfortunately these parts when united do not produce the water. The manner too in which these waters of different qualities rise up within a short distance of each other and continue to flow unchanged is to me inexplicable.

The present provision for the increasing numbers of visitors to these invaluable waters is inadequate for neither the invalid nor man of pleasure finds just those accommodations he could wish. Saratoga is crouded and dirty throughout and indeed the high rock & flat rock springs are inaccessible but through a dense and complex mixture of unanalised smells. There is a fine situation for a boarding house on the eastern side of the springs, By appropriating 10 or 20 acres of that unoccupied land which is already provided with a natural growth of small pines, a retreat from the dust and filth of the village might be afforded which is now no where to be found.

If one would see the world in miniature, let him go to Saratoga Springs

Elihu Hoyt

In the earliest years of the spa, many of its visitors came from small towns in New England, as did Elihu Hoyt (1771–1833) of Deerfield, Massachusetts, perennial state senator and representative. An antiquarian who lived in Deerfield's "Old Indian House" and published a short history of the town, he kept a careful memorandum during his August 1827 trip to New York State. Hoyt's comments mirrored those of many other New England visitors, particularly the surprise he registered at Betsey and Sally, two farm girls who boldly competed at games against young men. He does not quite say so, but the implication is similar to Alexander Coventry's that the multicultural New York State was a very strange place compared to good Old New England. A few years after Hoyt's visit, the Saratoga Bookstore advertised his book on the Indian Wars in the Connecticut Valley.[65]

Elihu Hoyt, "Journal of a Tour to Saratoga Springs, August 1827." Hoyt Family Papers, Box 6, Folder 2, Pocumtuck Valley Memorial Association Library, Deerfield, Mass. Transcribed by Field Horne with punctuation added. A faulty transcription prepared by Peter Rippe was published in *Supplement to the Heritage Foundation Quarterly*, 5 (July 1966), no. 19. Biography is found in George Sheldon, *A History of Deerfield, Massachusetts* (Deerfield, Mass.: The Author, 1896), 2: 216, and David W. Hoyt, *A Genealogical History of the Hoyt, Haight, and Hight Families* (Providence: The Author, 1871), 389.

Sunday 5th engaged a carriage to carry us to Saratoga Springs. left Albany in the morning there being five of us on board a four horse stage coach, we passed through Troy—Lansingburgh, Waterford thence to the Borough[66] (in Stillwater), then to Malta, to Downing Street[67], & to the Springs, we arrived about 5 o'clock P.M. & put up at *Montgomery Hall.*[68] kept by Mrs. Palmer, the distance from Albany to the springs is estimated at from 34 to 36 miles. it usually consumes about a day to go through. the weather was unusually warm when we came up, & it became necessary to make several stops, we usually dine on the way, generally at The Borough where they furnish a table well stored with a variety—the country through which we pass is generally on the borders of the Hudson, & many times in the vicinity of the Erie & Champlain Canals, which we pass by bridges four times, in the vicinity of the Hudson we fell in with many coaches bound from Albany to the springs, containing passengers from almost every State in the Union, we found the boarding-houses very full. said to be 1200 strangers at the springs, & that 12,000 in all had visited here during the present season.

Monday the 6th Began to take the waters soon after our arrival last night moderately. this morning commenced a regular trial of them, found them the same as formally. Spent the day attending to the use of the waters, & visiting various parts of the village, the various springs, &c. met many acquaintance from Mass. particularly from Boston.—

We have now introduced our fellow travellers to the principal places of resort in the Village, we begin to see the fashionable world as it displays itself at this place, we here see some of every condition in life. one would suppose that we should find every body here on the sick list—but it is far from being the case. seven tenths of the visitors come here probably in good sound health, for amusements & for the sake of spending a week or two among the fashionables, to see & be seen, here we see all the last fascions of the cities, intermixed with the more plain fascions of the Country. we have fascionable Balls, stated concerts, and all descriptions of amusements, which are calculated to take up the time & spend the money in our pockets. many matches have been negociated here, or at least many a negociation has been commenced here which has eventuated in wedlock.

I here insert as a specimen of the manners & habits of the farmers & their offsprings in this vicinity, we called at a place of resort for amusement called the "pine grove,"[69] where gentlemen resort to amuse themselves with a civil exercise at rolling nine pins, about sun set, here we found a farmer who belonged out a few miles with his dutch waggon[70], & his two daughters, who had called to see the fashionables play off the dull hours of care & mental fatigue, they were siting at the head of the game seemingly very much at their ease intermixed with the York State *Bloods* stripped to their shirts, & they were actually engaged in the game, *Betsey,* (for this was the name of one, & Sally the name of the other), managed her part so well that she †dished the best gent^m player on the green, after which they partook of a social glass of grog. apparently with much satisfaction at the result of the game, Betsey & Sally next took a game together; when this was ended, the two Ladies joined their forces, against the master player. when this being finished the Ladies & Gentlemen marched up to the barr, & the glass moved briskley round untill they were all hail *fellows* well met when the Father summon'd the young ladies to mount the waggon, & prepare for home, the Father had been present during the play apparently well pleased with the dexterity & skill of his daughters at the game of ninepins, this was done with an apparent well meant intention, & they seemed to be not aware that any impropriety could be attached to this transaction. drove off in an evident triumphant state of feeling at their success,—I know not what the gentle *swains* of Massachusetts would say if a feete of a similar kind should be exhibited in their own State,—we however venture to believe that no one female east of the green mountains would be found sufficiently *unbridled* to contend at the public games against the hardy sons of Newengland.—

Tuesday 7th weather warm, as has been the case since we left Deerfield, the first of every days work is to take freely of the Congress waters, then walk among the multitude untill the breakfast bell summons us to our repast, after which, this day we chartered a †barouch & took a ride to *Barhites,* a dutch farmers about two miles east of the springs, here we can generally procure a repast of fresh trout but this day the good lady was engaged preparing a trout dinner for a select party from the Springs, consisting of high blooded Jacksonians, at the head of whom was *Martin Vanburen,* a Senator in the Congress of the U. States, from the State of New York—celebrated for his decided opposition to the present administration of the United States, & considered by some at the head of opposition, in point of zeal if not of talents,—I must confess that a †*coup de cil* view of him, did not prepossess my mind much in his favour, I had several chances to see him, & of course made up a minds eye view of his character, he appears ar-

Barhydt's Pond. Engraving by W.H. Bartlett. *American Scenery* (1840).

dent, & determined to carry his points at all hazards, more from selfish views of aggrandisement, than from a well tempered zeal for the public good; this may be hard Judgment, wrongfully applied but such were the impressions made upon my mind—in the evening we attended an exhibition of sleight of hand &c &c by Mr Potter. I think he has not improved in his art, but on the other hand has evidently fallen off, age appears to be creaping on him, his nerves tremble.

Wednesday 8th But there seems to be a great sameness among the ladies in point of dress. I see very little difference in this respect between the Ladies of Boston, those on the Conecticut, or at the springs, except it be, at the springs the Bonnet is generally made of *grass cloth.*[71] There are no end to the Balls, Concerts & other exhibitions, which are continually brought forward here to amuse & to pick your almost exausted pockets.

In the evening we steped into Congress Hall to witness the brilliancy of the evening ball. yet I could not distinguish much difference between an elegant Ball at Saratoga Springs, & a Ball upon the banks of the Connecticut, except that it was more numerously attended & by people of allmost all ages, we stayed & saw them dance a †cotillion or two.

Thursday 9th went in the evening to Book auction. found nothing worth buying, the books were generally poor editions, of small unsaleable works, although they were sold very low, yet it was as much probably as they were worth, called in also to an english & fancy goods auction, & found dull sales, very little biding, & not much sold, every thing in operation in this place, if one should wish to see the world in miniature let him go to Saratoga Springs.

we passed in our walk this evening almost all kinds of amusements—at the Pavilion Mr & Mrs Knight were giving a vocal & instrumental Concert,—At the U. States Hotel there was a splendid fashionable Ball—Opposite, Mr Potter was displaying his powers of sleight of hand, & his art of Ventriloquism—& some where else Mr somebody was showing the wonderful faculties of his learned dog. & the purring qualities of his tabby cat while some few were rationally spending thir time at their boarding houses, but this number was small.

Such a fiddling and dancing
ELIZABETH RUFFIN

In the diary of Elizabeth Ruffin (1807–1849) of Evergreen Plantation, Prince George County, Virginia, we find a different approach from that of the conventional letter-journals addressed to sisters and other intimate friends. Ruffin was a contemplative who found in her diary someone to talk to; in fact we, her readers, are her audience, and she seems to be speaking directly to us.

She noted the routine, as most diarists did; she recorded her impressions of popular entertainments; especially she observed people. But it was "Brother" (Edmund Ruffin, 1794–1865) who plays the starring role in her writings. This (to her) bumbling eccentric was the South's most distinguished agricultural reformer and the fiery character who fired the first shot on Fort Sumter, then killed himself rather than face the reality of "the lost cause." Soon after her northern journey, Elizabeth Ruffin married her cousin, Harrison Henry Cocke (1794–1873), a commodore in the Navy; they had six children before her premature death from tuberculosis.

Elizabeth Ruffin, diary. Harrison Henry Cocke Papers, Southern Historical Collection, Wilson Library, University of North Carolina at Chapel Hill. Transcribed by Field Horne. It was published in Michael O'Brien, ed., *An Evening When Alone: Four Journals of Single Women in the South, 1827–67* (Charlottesville: University Press of Virginia, 1993). A particularly skillful exploration of her character and her writing is contained in O'Brien, 7–14, as is a genealogical chart.

THURSDAY [9 AUGUST]—Well here I am at the famous Saratoga Springs after having come 40 miles today (in addition to many others) to reach them in the stage too, smothered with dust tho' more agreeable (bad as it is) than the Steam-Boat to me, I am heartily tired of the dullness and identity of that mode of travelling it will do while a novelty, but one quickly becomes satisfied particularly where every thing like sociability and intercourse among passengers are not encouraged as is the case in these Boats, among these phlegmatic people; whether it proceeds from timidity, want of confidence, pride or any other cause I don't know, but so it is they all stand aloof as though they were afraid to make any advances—But is this the Elysium, my ears have so long heard? If so, how unwilling would I be to spend my days among this *happy* and *congenial set*; rather let me be glad my lot is cast among the many and nameless agreeables of the *little-Bed* in Mama's chamber but I'm too hasty in passing sentence we've just reached here and can only say out of a house full there is not an individual whom we've ever seen or to whom we can converse at all so the means of amusement and entertainment are very limited being confined within our own selves as yet this is pleasant, is it not? but enough to night: hope to report more favorably tomorrow. Brother has already fled to the circulating library and has (with me) become a subscriber, making provision in case of a *failure* of *present enjoyment*, which, 'tis to be hoped will not continue

Friday—Oh! Tis much more sufferable than was anticipated and can get along very well, true they are all strangers still but all ceremony must be waived at such places and indeed I find it the only way; I have made advances, they have met half way (some few) and between us have contrived to be tolerably sociable, but others I dare not approach, they look as chilling as isicles: we went in the morning to the library, lounged about awhile, overhauled the books and from there went to see the American Automaton Chessplayer[72], which every one says is an admirable and successful imitation of the European, 'tis to me a wonderful and unintelligible piece of mechanism and singular to see merely a human figure playing a game which requires the exercise of reasoning principle, genius and application; had I never have seen it most fully persuaded in my own mind should I always have been that there was human artifice at work within but the gentleman is particularly careful to open all places for inspection and the whole box appears filled with the machinery, so, if any one is concealed he must be a Lilliputian and withal terribly squeezed—Brother has most fortunately met an acquaintance, but he goes to-morrow; so, he will be as far to seek as ever, should he chance not to stumble on others—

Saturday—Better and better, I mean as it regards my feeling of ease and independence, but some of these customs I do abominate and shall never be reconciled to, for instance, this dressing regularly twice a day; most distressing in truth, and really 'tis such a general thing among the ladies that it causes you to be much more noticed than if you were to appear in the most costly suit, the gentlemen are not so foolish in that respect except the dandies and fops—We are all rung to our meals, assemble in the sitting room and there eye each other till tea is announced at which signal you are apt to fare rather badly without some one to assist you through the crowd; after tea is over you can stay in the public room with the company or retire which you may do without being missed and which is my choice—as you may suppose, tho' not so this evening for I had the pleasure of having my name asked me, after a day's intimacy with a young lady she ventured thus far which gratified me, and relieved me in the difficulty respecting her's, which of course she told me in return, this led to a formal introduction to her gentlemen acquaintance and among ourselves passed an agreeable evening—I believe I get on much better than brother, not withstanding his fondness for talking which should act as an assistant; he brought his *Virginia pride* along with him which does not so well relish an equal footing with any and every one; his first debut at Saratoga was to be enticed and introduced to the place by a †Black-leg which I rather suppose sat heavily on him, that together with the possibility of a nother equally agreeable deed keeps him aloof and to tell a good joke on him his solidity and venerableness pass him as my father! sad indeed! if he looks old what must I seem? one comfort is, all do not see alike—There is such a fiddling and dancing in my hearing now, my ears are almost deafened with the sound: all my fear is they will suffer from the exercise this hot night besides encroaching on the Sabbath which is not far ahead—(I forgot to say brother was entirely ignorant of the character of his then associate)

Sunday This morning went to church, can't say I admired the minister exceedingly not quite as much as brother whose admiration for him it seems consists altogether in the freedom and forwardness which he displays towards his people in lashing them for their coldness and backslidings. this evening went again lugging brother sorely against his will who says he's determined the sin of my not going shall not be chargeable to him, however, give him due credit for doing so directly contrary to inclination merely for my pleasure—I'm getting on very smartly and have been frequently accosted to-day by my name—which sound my ears always hail with gladness the widowers tho' I think have manifested more politeness and respect for me than any others; don't know why unless my gravity and matronliness entitle me to it, very old ones particularly, but these grown daughters here are much in his way: in his favor the best policy would be to leave them at home—unfortunately for me just as confidence has come to my assistance a violent cold has made me as hoarse as a raven and so spoils my fun for the present, occasioned by my sleeping with the windows open; 'tis now so cold every body is shawled up, tho' the first of August.

Tuesday—This day has been so cold, rainy, and comfortless I've not been out the house and scarcely out my chamber tho' found abundant amusement from my books: wrote a letter home and have become so excessively genteel that the sewing is laid aside entirely, wish the use of the needle may not be quite forgotten during this trip of fashion: had a fresh importation of people in the place of late vacancies: we have here a variety of face, manner, character, and disposition; some inaccessible by every means as haughty, highminded and proud as Lucifer from such turn away with all possible quickness—others agreeable, affable and advancing even Old Maidism is not excluded from this scene of enjoyment but reigns but reigns in all the "bloom of antiquated virginity." The Quakers and clergymen form no inconsiderable part of our company whom I overhear occasionally discussing some theological question; not forgetting to mention disease in a multitude of shapes, such as dropsies, loose jointedness, spiny affections and eruptions which make our establishment quite an infirmary—Some of the oddest and most ill-matched couples; young husbands groaning under the galling rein of an old wife who hen pecks him to the nines: young wives making their old husbands look as suitable and young by brushing up his hair and smarttening him up for dinner, sorely against his will—newly married ones billing and cooing like doves, and old pairs so completely outgrown the novelty of matrimony, they might well pass for some of the venerable sisterhood—

We are tired to death and half choked with dust

BASIL HALL

Basil Hall (1788–1844), naval captain and author, was a world traveler, having served in the Royal Navy in North and South America, India, the East Indies, China, and even Korea. In 1827, he proposed a journey to the United States to his wife of two years. His published account is constructed in the past tense, but it must have been written en route (as indeed his wife suggested in her description of their activities) with revisions after returning to Scotland, or written soon afterward from extensive notes. In Captain Hall's account is found mention of a stage proprietor in Saratoga Springs whom he later encountered, presumably in the winter, at Charleston, South Carolina, an early and reliable reference to the itinerant lives of resort workers, which becomes more evident after the Civil War, particularly among the large cadre of African American waiters.

Basil Hall, *Travels in North American in the Years 1827 and 1828* (Edinburgh, 1829), 7–28.

ON THE 9th of September, we drove to Saratoga Springs from Caldwell[73], a distance of twenty-seven miles, which cost us nine hours jolty travelling over hilly roads, in a most intensely hot and dusty day. On driving up to the door of an immense hotel, called the Congress Hall, the steps of the carriage were let down by a very civil sort of gentleman, whom we took for the master of the house, or at least the head waiter, and were much flattered accordingly; but the question he asked dispelled these visions of prompt reception. "Pray, sir," he asked in great haste, "do you go away tomorrow morning?"

"To-morrow morning? No! what put that in your head?"

"Do you go in the afternoon then, sir?"

"Not I, certainly," was my answer; "but what makes you in such a hurry to set us a-going again, when we are tired to death and half choked with dust?"

Before he could muster a reply, or put another question, a smart, brushing kind of man, with a full drab coat reaching to the dust, stepped in between us, and with more bows in two minutes than I had seen altogether since landing in America, wished us a dozen good days and congratulations on our return from Canada, and reminded me of a promise I had made to employ him if I should want his assistance.

"Well!" said I, trying to get past, "what is it you would be at? I don't want any thing but a little rest and some dinner."

"O yes, to be sure, sir," said both these busy gentlemen at once; and pulling out cards from their pockets, let me understand that they were rival stage proprietors on the line of road between the Springs and Albany. In our subsequent journeys amongst the woods, we often thought, with a sigh, of this solitary instance of †empressement, and would have given a great deal, sometimes, to have been thus encumbered with help. It did so happen, by the way, that we met one of these obliging personages again, far away in the south, after we had travelled more than a thousand miles from this spot; when we learnt that he was a complete bird of passage,—carrying his horses and carriages to the south in the winter; and accompanying the flock of travellers back again in the north as soon as the sickly season set in at Charleston.

As the dinner hour was past, we had to wait a long while before we got any thing to eat. This we had expected; but our disappointment was more serious and lasting when we found that nearly all the company had gone away not only from this watering-place, but also from Ballston, another fashionable resort of great celebrity in the neighbourhood. During the hot season of the year—when the greater part of the United States becomes unhealthy, or otherwise disagreeable as a residence, even to the most acclimated natives, as the local expression is—the inhabitants repair to the North, to these two spots in particular, which are consequently much crowded during July and August, and sometimes during September. A few days of cool weather, however, had occurred just before we arrived, which acted as a signal for breaking up the company, so that when the great bell rung for supper, the whole party consisted of only fourteen, instead of a hundred and fifty, who had sat down ten days before.

Had we been sooner aware of the chance of missing the company at the Springs, we might perhaps have managed to pay our visit at a better moment, as such a meeting of the inhabitants from all the different States would have been a sight extremely interesting to strangers. I was also curious to see how the Americans, a people so eternally occupied and wound up to business, would manage to let themselves down into a state of professed idleness.

The hotel in which we found ourselves lodged at the Springs of Saratoga, was of great magnitude, as may be inferred from the size of the verandah or piazza in front, which measured eighty paces in length, and twenty-five feet in height. The public rooms, also, were large and handsome, and no fewer than 120 beds were made up in this one building. But with all this show, there was still some want of keeping, and many symptoms of haste, in every thing, indicated chiefly by the absence of innumerable minor luxuries. On the day we arrived, for example, we wished one of the windows of the dining-room kept open; but there had not yet been time to place any counterpoises, nor even any bolts or buttons to hold it up. The waiter, however, as usual, had a resource at hand, and without apology or excuse, caught up the nearest chair, and placing it upon the window sole, allowed the sash to rest upon it. The bed-rooms, too, were uncomfortable little raw sorts of places, fourteen feet by ten, without a bit of paper or carpeting, and the glass of the windows was so thin it was apt to break with the slightest jar. Not one of these cabins was furnished with a bell, so that when the chambermaid was wanted, the only resource was to proceed to the top of the stair, and there pull a bell-rope, common to the whole range of apartments.

It is true, we were at the Springs after the season was over; and, therefore, saw nothing in the best style. But I must describe things as I found them, in spite of the explanations and apologies which were showered upon me whenever any thing, no matter how small or how great, was objected to. I grant that it would be unreasonable to make these trifles and many other and graver things, matters of criticism in so young a nation, were not claims put forth by the inhabitants to the highest degrees of excellence.

On the 11th of September, we observed in the Piazza of the Hotel at Saratoga, a piece of paper stuck up with this notice,—"This house will be closed for the season, on Saturday next, the 15th inst." Accordingly, taking the hint, we resolved to move off, though we found the quietness of the Springs—now entirely deserted—very agreeable, after the turmoil and excitement we had recently been exposed to.

We had come abroad to see what is curious

MARGARET HUNTER HALL

Edinburgh native Margaret Hunter Hall (1799–1876) was the daughter of the British Consul-General in Spain and thus grew up traveling. In 1827, her husband, Captain Basil Hall, suggested that they tour the United States; she welcomed the idea. She wrote a running commentary in the form of letters to her sister Jane and, as a result, her remarks are intimate, witty, and personal.

Arriving at Congress Hall in early September with their 15-month-old daughter, Eliza, and a Scottish nurse, they found the village almost deserted, but they did have an opportunity to attend an Indian exhibition, of a sort later formalized as an attraction by the Indian Encampment. Like most Europeans, she was dismayed by signs of civilization among the indigenous people, in this case a rather high-style coat and a repertoire of Scots and Irish fiddle tunes.

Mrs. Hall found America something of a wilderness, as did many upper-class English travelers. As her editor wrote a century later, "Both Captain and Mrs. Hall disapproved on principle of everything that America presented of equality and fraternity and were completely out of their bearings in a society unmapped by class distinctions. They held democracy to be a demoralizing blight from which, however, it was always possible a country might recover."

Una Pope-Hennessey, ed., *The Aristocratic Journey* (New York: G. P. Putnam's Sons, 1931), 59–61. Biography is found in the preface, 3–9.

SARATOGA SPRINGS, September 10:—It is singular enough that at this place where probably in the season there is a greater racket than anywhere in the States we should have an opportunity of enjoying the only quiet days we have been able to secure since we landed in America, and we are taking the advantage of the leisure to do many little odds and ends that we have not before had time to manage. We left Caldwell on Sunday at nine o'clock in the morning. It was our wish to have remained there for church, but had we let slip the jog trot course of getting on we could not have left Caldwell for three or four days, so we did as we were obliged by circumstances and made out a dusty, hot journey of twenty-seven miles by half past four o'clock, in the course of which we visited Glen's Falls and Baker's Falls[74], both on the river Hudson and very pretty in spite of the persons from whom they derive their respective names having done their utmost to spoil them by turning off the water to their ugly mills. If we live long enough I doubt not we shall see Niagara itself turned all into mill dams. We were told that the Congress Hall was the boarding house at which we had the best chance for seeing company at so late a season, so to it we drove and are here established. At tea that evening we sat down with fifteen persons, nine of whom took their departure next morning after breakfast, since when we have been a party of six, breakfasting, dining, and drinking tea, in a room eighty feet long and in a house capable of accommodating a hundred and fifty persons. We have a comfortable fire in our own room where we sit the greater part of the day writing, reading, arranging our accounts. Yesterday evening, as we were walking along we saw a bill pasted on a wall of a house intimating that in that house at seven oclock there was to be an exhibition by some Indians who were to dance the war dance, give the war whoop, go through the scalping manœuvres, and various other feats. As we had come abroad to see what is curious, this was of course too valuable an opportunity of gratifying curiosity to lose, and, accordingly, we swallowed our tea and set off forthwith to the appointed place. The exhibition was certainly sufficiently savage and strange to be quite natural, but for the scalping part of it I confess that my nerves were not strong enough to admit of looking even at the mere pretence of this barbarous practice. We were told by the handbill that part of the entertainment was to consist of playing on the violin by an Indian, and this proved certainly not the least curious part of the scene, for this Indian, dressed in a †surtout coat between the acts of their barbarous dances and war whoops, filled up the intervals by playing Scotch reels, †Strathspeys, Paddy O'Rafferty, and such like civilized tunes. Since beginning to write we have been to dinner and sat down a †*partie quarée* in the room before mentioned. I rather think the couple who formed the quartet go to-morrow, and then we shall be left to the enjoyment of the eighty feet long room to ourselves.

A fine broad street fringed with trees
JAMES STUART

By the 1820s the War of 1812 was receding into history, and increasing numbers of British travelers visited the United States, some of whom published very fine travel books. One such writer was James Stuart (1775–1849) of Dunearn, Fifeshire. Educated at the Edinburgh high school, he was admitted as a member of the Society of Writers to the Signet in 1798. After a somewhat contentious political career in which he took the Whig side, he found his finances "embarrassed" and, in 1828, resigned his position of collector of the widows' fund and set off on a journey to America that lasted nearly three years. Unlike Basil and Margaret Hall, the Whiggish Stuart strongly favored the Americans. In consequence, the book he published two years after his return attracted favorable attention, and it seems to have been the best-known of the books describing Saratoga Springs from a foreigner's perspective. It is, indeed, a finely-crafted travel narrative, filled with detailed first-hand observation yet unemotional and objective. After his return to Britain, Stuart became editor of a London newspaper and then, in 1836, an inspector of factories.

James Stuart, *Three Years in North America,* 2 vols. (Edinburgh: R. Cadell, 1833), 1: 189–201.

SARATOGA SPRINGS, the great watering-place of the United States, is situated on high dry ground, at the distance of seventeen miles southward from Glen's Falls. We came here on 20th September. The weather had previously become comparatively cool, and the multitude had taken their departure. The great hotels were about to close. Intending to remain for some time here, we went to one of the lesser houses open for visitors during the whole year, and afterwards to a private boarding-house. The gentleman who had accompanied us from Britain left us to our regret on his return, a few days after we reached this village. It consists of one fine broad street, fringed with trees,[75] on the sides of which are so many large and splendid hotels, that it appeared to me that there was more extensive accommodation for company here than at Harrowgate.[76] Fifteen hundred people have been known to arrive in a week. They come from all parts of the states, even from New Orleans, at the distance of between 2000 and 3000 miles, to avoid the heat and unhealthy weather, which prevail in the southern part of the states during the end of the summer, and to enjoy the very wholesome and pleasant mineral waters of Saratoga.

There are four great hotels. Congress Hall, the largest, is 200 feet long, with two immense wings. The United States Hotel contains as much accommodation. This is the hotel to which the Ex-king Joseph Bonaparte resorts when he pays an annual visit to the springs. He now associates at the public table as an American citizen, which he did not do at first on coming to this country. There are of course public reading-rooms, library, and ball-rooms, and a newspaper press. Backgammon boards, and draft or checquer boards, as they are called here, are in the bar-rooms generally all over the country, and the bar-keeper not unfrequently playing at checquers with the people, who appear as respectable as any in the house. Backgammon is not so often played here. Cards seldom seen.

Apples are very abundant in this neighbourhood, sold at 3d. Sterling per bushel. We see large quantities of them dried by exposure to the sun, first pared, and cut in quarters, and then laid in any convenient situation, frequently on the house tops. Peaches are dried in the same way. Apple sauce is made of the apples thus prepared, which is used with roast beef and many other dishes, without any mixture of sugar.

The whole appearance of the place is cheerful,—the population residing in the village between 2000 and 3000. There are four or five churches, with spires covered with tin glittering through the trees, Presbyterian, Baptist, Methodist, and Universalist; the two first rather handsome houses of some size. There was not public worship regularly in all the churches, the crowded season being over; but two of the churches at least were open every Sunday; the sermons good plain discourses, but there was no eminent preacher when we were here. In the Methodist and Universalist churches, the males occupy the pews on the one side of the church, and the females on the other. This practice we afterwards found not to be unusual in the Methodist churches in the United States. The Methodists generally kneel at prayer, and stand while singing, but the practice varies in different churches. Ladles are common, as they used to be in Scotland, handed about by the church officers or deacons for offerings of money, previous to the last prayers; the singing good, usually accompanied by instrumental music, and but few of the congregation joining. Everywhere there is a band of singers. The deacons and congregation very attentive in giving seats to strangers. There is never any whispering nor speaking in the church before the clergyman comes in. Few people of colour in the churches, and such of them as are there assemble in a corner separate from the rest of the people. Such of the inhabitants as do not go to church, seem to be under no restrictions. They shoot or work, or amuse themselves as they choose. We saw a house get a thorough repair on two Sundays, but this is not usual.

Saratoga Lake, about five miles from the springs, is a fine sheet of water, where there is good fishing, and where pleasure-boats can be had. There is also a fishing pond conveniently situated, only two miles from the springs, the proprietor of which, Mr. Barhyte, of German extraction, makes strangers very welcome to enjoy the sport. Although he has a considerable property, not of trifling value, we found the first time that we called in the evening to see the place, that he was at work with the necessary implements, mending his shoes. I positively at first took him for a shoemaker, but he received us so hospitably, that I soon was convinced of the mistake I had so nearly committed. Every one in this country is taught to do much more for himself than with us. I have never met an American, who, when put to it, could not use the needle well. Mr Barhyte set down cyder, and peach-brandy, and forced us to partake, before he would show us his grounds. The pond is not of great extent, but the scenery about it, though on a small scale, is sweet. It pleased Joseph Bonaparte so much, that Mr Barhyte told us, he would have been very glad to acquire it as a retired situation for himself on his annual visit to the springs; but Mr Barhyte was not inclined to sell. King Joseph got the first lesson to fish from Mr Barhyte, in which, however, he says, he is by no means a proficient.

Some other Miss Van Whangohoven or other

IRA A. BEAN

The strangeness of the Anglo-Dutch culture to the residents of New England is striking to us moderns, accustomed as we are to far greater ethnic diversity. But in the Jacksonian period, there was something other-worldly about the Hudson Valley. A letter sent home by a New Hampshire man makes this clear in his parody of Dutch names. Ira A. Bean (1797–1869) was a lawyer in

Sandwich, New Hampshire, and lived in a handsome house inherited from his wife Eliza's father. But they later went west to live in Urbana, Ohio, then returned to Sandwich; after Eliza's death, Ira Bean went west again and died in Olney, Illinois. His 1830 visit seems to have been strictly for health; he took the waters and experienced prompt relief for what may have been gout. He certainly wasn't in Saratoga for amusement, as his affectionate letter to his wife makes clear. He promised to bring her along on his next visit. But, as a first-time visitor, he set down wonderful details for his wife's enjoyment, especially the raucous welcome by stage agents.

Ira A. Bean, letter to Eliza Hoit Bean, 6 June 1830. New York State Library, Manuscripts and Special Collections. Ira Bean was identified with the assistance of Craig F. Evans, director, Sandwich Historical Society; genealogical data is found in "The Genealogy of the Moody Bean Family of Center Harbor, N.H.," by Ira A. Bean, ms., Sandwich Historical Society.

New York City June 6 1830

My Dear E

The Springs at Saratoga are situated in a wet marshy valley something in the form of a semicircle upon the Northeast of which is a bold abrupt bank covered with shrubbery, upon the southeastern side the land rises gently from the springs for many †rods and terminates in a beautiful plain. The village which is now incorporated here by the name of Saratoga Springs, is situated immediately upon the margin of this valley upon the west side and is truly a neat and beautiful village. The Main Street is straight and broad with a handsome row of trees upon each side the whole length of the village. The houses are regularly built and neat and many of them handsome. Washington Spring[77] and bathhouse are upon the west side of the street. Within two rods of the same at the south end of the village, about one rod south of the spring, is a beautiful fish pond recently and elegantly finished and furnished with plenty of trout. Around the pond there is a natural grove neatly trimmed and fenced. In the middle and almost concealed by it are two bowling allies elegantly furnished. At the westerly end of this is a club room designed for †whist parties which is said to be furnished in a splendid manner. I did not go into it. South of this room and under the same roof is an aisle about 8 feet wide leading East to the bowling alley and westward by a circular route to the highway near Washington Bathhouse. South of this aisle and under the same roof is a fruit shop designed to furnish parties of pleasure with any refreshment they need without

Washington Garden. Engraving by G. Endicott. *Endicott's Picture of Saratoga* (1843). The amusement park surrounding the Washington Spring, it was more often called the Recreative Garden.

returning to their boarding houses. In the center of this fish pond is a stand about 10 feet in diameter for the accommodation of fishermen. Congress Spring is situated a few rods further west upon a cross street between Main Street and North Street.[78] This spring is the most celebrated of any spring in the United States. The water tastes much like soda and will foam as well by mixing with acid. The next spring encountered is Hamilton Spring Bath House; next Flat Rock Spring Bath House; next High Rock; next Red Spring.[79] All you can see of High Rock Spring is the water boiling about one foot from the top of a rock three feet high with a round hole in the center into which you look to see the water which never rises any higher or sinks any lower. There are other handsome groves in the village with bowling allies similar to that first described. Some of the gardens and ornamental flower beds with the the retreats attached to them are not rivaled by anything of the kind in New England. The principal boarding houses are Congress Hall, Union Hall, Pavilion, the U.S. Hotel, Northern Hotel, Montgomery Hall (where we boarded), Columbian Hotel, Hullet's Mansion House, Congress Spring Hotel, Saddler's Tavern and Monroe's Hotel. The four first named are entirely surrounded by ornamental trees, shrubbery and evergreens. For a more particular description of this place I must refer you to Saratoga

Springs where I hope during the next season to point out to you the various beauties and amusements at the greatest watering place in the world.

But before I leave this subject I must say something of the customs here and of the miseries to which visitors are subjected here. When the stage stops at the public house, you are politely handed down into the stoop with which all the taverns are furnished and before you have time to give any directions about your baggage you are accosted by a stage agent (who by the way are all respectable looking men). I will give you the commencement of the stage man's story as near as I can in his own words, but I cannot so complacently—Are you going South Sir, will you take a seat for Albany in the Telegraph line, new splendid red coaches, 4 dapple gray horses, 2 passengers only engaged, the Miss Vanvectons, Judge Vanscoonhoven and daughter, the Miss Vanderpools, (or some other Miss Van Whangohoven or other) careful drivers go through in five hours no mistake. By this time you can get an opportunity to tell him you are not going that way and only have time to turn about when you are met by the agent of the old line and accosted as follows—will you patronize the Old Dispatch Line sir, new splendid yellow coaches, five bay horses, only 2 passengers engaged are Col. A. and Chancellor B. or the famous Miss Aster from New York City, we go by Ballstown Spa will give time to get some water from Jack Spring or the Spring lately discovered there. We have experienced drivers and go through in 6 hours, your answer is the same as before and you begin to look for your trunk when a third comes up, "going west sir, if you will take a seat in the pioneer line we will set you down at Skenectady or Caughgawaughy[80] at 6 o'clock tonight. New green coaches, 4 Arabian horses and good drivers go through every day except Sunday.[81] By this time he got a short answer, you tell you are going no where at present, this said landlord steps up and offers to show you a chamber and carry your baggage into it. Enquiry is then made whether you will have some of the Congress Water or Hamilton flat rock or high rock, and during the time you stay you will have as much attention as you wish. A porter is always in readiness and will expect

MAIL STAGE

From Saratoga Springs to Ballston.

THE subscriber has commenced running every day (Fridays and Sundays excepted) a mail stage from Saratoga Springs to Ballston, for the accommodation of passengers. The Carriage has spring seats, a razee top, and is otherwise rendered easy and convenient.

The Stage leaves Saratoga Springs, on Monday, Tuesday, Wednesday, Thursday, and Saturday, at half past 9 A. M. and arrives at Ballston at 11. Leaves Ballston same days at 4 P. M. and arrives at Saratoga Springs at 6 P. M.

Good horses are provided, and no pains will be spared to render the accommodations pleasant.

Application for seats to be made to the keepers of the Congress Hall, Union Hall, Pavilion, Columbian Hotel, Congress Spring Hotel, or Saddler's Inn, Saratoga Springs; and at the Village Hotel, M'Bain's, Clark's, or Cook's Inn, Ballston-Spa.

Asa How.

July 20, 1819. 9tf

N. B. A Stage will leave Saratoga Springs, every Friday, at 6 A. M. for Sandy *Hill*, and return the same day, at 5 P. M. Passengers can apply as above.

Mail Stage. *Saratoga Sentinel*, 30 September 1828.

his fee when you leave. Our Landlord and lady were very pleasant and genteel people, no children. Kept a niece there who played the piano fort for the amusement of the boarders, they kept a good house remarkable for neatness throughout.

I drank fully of Congress Water and bathed twice in a warm bath at Hamilton Spring and after the first day I was so weake I could hardly go about the street. I came near fainting when I first went into the Bath but in minute it threw into a profuse perspiration which lasted the remainder of the day and altogether has helped me very much. I could not have believed that so great a change could have been wrought in so short a time. I now wear two boots since yesterday and I often forget to take my cane and my health is improved miraculously upon the whole I should enjoy my touring very much if Eliza went along with me and I am now determined to have it so next time and I think I should hardly treat her as I saw a beautiful young lady treated a few days since, while at Saratoga as I was standing in the door of my boarding house I saw an old man about 55 walking down Street in company with a genteel looking young lady which I first took to be his daughter. They were both well dressed and the lady was called beautiful by those who had seen her. As they came near I thought she was his wife. They went down to the Spring together. Sometimes she would get his arm at other times she had to follow as well as she could. He appeared to pay no attention to her.—and found that she was a rich Ohio—that she was his wife and about 24 been married 2 yrs that her father had been rich but failed in business about a year before her marriage. She was well educated it seems and very much esteemed and that she was induced to marry this old man by his wealth. He was then a widower. I also learned that he was about to send her out 60 miles in the stage next morning to stay a week at a public house while he staid there and amused himself. Thinks I to myself young lady you pay dear for the †whistle called cash and you may keep it, give me a companion who is willing to stay where I stay and who never enjoys the amusements of this life more than when I am present and thinks it a privilege to have me attend her at home or abroad. Only think a beautiful intelligent young lady of 20 united to an old lame intemperate odious looking man of 60. Those who have this choice from all the world may well rejoice that they have been so fortunate in a matter of so much consequence and this will generally be the case if they act by their impulse of their judgment—

Ira A. Bean

I rode into Saratoga Springs on a wagon load of furniture
EDMUND JAMES HULING

Late in life, Edmund J. Huling (1820–1891) was "the veteran newspaper man of Saratoga County." Born on a farm at North Milton, about five miles west of Saratoga Springs, he moved with his parents to Federal Street in 1831. In 1882, he set down his recollections of the village as it was when he arrived, publishing the account in a village directory he issued. The full document is an important one and makes interesting reading; an extract follows.

At the age of 14, Huling became a clerk in Rockwell Putnam's store where he spent three years; he spent the summer of 1838 as a clerk in Union Hall, the predecessor of the Grand Union Hotel. In the following year he joined the staff of the Saratoga Whig. *He was a newspaperman for the rest of his life, although from 1842 to 1851 he also operated a drugstore. He was editor or publisher of a series of newspapers, notably the* Saratoga Sentinel *(1872–1886), and he was also a correspondent for Troy and New York papers and for the Associated Press.*

Huling took a truculent tone in his editorials, often attacking the editor of The Saratogian, *a hostility based in part on the latter's Baptist faith. Huling was raised in the Universalist Church, then still considered a Christian denomination though liberal in comparison to others of its time. In later life he was a rabid Spiritualist and a member of Saratoga Springs' First Society of Spiritualists.*

Edmund J. Huling, "Saratoga in 1831, a Chapter of Personal Reminiscences," in *Huling's Directory of Saratoga Springs, 1882–83* (Saratoga Springs: Huling and Company, 1882), 17–34. Biography is found in obituaries from the *Saratoga Sun*, 12 February 1891, the *Saratoga Union*, 9 February 1891, and other news clippings pasted in a small scrapbook, xerox copies of which are in the Huling file, Saratoga Room, Saratoga Springs Public Library.

ON TUESDAY, March 29, 1831, the writer of this, then a lad of ten years old, rode into Saratoga Springs on a wagon load of furniture, from the farm near the stone church in the adjoining town of Milton (where he was born), and became a resident of the place. The season was an early one, and the weather pleasant and almost summery as the family stopped at the house on Federal street, purchased by my father of the Rev. John Freeman[82], standing on a lot a portion of which is now included in the grounds of the Grand Union hotel. I had been an occasional visitor in the village in former years, attending meetings at the Universalist meeting house on Church street[83], still standing (occupied by Dennis Hayes, grocer); also coming sometimes on trading visits here with my parents. Ballston Spa was yet, however, the principal business center of the county and I had more of an acquaintance there than at this place before coming here to live.

Having assisted in unloading and storing the household goods I started out to the main street (laid down on the early maps as "Broad street," now known as Broadway), and I well remember the appearance of some of the places of business. Saratoga then had but four streets in the corporation bounds running north and south, viz, Broad street, (then ending on the north at Rock street,) Putnam-Front street, running as now, from Congress to the north part of the upper village, Matilda street, running from Division to Church street, and Federal street, connecting Congress and Washington streets; (what is now known as Nelson street was then altogether out of the village, being a somewhat narrow country road, with fields on both sides, cultivated for farming purposes.) The streets running east and west were Congress street, then as now, extending both sides of Broadway; Washington, extending from Broadway west to little Beekman street, beyond the Continental hotel; Division street, from Broadway to Matilda street; Church street, from Broadway west as now; Van Dam street, crossing Broadway as at present, and Rock street. On the east side of Broadway were Geneva street, from Front street to the ten springs; Grove street as at present, connecting Broadway and Front street; Lake avenue as at present; Caroline street stopped at Front street, all being swamp between Front street and the sand bank, where is now Circular street; Bath street, north of Congress Hall, from Broadway to Putnam street. On the east side of Putnam street, where Phila street now runs, A.A. Kellogg had a brick yard.

The whole town, according to the census of 1830, had only 2,204 inhabitants.

The springs which were tubed and in use in 1831 were the Congress, Columbian, Washington, Hamilton, President, Monroe, Flat Rock, High Rock, and Red, in the village, and the Ten Springs in the field about where the Excelsior is now, also the Ellis[84], at the mill.

The Congress spring, owned by Lynch & Clarke, stood as now on the south side of Congress street, but the surroundings were altogether different. There was a substantial platform with a frame about it with rafters which were covered with an awning in hot days in summer, being removed on rainy days. Four dipper boys were on duty every morning, and after breakfast two of the boys brought bottles across the street from the bottling house in racks to be filled, returning the same filled. One boy sat on a stool with two tin fillers into one of which he put an empty bottle and dropped it into the spring, pulling up as he dropped one filler in the other with a bottle of water. Ashbel H. Andrews stood to take the bottle and pound in the cork as the bottle was drawn up. The fourth boy fitted corks into the empty bottles and waited on chance callers for water. The office, being nearly the same as at present, was in charge of Russell C. Carpenter, and Cephas Parker superintended the packing and boxing of the water, which was carried off in every direction by teams. The grounds now so tastefully laid out inside of the hills surrounding Congress Spring park were then a swamp where cows sometimes pastured in dry seasons and were mired if they strayed in wet seasons.

The High Rock stood as now in the valley at the foot of the high stairs descending from Front street, a few †rods from it was a building for the use of a woman who had charge of it in the visiting season and sold candies and lemonade. It was owned by Dr. John Clarke. It was more visited from curiosity than from any other cause.

A few words here in regard to the freight business of the place before the day of railroads may be appropriate. The principal portion of freighting was done by three men, each owning a span of horses and lumber wagon: Jacob Reed, living on Congress street, Rufus Carryl, a man with a wooden leg, and Samuel Rakins, a colored man. These men made frequent trips in the spring and fall to Troy (where all the merchants had their goods brought by sloop from New York) taking down loads of Congress water and bringing up goods for the merchants, delivering the same at the uniform rate of twenty-five cents per hundred pounds. Occasionally these men would bring up some fresh fish or clams on their own account for sale. In the fall of the year farmers going to Troy with grain or pork would canvass the merchants here to secure loads on their return. Several men made a business of purchasing Congress water in bottles at the spring and peddling it about the country.

These were the days of stage coaching almost exclusively for public travel by land. Lines of four horse coaches ran daily in the visiting season from Albany to Saratoga, also from Whitehall, and I think a third line ran from Bennington and the east. The great northern mail from New York city to Montreal was carried by a line of stages which went up the turnpike through Schuylerville. Loomis & Wilkins, I think, were the proprietors of the line south to Albany, and as near as I can remember Baker & Walbridge, or Reed & Baker, had to do with the line north.

The Saratoga and Schenectady railroad had been chartered in February 1831, and being only the second one in the state (the Mohawk and Hudson, from Albany to Schenectady being just opened), there was much speculation regarding its operation. The hardware store of W.A. Langworthy was one of the places for gossippers to meet, and it was concluded there that a large circular track would have to be built to turn the cars upon. Ground was broken with considerable ceremony for this road August 19, 1831, by Churchill C. Cambreling, president of the road, a leading merchant of New York. There was a great assemblage of people to witness the ceremony, and a collation was served on the field. I may here remark that the road was opened for travel in 1832, except a portion running through Ballston Spa, which was not completed until the year following. The cars were run entirely by horsepower, and travelers were carried by stages from the Blue mill in Ballston to where is now the station. The cars were built after the English fashion in three compartments, holding six or eight persons each or eighteen to twenty-four in a car. Two horses driven tandem drew two cars, the baggage being carried on top of the cars. The conductor went on the outside around a foot board to collect the tickets. The ticket office in 1832 was in a rough shanty and the waiting room was only a shed, on Washington street, about where the railroad now crosses.

There was a custom of what is called "house room boarding" then much in vogue; country folks from the north and east would come bringing some bedding and perhaps some provisions also, and pay one shilling per day for each person for a room in which to sleep, with a privilege of doing the cooking at the family fire. I have seen some quite large parties thus cared for by residents on the streets outside Broadway.

Mechanics wages in those days were $1 per day with board or $1.25 to $1.50[85] without board. Common laborers received fifty cents with board or seventy-five cents without. John Balcom, who kept a mechanics' boarding house on Front street, charged $1.75 per week. Salt pork and potatoes were generally served at these houses twice or three times per day.

In writing the foregoing I have had to depend almost entirely upon recollection, as I have had no documents or papers for reference, and there are very few people yet living here who could aid me, except by close questioning regarding particular facts.

Delightful in summer to be between air and water

WASHINGTON IRVING

It is happy chance that two of the travelers who recorded their experience with the new railroad in the summer of 1832 were distinguished men of letters. Philip Hone (1780–1851), New York City's greatest diarist, wrote "This is a pleasant mode of traveling, not very rapid but free from fatigue or inconvenience of any kind."[86] *A less formal journal was kept by Washington Irving (1783–1859). Irving's telegraphic text is interesting primarily because of its author's prominence and for certain touches of colorful perspective.*

Sue Fields Ross, ed., *Washington Irving's Journals and Notebooks 1832-1859: The Complete Works of Washington Irving* (Boston: Twayne Publishers, 1986), 5: 7–10. Copyright 1986 by Twayne Publishers. Reprinted by permission of The Gale Group. In the short section presented here, Irving's own deletions are shown struck through, while superscript insertions have been brought down to the line.

SATURDAY, AUG 4 at ~~8~~ 9 oclock. Albany half deserted on a/c of the cholera.[87] ~~Dinner~~ meet Mr Marcey (Senator) &c—Dine at Gills—leave in rail road line ~~½ past~~ 3 oclock. at 7 arrive at Saratoga & put up at Congress Hall where I find Chas Graham—Maxwell—Mr Cutting & family—Mr Greenway & &c— ~~meet~~

Sunday, August 5 Meet with Latrobe & Pourtales[88]—In the afternoon drive to Saratoga lake [—] fish—

Monday, August 6 at ½ past 6. Set off with Latrobe & Pourtales for Saratoga lake Breakfast at Williams—. ~~Wo~~[?] ~~Broi~~[?] Perch—Pickerell. Broiled wood-duck &c embark on the lake with Latrobe—attended by "David" a boatman & Alonzo Stickney, a boy—catch perch & Bullhead[?] & pickerel—pleasant air—awning[?] to boat[?] ~~it~~[?] delightful in summer to be thus between sky and water—Sound of wood cutter axe—King fisher—with his ~~ha~~ plunging & swaying[?] flight wood duck—. Locust his sultry note like spinning—crow barking.

~~Mid day~~ —noon—Horns sounding from distant farm house for dinner Skiff shooting across the lake—light blue ~~tint~~ airy tint of distant *islands* & promontories—Silver waves with dark ripples †laving the sandy shore—pond lilies— ~~*illegible*~~ Marsh long blades[?] of water winds[?] with diamond drops— ~~fa~~[?]

Luke Moore[89] who ~~lives in~~ fishes & shoots about the lake & makes 20 to 30 $ per month—Sells fish at Saratoga—at present employed by Williams—about 40 years of age. Has small ~~*illegible*~~ house on little river that runs into lake—wife, cow & potato patch. Knows all the deep holes and fishing places—what places what streams—what creeks & bait to choose—

After dinner meet a Scotchman and an Englishman—The former claims cousinship with Campbell

On the way homeward stop at old [Barhydts]—a mill wright who fixed himself 2 miles from the springs 35 years since—His millpond abounds with trout & trees[?] ~~to~~ became a source of wealth bringing company to his farm[?]. He is of dutch or flemish extraction—His wife of German—her parents from Hamburgh. She speaks a little German & reads more[?]. Has an old German bible & prayer book—[Barhydt] tall, thin white headed. ~~*illegible*~~ His farm 200 acres—60 cleared—but does not consider himself a farmer. Independent—sometimes cross—though to us very civil. His wife a decent matronly old woman seated with spectacles—mendg stockings. Their house in the forest—tall primitive pines & oaks about it deep dark mill pools—view in one direction of distant mountains—Joseph Bonapart wanted to buy the land of old [Barhydt] but the old man asked too high.

A motley crowd of women and men of all degrees

CHARLES JOSEPH LATROBE

Englishman Charles J. Latrobe (1801–1875) was Irving's traveling companion at Saratoga. Latrobe journeyed through the United States and Mexico in 1832 and 1833, visiting Saratoga Springs in both summers. In his rather

formal travel book he records his impressions of the spa, perceptive, critical, but not hostile in the manner of some of his countryman.

Charles J. Latrobe, *The Rambler in North America, 1832–33* (New York: Harper and Brothers, 1835), 2: 98–100.

THE NUMBER of well-dressed idlers compressed within the bounds of the little village was computed upon the year of our second visit to amount to upwards of three thousand,—a motley crowd of men and women of all degrees;—patricians, plebeians, first-rates, second-rates, third-rates: gentlemen whose manners savoured of the good old school, and others whose manners indicated their being copied from some new school, or—no school at all: legislators, travellers, others of literary name; men with name but little money; others who had money and no name;—citizens and families from every State in the Union—beaux and belles—the belles of this year, of last year, and the belles of the year to come; hosts of cheerful pretty faces of the softer sex, and hordes of young aspirants to their good graces, rioting in the fair sunshine of the morning of life; with a very partial sprinkling of responsible matrons, and irresponsible old gentlemen, to keep them in order. As to the real votaries of the nymphs of the crystal fountains, (for the Springs are many,) they were as usual comparatively few in number; though hundreds of both sexes would rise at early dawn, and, enveloped in shawls and surtouts, glance through the colonnades—trip down to the principal fountain of Congress Spring,—take a sparkling draught, and then return to dress for breakfast; yet save a few regular †old stagers, who might be seen with pale †dyspeptic faces, with their collars pulled up over their ears, pacing backwards and forwards on the little enclosure by the spring, alternately sipping and marching till they had imbibed the prescribed quantity—and a number of invalids of the softer sex, who I was informed drank with the same steady purpose in their small chambers,—but few indications of suffering were visible, and Saratoga was a scene of as perfect freedom from worldly woe and care as you can conceive. I would not however deny that it appeared as though there was a considerable hollowness in much of this gaiety, for the dust and the heat, and the ennui, and the yawning which pervaded the reign of pleasure and fashion,—not to speak of the squeezing and the elbowing at meal-times,—was far from being agreeable; and though I believe many, if not most of the young people esteemed Saratoga a paradise of delights, yet among those whose halcyon days had passed, there were a good number of faces whose expression was evidently that of "smiling at grief."

The public accommodations for the visitors at the Springs are certainly on a splendid scale, the private do not correspond. As not unusual in the dispositions of hotels, even in the most civilized parts of the Union, every thing is sacrificed to the accommodation of the mass. Thus the drawing and dining-rooms, the spacious and elegant piazzas are strikingly commodious, but the bed-chambers are confined, ill-furnished, and inconvenient; and as to private sitting-rooms, it would be unreasonable to expect them. There are four large and as many small hotels or boarding houses, if I recollect right;—all tasteful buildings built of clapboard or brick, surrounded by trees and shrubberies, and most, if not all, having piazzas of tasteful proportions attached to them. That in front of our hotel, Congress Hall, was two hundred feet long, and twenty wide, with a very elevated roof, supported by seventeen trees, wrought into columns and garlanded with creepers. The house accommodated probably in one way or another four hundred boarders.

They take a glass every other day
CARL DAVID ARFWEDSON

When the railroad gave easy access to Saratoga Springs in the summer of 1832, a flood of visitors descended on the spa. Europeans, of course, were not often dissuaded from the journey up the Hudson, having already crossed the ocean by sailing vessel. Among them was a Swede, Carl David Arfwedson (1806–1881). A member of a well-known and wealthy family of shipowners and merchants, he traveled a great deal. In 1834, he published a literary account of his travels in America, containing many of the usual comments, but with sparkling characterization of the "types" he met at the springs. A businessman as well as author, he served as the American consul in Stockholm from 1838 to 1855 and, after his father's death, headed the family firm until it was dissolved. He died in Wiesbaden, Germany.

Carl David Arfwedson, *The United States and Canada in 1832, 1833 and 1834,* 2 vols. (London: R. Bentley, 1834), 2: 268–276. Biography is found in *Svenska Män och*

Kvinnor: Biografisk Uppslagsbok (Stockholm: Albert Bonniers, 1942), 1: 126, located through the courtesy of Virginia Laursen of Det Kongelige Bibliotek.

I MOVED at once from one coach to another, and set off on the just-finished railroad to Saratoga. The country through which it passes consists almost exclusively of sand, which renders this trip less pleasant and varied than the former; but, although five miles longer than that from Albany to Schenectady, it cost the company less than the other. According to statements shown to me, the Mohawk and Hudson railroad is said to have cost not less than from eight to nine hundred thousand dollars; whereas, that to Saratoga was completed at an expence not exceeding two hundred and seventy thousand dollars. The shares of the former were, nevertheless, lower than those of the latter. In the course of the three summer months, June, July, and August, no fewer than thirty thousand five hundred and sixty-five persons travelled on the railroad between Saratoga and Schenectady.

At these watering places there are several hotels, whose charges vary according to the prevalence of fashion and the class of visiters. Hence arises a certain distance between the guests, who seldom associate except with boarders living in the same hotel. Here, more than elsewhere, may be discovered the distinction that really prevails among persons of different classes in America. I heard, for instance, on various occasions, individuals, boarding at the fashionable Congress Hall, speak of those who had taken up their quarters at the Union, or United States Hotel, in a way which clearly indicated their own presumed superiority in point of rank. This aristocratic tendency in Republican States may be condemned or not; certain it is, that exorbitant prices, combined with a ridiculous extravagance in dress, have jointly succeeded in causing Congress Hall hotel to be frequented by the first company in the Union. In the month of August, in particular, people resort to it from the South and from the North; all who can lay claim to beauty, genius, and talents, are to be found here. They do

Saratoga & Schenectady Rail Road,
1839.

On and after Monday, April first, and until further notice, there will be TWO daily departures and arrivals by STEAM-POWER. Viz.

Leave Saratoga Springs at 7 1-2 o'clock A. M.
" " 4 1-2 " " P. M.
Leave Albany at 9 1-2 o'clock A. M.
" " 2 1-2 " P. M.

N. B. The same coaches, baggage and freight cars, will be run through the whole distance, without any *change or detention* at Schenectady.

☞ There are daily lines of stages in connection with the Rail Road, between Saratoga Springs and Whitehall, on Lake Champlain. Passengers going north, should take the morning train from Albany.

A stage will start from Saratoga Springs daily at 5 o'clock A. M. to convey passengers to Whitehall in time to take the Champlain steamboat the same day. Travellers to the eastwart, by selecting this line, will arrive at Rutland, Vt., early in the evening.

All baggage positively at the risk of the owner thereof.

JOHN COSTIGAN, *Superintendent.*
April 26th, 1839.

Rail Road Cars. *Saratoga Sentinel,* 11 June 1839.

not repair hither for the sake of health—far from it. Their sparkling eyes and smiling faces prove that they do not labour under great infirmity. Those who, unfortunately, are real invalids, take up their residence at more quiet hotels, seldom mingling with those who are in possession of good health. Most of the individuals here met with say that "they come to drink the water," that is, to "take a glass every other day." Their particular object is amusement, and to kill time in every possible way. When such visiters arrive at a watering place, extravagance, as a matter of course, reaches its climax, and they try to surpass each other in expenditure.

The fair sex have here a fine opportunity of displaying their taste and elegance in dress. I shall not venture to †advert to the studied cut of the coats and waistcoats of the beaux, fashioned as they are after the last patterns from London or Paris. The most fashionable ladies have a peculiar dress, adapted for the process of drinking the water, a kind of *demi-†négligé*, another for the ceremony of breakfast, a third for the recreation of riding or driving, a fourth for display at dinner, and a fifth and last for exhibition at a concert or ball in the evening, which concludes the day. Health appears to be the last consideration. On rising in the morning, the prevailing rule is to devote the whole day to eating, sleeping, and the display of dress; and when evening, or rather midnight, arrives, they retire to rest, satisfied with having got over an agreeable *soirée*—young ladies dreaming of the conquests they fancy they have made, and which they calculate will be followed up by a matrimonial alliance in the ensuing winter; young dandies, again, delighted with the figure they have made, and some chance witticisms which they have uttered, and which have been graciously and smilingly received by the belles.

But, before we bid adieu to Saratoga, let us once more visit the springs, and take a review of those who drink the "wholesome waters." Who is that handsome lady, who, with rosy cheeks, approaches the iron railing near the spring, and with a feeble voice asks the little boy standing inside for a glass of water? She is from New York, having visited Saratoga four successive years, to get cured of an inward disease which no person can define, and which, strange enough, every year shows itself in different forms and symptoms. What extraordinary and beneficial effect the water has upon her! In the fall, she resumes all the frivolities and pleasures of the city, dancing and happy; for she has already given her heart to a swain, who has promised, before the end of winter, to offer her his hand. Not far from her stands a man in the prime of life, with a goblet to his mouth; he is pale, but it is not a sickly paleness; he is silent, but it is not suffering that imposes this silence. With what delight does he drink the brackish water! with what devotion does he empty the last drop! He appears almost to bless the water, that gift of Heaven, and at last takes his departure to a neighbouring field, the resort of cattle and musquitoes, to ruminate and philosophize. He is one of the "cold, watery, fish-blooded young men, incapable of a glass or two,"[90] who, foolishly enough, either from want of means, or in consequence of a debilitated constitution, has joined an excellent society, which drinks nothing but water, and wages war against wine and brandy. How he enjoys it, poor fellow, this ice-cold, clear, and medicinal beverage! It is an instructive lesson to contemplate his contented face. Are his philosophical ravings equally instructive? Know that the individual is a genius, who has written many romances, which have been printed and admired by contemporary authors.

This bustling, noisy, and talkative man, who makes wry faces at every drop he seems to force down—who is he? Philadelphia is his birthplace, and in New York he has received the rudiments of his education—a perfect fool! None is a better judge of a bad tragedy, or a vapid novel; and none can excel him in the knowledge of the history, qualities, and fortune, of every lady. He pretends to labour under some serious infirmity, and tells every young lady, smilingly, that his disease consists in continual heartaches, in an enlargement of the heart. He says that he has only one enemy in the world, which is morning, always coming too early, and on which, before rising from bed, he invariably bestows a certain quantity of invectives. That the waters have very little effect on his constitution is not matter of surprise, as he never takes more than one glass immediately after a hearty breakfast. He complains of being poorly.

But who is that original, who, despising water, always appears with a glass of julep, swearing at every thing, so as to frighten the old ladies? Born in the South, he has from infancy been accustomed to be attended by slaves, and forgets himself every moment, thinking that all the free and independent servants in the house are slaves, who ought to understand and obey his commands at the first signal. His dress is composed of summer trousers, in size resembling those of a Turk, and a jacket of the same stuff, the sleeves of which are regular bishop's sleeves. With a face covered with hair, he stares at the company, to the no small terror and annoyance of the ladies. A stick, cut out of an orange tree, and called the snake-killer, is likewise an object of such terror, that none of the fair sex dared approach him. He was, however, constantly surrounded by men, who discussed the favourite subject, "Nullification."[91] Alone, he advocated the cause of South Carolina, with a warmth which compelled many of his opponents to give way, leaving the field to the champion of the South. But whither am I wandering? A volume would hardly suffice to depict the different characters I had occasion to observe during a residence of a few days at Saratoga: but this is not my intention; therefore, peace be with them for the present!

Couldn't compare them to anything but snowbirds hopping about

CHARLES D. GRIFFIN

Charles D. Griffin (1811–1887) was 22 years old, high-spirited and witty, when he left his home in Stamford, Delaware County, to visit Saratoga Springs in the spring of 1833. His account is filled with humorous descriptions such as the one of his stagecoach ride over the western Catskills with which he began. Even better is his detailed account of taking a shower bath. Traveling as he did in the spring of 1833, he took the horse-drawn railroad prior to its conversion to steam power.

At the time of his trip, he was already keeping a store across from the Delaware House in Stamford; he continued in business, becoming postmaster as well, until 1858, when he quit to become a farmer. He served in the militia, as school inspector, village trustee, railroad commissioner, and as president of the Stamford Fire Insurance Company. About 1880 he wrote a history of his town that was printed at the Stamford Mirror *and was put on the train to go to a city bindery, but the train was wrecked and the pages were scattered along the railroad. Some were saved and placed in the* Mirror *attic where they remained until 1950, when a copy was given to the library. The history was finally published in 1988. But his delightful diary of his trip to the spa remained unpublished until now.*

Charles D. Griffin, diary. Collection of the Stamford Village Historian; a typescript prepared by Alice Willis McCauley is in The Saratoga Room, Saratoga Springs Public Library. The quotations are taken from the typescript. Biography is found at the front of Charles D. Griffin, *A History of Stamford* (Stamford: Stamford Historical Society, 1988), and in *History of Delaware County* (New York: W W Munsell, 1880), 304–305.

TOOK PASSAGE for Saratoga Springs in A. Watkins line of coaches at the head of the Delaware[92], May 8th 1833. The first coach was an elegant one, built I concluded for the service of some lumberman, probably since the french revolution, or perhaps during the American revolution for a baggage waggon—made of good timber with a tongue and four wheels with a twelve-foot square box, eighteen inches high which contained two spring seats built for durability with springs somewhat less than foot square, likely made so on purpose so as not endanger the passengers being thrown out of the coach in travelling over rough pieces by its springiness. The coach was built in a fashionable style without top to the annoyance of the passengers heads, hats and bonnets, a convenience well thought of especially in foul and rainy weather. It was drawn by a numerous retinue of horses, the whole number before it at once being composed of two, well oated so that their tongues hung out a foot in consequence of eating too many and their ribs stuck out a †rod—a bad remedy for speed because it made them puff so going up hill.

After a very agreeable ride over Chimborazo, Volpichinca, the rocky mountains and the ravines of the Alps and Appenines we arrived at Patchens[93] Schoharie Co.

[After more rough travel, Griffin arrived at Albany, took the railroad to Schenectady and changed trains for Saratoga Springs.]

The wirks are covered or housed and built very strong. The cars are drawn by horses on the railroad from Schenectady to Saratoga. They go at good speed and it is pleasant riding. They are drawn by two horses one placed before the other. Sometimes only one car goes from Schenectady to Saratoga which is sufficiently large to accommodate twenty four passengers.

Took a walk down to Congress spring to see the folks as they flocked in after water after the rain. Didn't know but I might see Leal there. Got well paid for going by just seeing a couple of [?folks] come and drink. Enquired some about 'em if they lived in the village and found out they didn't. Were a couple boarders just come in. Don't know where they come from but couldn't think they belonged anywhere in this country. Never see anybody act so before. They'd get a glass of water then run off two or three †rods to drink it—would take a swallow or two then hop about and turn around and take another and give a kind of scratch with their feet and kept working till they made out to get down two glasses apiece when they pulled off a little ways where they stood viewing. They'd hop up on a log then down again, and cut up all manner of capers that I never see before. Couldn't compare them to anything but snowbirds hopping about and scratching. One of 'em was quite a heavy man and had a belly that looked just as mine would with the top of a haystack set on it with the peak out. Never see such a belly before—thought it was no wonder he acted as he did cause he looked so. The other looked as much like a choked mouse with corsets on as anything, and I thought he walked a good deal as Jackson danced when he first begun to get under motion. And I tell you he felt three times as big as anybody I ever see before. But I never see modesty dashed out of countenance before then.

There was a gentleman and two ladies come to the springs, the gentleman and one lady were middle aged people and the other was quite a young modest thing. I took a considerable notice of her before she got to the spring. She had her clothes made pretty short and as she came down towards the spring I could see about half way up to her knees. She took mighty short cut up steps and looked just as though she was walking on stilts. She was most terribly bothered to get along. She tried to tip off on her toes but she had pumps on and once and awhile she would make a misstep and put her heel down before her toe and it troubled her very much, but finally she got to the spring.

The boy at the spring dipped up some water and handed them and the girl and all began to drink. I happened to sit about a rod in front of her taking observations. I thought I'd see how she made out getting down the water for I reckoned it must hurt her, if it troubled her as much as it did to walk. She had taken about three or four swallows and was getting along very well, when a sense of modesty come over her and she raised her eyes to see if anybody was looking at her when behold I was looking right in her mouth. What an awful thing it was to have a gentleman see her drink. She cut it off quick—took very small swallows then and nipped and tucked and puffed until she made out to get down about half a glass when she walked to the outside of the platform and threw it out of the glass. Then thought I that modesty was worse than the †gravel, and if it hurt her to make water as bad as it did to drink it she must be in extreme pain.

Dipper boy at Congress Spring. Stereoscope view. Robert Joki Collection.

I thought I had got very well paid for my walk and went up to Washington Spring the one I drank of and then to my board.

Monday, May 13th. The weather being pretty warm concluded I'd be showered.

Went to the door and didn't see anybody but a couple of gals in the house, and told one of 'em I wanted to be showered. And by golly she took me into the bath house pretty quick. Hadn't never been showered and thinks I, darn her, maybe she's going to shower me a new way, but I plucked up courage and followed on after her. She led me into a dark room in the centre of the house with one dark window in it between that and another room and said that was the spot, and she staid there yet, and thinks I by thunder if I must I must, so I off with my cloak quicker and threw it down into a chair and begun to strip, and sais she, perhaps you'd better lay your cloak in a chair in the other room, so I carried my cloak into the other room and went back and then she cleared, so I got her off better than I expected.

I begun to undress and she begun to carry water upstairs and pour it into something overhead; I got my clothes all off and I looked and see a paper stuck up on the wall with some writing on it. I stepped up to it and read as follows: when you want a shower just step in the box and pull the wire, so I jumped into the box and gave the wire a twitch and O havens and arth how I jumped! I sithed, I winked, I catched for breath, I shook all over, and I thought sartinly I should die and I guess I should if it hadn't stopped just as it did, for I was just a going too and it stopped right off short all at once.

Then I begun to wipe the water out of my face and eyes and catch once and awhile a breath or two, and after I got so I could see I looked up to see if there was any more coming but didn't see any and was glad enough for that too. Thought I had seen it shower pretty hard before but never got caught in such a shower as that was. However I survived it and put on my clothes and went out and †axed the gal what was to pay and she said eight cents so I paid her and come off and begun to feel warm and nice.

Wednesday, May 15th. After tea Barber and I took a walk down through the village to high rock spring. As we came back we called into the store where the post office is kept to get a letter for Miss Miller. The store contained a large assortment of goods, and we had been there but a few minutes before in came two women to trade who lived some miles out of the village. They called for such articles as they wanted, and the gentleman in the store flushed with the idea of getting a handful of money pulled down and unfolded, praised, argued, examined, and reasoned with them, when all at once they wheeled, spread sails and floated away without even purchasing so much as a box of snuff. As they turned from the counter, he cocked up his nose and tried to whistle, but vexation overruled musical taste and he puckered his mouth back again and went to replacing his goods. I couldn't help laughing at his vexation and disappointment and the sarcastic look he gave as they departed as a token of his thanks to them for their call. Then thought I to myself, that women were women, and †eytooth skinners at Saratoga as well as in my section.

Thursday, May 16th. After dinner I started down through the village as far as Mr. Spauldings cabinet shop[94] about half a mile. Staid there a spell and came up back as far as Washington Street and turned up that and wend down the railroad into the village again and waited there till the cars came in from Schenectady which was about three o'clock with about thirty passengers, but nobody that I knew. The gentleman that oversees them told me that the day before thirteen cars left Albany for Schenectady at one time all filled with passengers, that ten of the cars were drawn by the steam engine and three by horses. The cars leave Albany four times a day. There were some real †tippers came in the cars, there was no mistake in 'em.

Take 2 or 3 tumblers full before breakfast

ANONYMOUS CORRESPONDENT, DATE UNKNOWN

A celebrated beauty, Eliza Pintard was the wife of John Pintard (1759–1844), a New York merchant who made a great fortune before becoming bankrupt in 1792. He never recovered fully, but he remained a prominent citizen, as demonstrated by his role as a founder of The New-York Historical Society in 1804. In the undated letter that follows, Mrs. Pintard was advised on the correct procedure for drinking and bathing at Saratoga.

Letter, [? W L] to Mrs. John Pintard. Pintard Papers, Box 11, Folder 6, The New-York Historical Society. Transcribed by Field Horne.

Dear Madam

THERE ARE two kinds of waters more especially used as the Springs at Saratoga. The Congress water—and that of the flat Rock. Both these waters are exciting and induce congestion unless the system is first made freely open. In your case the better plan is to take a little epsom and magnesia— or the common rhubarb and magnesia mixture, which you have occasionally done— or to take salts and occasionally a couple of the pills, night and morning— These pills will induce the state you desire— If not by the above number you must take more.

After you have unlocked the system a day or so then you begin with the Congress water which is generally taken at the font early in the morning— But a better way is to have it draw off over night and let it stand in your room bottled— In the morning take 2 or 3 tumblers full before breakfast— this is not too much and if it should be a little difficult then make 2 answer for a morning or so. afterwards take 3— So go on— taking breakfast shortly after—some two hours after breakfast take a couple of tumblers at the Well. It is more sparkling and more exciting but will well do.—These waters do not oppress unless the bowels are confined or torpid—

So go on daily—never take the waters in the afternoon—unless save a glass in walking about the well—

The flat rock waters—these are to be taken when you have been some little while at the Springs—and when the system is free of all irritations—as they are more sparkling—and more †tonic.—But after all they are only taken occasionally—

The same remarks apply to the waters at ~~Saratoga~~ Ballston. They must never be taken unless the system is open—and free of all irritations of the lungs, liver &c.—They are †chalybeate—and will do to take in cases of great exhaustion free of pain—and after the waters of Saratoga have depleted the system—

One or two tumblers at a time—

As to bathing—you if desirous of bathing can so do at the Springs—having the temperature regulated at a moderate rate say about 90—But I would not advise the *cold shower bath*—the shock would do you no good

Most resp[? W L]

A glass door opens into a handsomely decorated garden

MARGARET MILLER DAVIDSON

Margaret Miller Davidson (1823–1838) was only 10 years old when she used a little marbled notebook to keep a travel diary of her journey from her Plattsburgh home to New York City. Its lines give an indication of her precocious talent; she began writing poetry at the age of eight, and when she died, she left more than 200 pages of poetry, some of which was edited for publication by Washington Irving three years later. Young Margaret Davidson, dead of tuberculosis at 15, was one of the best-known poets in America.

Margaret Miller Davidson, travel diary. Rutgers University Library. Transcribed by Field Horne. It was published as "Sentimental Journey," ed. by Walter R. Harding, in *Rutgers University Library Journal* 13 (1949): 19–24, which also contains a brief biography. For her poems, see Washington Irving, *Biography and Poetical Remains of the Late Margaret Miller Davidson* (Philadelphia: Lea and Blanchard, 1841).

WE ARRIVED at the Springs at about 8 o'Clock in the evening, after having enjoyed in the highest degree the beautiful and varied scenes which presented themselves to the eye, mountain riseing above mountain plain succeeding plain and all not in my opinion to be equaled except in sailing from Albany to Newyork on the north River—my dear Mother was taken from the Coach nearly fainting with fatigue and debility—our first care was [to] procure a quiet room and refreshment for [her], and after a good nights rest she awoke much recruited in strength and spirits—

June 7th. My mother is unable to go down—I went down to breakfast with my father, and after the ceremonies of that repast were over, I had an opportunity of examining and making my observations on this stately edifice—Union Hall is kept by a Mr. Putnam a descendant of old Genl Putnam[95]—a large piazza in front, ornamented with Shrubbery gives it quite a rural appearance, the entrance is into a spacious Hall which opens with folding doors into a Splendid Saloon which is ornamented with elegant paintings—in the centre is suspended a large lamp which when lighted gives it a most brilliant appearance, a centre table contains various implements of amusement, and exercise for the entertainment of the votaries of pleasure, who constantly flock to this place; two pair of folding doors opens from the Saloon, one pair admits you to the drawing, the other to the dining room—the former is a very elegant apartment splendidly furnished, the walls are ornamented with beautiful engravings representing various scenes in *Ivanhoe*[96]—one representing the young hero as offering himself as a Champion to the suffering Rebecca; the lady Rowena crowning the magnanimous Ivanhoe with the dear bought wreath of victory, Rebecca in the prison, and others, equally interesting—a sofa stands on one side the door, a piano, on the other, on the East Side of the room—a glass door, opens into a handsomely decorated garden Lichens, pinks, lillies, geraneums, and other choice flowers tastefully arranged in rich profusion ornament the Spot, on the mantle piece stands a flower pot filled with these toys of nature and a large mirror reflects the splendor of every object.

8th this day being the Sabbath, I spent chiefly in my mothers room; I rose and drank the water breakfasted with a good appetite and while in the drawing room attached myself chiefly to a Mrs Hart, a lady from Utica who treats me with much attention, and I am become quite attached to her, with a few exceptions there is no very interesting Company here but my time passes very pleasantly—After dinner papa went with me to the rock Spring. Oh! what a curiosity it is, from a fissure in a large rock Spings [*sic*] the water of health, when I viewed it reminded me of the refreshing fountain which flowed in the wilderness[97], to refresh the wearied, and half fainting Sons of Israel, the chosen of heaven; I intend to attempt a sketch of this rock, that my friends in Newyork may see it; we returned and drank tea—and went to church with Papa, heard a good plain practical Sermon, from the words, "What shall I do to be saved" returned home and retired to rest, and soon lost all recollection of the events of the day in refreshing slumber.

There is an adequate supply of churches
ANDREW REED

An independent (we would say Congregational) minister, Andrew Reed (1787–1862) of London visited the United States in 1834 along with a colleague, James Matheson, sent by the Congregational Union of England and Wales to promote friendship between the two communities. Visiting Saratoga Springs in mid-August, they not surprisingly sought a more serious side of the village than most visitors did, and they found it in the so-called "Religious Hotel," which was Union Hall. But they also noted that gambling was present, and unwittingly provided us with the earliest documentation of the vice that came to dominate the spa.

Andrew Reed and James Matheson, *A Narrative of a Visit to the American Churches from the Congregational Union of England and Wales* (London: Jackson and Walford, 1835), 318–321.

SARATOGA IS the most fashionable watering-place in the States. Like most of their watering places it is inland. The people here all run from the sea in the summer; while with us they are all ready to run into it. The sea coast, and the river sides, at this season, are deemed unwholesome. The town is composed rather of several enormous inns than of streets and houses. The principal are, the Congress, the Pavilion, the Union, and the United States. From their size, and from the large porticoes which run in their front, ornamented by flowering shrubs, they have a good and imposing appearance. They will accommodate from 200 to 300 persons; and at this time there were upwards of 2000 visitors. The refectories and the withdrawing-rooms, as they gather all the occupants together at certain times, have an animated and striking effect. Our waiter observed to me, with great complacency, of the dining-room, that it was the largest room in the States. I admired his modesty, that he did not say—in the world.

Altogether, though the place is the centre of transatlantic fashion, it has the air of having been just redeemed from the forest. The main avenue, or street, is just a clearance from the woods, with its centre cut up by the carriages, and filled with the native dust and sand, and the margins are overrun with grass; and the Pavilion, which was completing[98], is at present enveloped in the original and verdant spruce pine.

The chief amusements of the place are, a visit to Lake George;

fishing at Balston; a drive out and in again; and an occasional ball, got up at one hotel, by a subscription made at all. The only sight was a Panorama of Geneva[99], which I had seen in London, and was glad to see again, that I might be transported to Europe and Leicester-square. There is certainly gambling going on here; but, if seen, it must be sought for. On the contrary, there is one hotel, and that first-rate, which has the denomination of the Religious Hotel.[100] Its name preserves its character; the religious are attracted by it; and as clergy-men are usually staying here, domestic worship is observed, and not only most of the occupants, but many from the other inns, attend. It is also worthy of remark, that in this place, so lately risen from the forest, and raised for purposes of fashion, and having so very small a resident population, there is an adequate supply of churches, even when the company is largest.

I desired to improve the evening by uniting with some congregation in worship and at last entered somewhat later than we wished the Episcopal Church.[101] There is in this plain church a pew which attracts attention, and is meant to do so. It is composed of two, and is as large and splendid as a mayor's; and has a showy lamp chandelier suspended over it. When the owner of this dress box attends, it is lighted, to notify his presence to the gazing congregation. He was present on this occasion, and exhibited a gold chain, like our sheriffs. This gentleman[102] is from England, they say; he makes large gifts and large charges; and has succeeded by *dash*. How many have done so both in the old and new world! But is it not a profanity, as well as a folly, when these vanities are carried into our temples, and are made to give to the house of God the aspect of the theatre?

A circular track on which elderly children may take a ride

HARRIET MARTINEAU

Harriet Martineau (1802–1876) was one of the best-known English commentators on the American scene, particularly as a result of her book, Society in America *(1837), the product of the same trip that, in the year following, produced the volumes from which the following passage is taken. An advocate for the abolition of slavery, for women's rights, and for other progressive causes of the day, her reputation for social commentary was well deserved. On her almost breathless visit to the spa, lasting apparently all of one afternoon, she managed to observe the process of bottling and provided us with the earliest description of the much-loved Circular Railroad. But the waterfall at Glens Falls — today almost unnoticed — "astonished" her with its "splendour," and contrasted with the absence of scenery at Saratoga Springs.*

Harriet Martineau, *Retrospect of Western Travel*, 3 vols. (London: Saunders and Otley, 1838), 3: 260–263. Biography is found in *Women in World History*, 10: 479–486.

IT WAS about noon on the 12th of May when we alighted shivering from the rail-car at Saratoga. We hastened to the Adelphi[103]; and there found the author[104] of Major Jack Downing's Letters, and two other gentlemen, reading the newspapers round a stove. We had but little time to spare; and as soon as we had warmed ourselves, and ascertained the dinner hour, we set forth to view the place, and taste the Congress Water. There is nothing to be seen but large white frame-houses, with handsome piazzas, festooned with creepers, — (at this time only the sapless remains of the garlands of the last season). These houses and the wooden temple over the principal spring are all that is to be seen, — at least by the bodily eye. The imagination may amuse itself with conjuring up the place as it was less than half a century ago, when these springs bubbled up amidst the brush of the forest, — their qualities being discovered by the path through the woods worn by the deer in their resort to it. In those days, the only edifices were a single log-hut and a bear-pound; a space enclosed with four high walls, with an extremely narrow entrance, where it was hoped that bears might get in during the dark hours, and be unable to find their way out

Circular Rail-Way. Stereoscope view by Barnum, photographer. Robert Joki Collection.

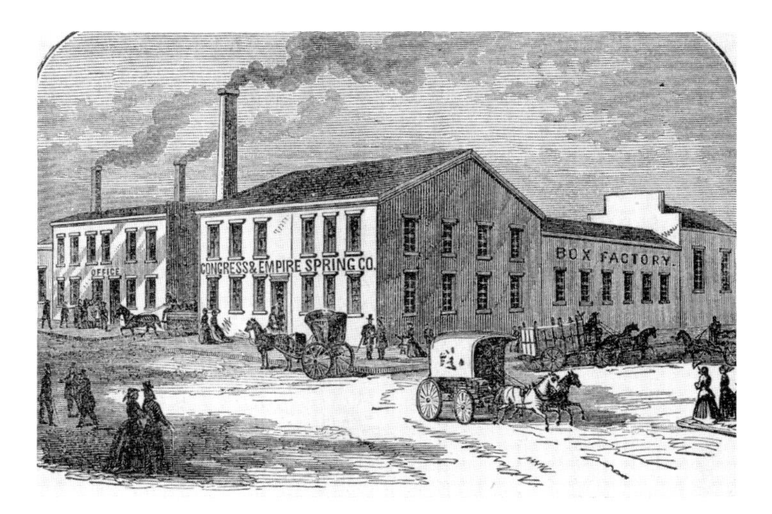

Congress Spring Bottling House and Box Factory. *Saratoga, and How to See It* (1873)

again.[105] Times are much changed now. There are no bears at Saratoga but a two-legged species from Europe, dropping in, one or two in a season, among the gentry at the Springs.

The process of bottling the Congress Water was in full activity when we took our first draught of it. Though the utmost celerity is used, the water loses much of its virtue and briskness by bottling. The man and boy whom we saw filling and corking bottles, with a dexterity which only practice can give, are able to dispatch a hundred dozen per day. There are several other springs, shedding waters of various medicinal virtues; but the Congress fountain is the only one from which the stranger would drink as a matter of taste.

The water-works are just at hand, looking like a giant's shower-bath.[106] At the top of the eminence close by, there is a pleasure rail-road,—a circular track, on which elderly children may take a ride round and round in a self-moving chair; an amusement a step above the old merry-go-round in gravity and scientific pretension.[107] But for its vicinity to some tracts of beautiful scenery, Saratoga must be a very dull place to persons shaken out of their domestic habits, and deprived of their usual occupations; and the beauties of the scenery must be sought, Saratoga Lake lying three miles, Glen's Falls eighteen, and Lake George twenty-seven miles from the Springs.

When boats are safe, and waters clear, and skies blue

CAROLINE HOWARD GILMAN

Caroline Howard Gilman (1794–1888) was a Bostonian transplanted, by her marriage in 1819 to Samuel Gilman, to Charleston, where the Unitarian congregation had invited her husband to be its minister. She came to think of herself as a Southerner, but always retained a fondness for her native New England. She considered the "family home" to be the center of the Union and she became the poet of the domestic bond cherished by both North and South. Her literary career began in 1832 with pieces for a children's magazine. Six years later, she published her Poetry of Travelling in the United States, *with its sentimental account of a visit to the spa. Like many visitors, she was somewhat preoccupied with the respectability of the other visitors; and like all those who were churchgoers in her era, she attended services without regard to denomination, taking pleasure in the sermon if not always in the congregation.*

Caroline Gilman, *The Poetry of Travelling in the United States* (New York: S. Colman, 1838), 84–87. Biography is found in *Notable American Women*, and mention of her is in Mary Scott Saint-Amand, *A Balcony in Charleston* (Richmond: Garrett and Massie, 1941), 1–3.

WE LEFT Troy at 10 o'clock in the commodious cars for this place. What a contrast are these airy and convenient conveyances to the Camden and Amboy rail-road cars! The rush of porters on our arrival, exceeded any thing I have met with elsewhere; the shouts were perfectly bewildering, as they recommended the different hotels to which they were attached. The U.S. hotel, in which we are located, is at present the most crowded, and perhaps fashionable; though I understand some of the others have better sleeping rooms and better fare. It is in vain to write here; there is something in the tone of things that prevents all fixedness of attention. It is enough to look at people dressed up for show.—There is a lovely demi-French family of celebrity, with five attendants and their foreign friends,—a Northern Senator, "the observed of all observers," about whom the Bostonians cluster; there is a Carolina party, &c., &c. A foreigner sits in front of me, who appears to associate with respectable people, wearing a dark check shirt, without a vest, and whose mustachioes surpass by many degrees the most extravagant American standard. Near me is an American lady, with *gold* cable watch-chain and ear-rings, and *silver* comb and buckle; but generally speaking, there is an air of propriety throughout this large concourse, the manners of the ladies are discreet, their dresses modest, and the men are unassuming.

A paper was circulated yesterday, at dinner, proposing a "hop" in the evening; signatures appeared to be easily gained, and at eight o'clock our fine hall was lit up brilliantly, and a full band began the preliminary notes. The affair went off languidly, no one group was large enough to form sets, and none amalgamated. The demi-French and foreigners only danced, and they made but one †cotillion. It was very warm, to be sure, but that had not prevented the joyous unceremonious couples at Fishkill from "tiring each other down," as gaily as if it had been Christmas eve. Notwithstanding the lively exterior of things at Saratoga, there are more forlorn looking people than I ever met with, if you watch faces; and there is nothing in the whole compass of yawns like a Saratoga yawn, if you hear one when a gaper is off his guard. The whole man is stretched, inwardly and outwardly. Let no one who values a small mouth risk a gape at the Springs. Still, it is a glorious place, and in fifty years, palaces, and fountains, and gardens will burst forth on its now rude location, and rival in beauty the healing power with which God has blessed it so richly. The site of the Congress springs, naturally beautiful, is beginning now to assume an air of improvement.[108] It is capable of tasteful ornament. A circular pleasure rail-road surrounds a grove on the hill, with a car, where two persons can sit together, and propel themselves.

We strayed out yesterday to the nearest church. The Sabbath is very dear to me amid the throng of strangers, and I would not miss its privileges. The church, neat externally, proved to be of the Baptist denomination, and was attended by the more laborious classes. A stranger preached with animation and earnestness; but as I glanced my eye round, I found two thirds of the men and several women asleep; they were probably rendered drowsy by their unaccustomed quiet attitude. Being wide awake, and most of our party, from principle and feeling, having the habit of attention at church, the pastor's attention was attracted to us, and he literally fixed his eyes upon our group until some of us were embarrassed. The style of music and the bass-viol reminded me of my early years, and the sounding of the key-note awoke a long strain of the melody of memory.

We left the drawing-room of the hotel as crowded after dinner as if there were no bell summoning us to the house of prayer, and went to the Presbyterian church. A South Carolinian preached on the admirable theme, a well-balanced Christian character. In the course of his discourse, he said there was no such thing as a particular Church of Christ on earth. The Church of Christ was composed of individuals of every denomination, who obeyed his precepts. Neither of the gentlemen alluded to the character of the place. They had probably good reasons to decline appropriating the healing power of the Springs to the illustration of religious truth.

We visited, this evening, Saratoga Lake. It is a placid spot, about five miles from the Springs. A boat lies temptingly ready for ladies of the lake and their Douglasses.[109] Our party entered one, and rowed across to a floating fishing-house, where, unexpectedly to ourselves, we became engaged, and successfully, as a †"piscatorial party." The first fish one of us caught was of that species which Cuvier[110] has named after Dr. Holbrook of our city. I forget what the name is. What can be said in a journal when one's carriages roll along over good roads, when boats are safe, and waters clear, and skies blue, and fish willing to come to the hook, and company good-humoured? Absolutely nothing.

More like a moveable gallery than a train of rail road cars

FREEMAN HUNT

Freeman Hunt (1804–1858) published a number of significant magazines in the mid 19th century. As a young man of 24, he continued the Juvenile Miscellany, *whose editor had been the famed cookbook author Lydia Child, and he began the first American women's magazine of any importance, the* Ladies' Magazine. *His life's work was the* Merchants' Magazine and Commercial Review, *which he directed for 19 years until his death. One of his most popular publications – it went through three editions—was his own* Letters About the Hudson River and its Vicinity. *In it he does not comment on Saratoga Springs; but on 10 May 1836 he took the "new rail road" (the Rensselaer and Saratoga) to Ballston Spa and the next day, in his room at Troy's Mansion House, he penned an extraordinary account of the train. These early railroad outfits were rather like stagecoaches on tracks and, from Hunt's description, the company had expended great effort and money to create beautiful objects.*

Freeman Hunt, *Letters About the Hudson River and its Vicinity* (New York: Freeman Hunt and Company, 1837), 79–81.

YESTERDAY, I took a seat in one of the passage cars, on the new rail road, for Balston. The road now extends to Saratoga, and will, I venture to predict, become the most fashionable route, as indeed it is the most interesting, to the "Springs." The arrangements for carrying passengers are quite extensive. There are twenty-four cars belonging to the company—at once spacious, elegant, and convenient. They are twenty-four feet in length by eight in breadth, and sufficiently high within for the passengers to stand erect, the whole divided into three apartments; the seats of which are cushioned and backed with crimson morocco, trimmed with †coach lace; each apartment is surrounded by moveable panels, thus affording the comforts and facilities of either a close or open carriage, to suit the convenience of the passengers. The outside of the cars is painted of a beautiful fawn colour, with buff shading, painted in "picture panels," with rose, pink, and gold borders, and deep lake shading; the small mouldings of delicate stripes of vermilion and opaque black. Within the panels are *"transferred"* some of the most splendid productions of the ancient and modern masters, among which are copies from "Leonardo da Vinci," "Horace Vernet," "David," (the celebrated painter to Napoleon,) "Stuart," and many more of the modern school. The whole number of the subjects of the twenty-four cars, cannot fall far short of two hundred, as each car averages from six to ten subjects: among which may be enumerated, several copies from the antique, Napoleon crossing the Alps, the two splendid scenes in Byron's Mazeppa[111], the Hospital Mount St. Bernard, portraits of most of the distinguished men of our own country, among whom Washington (from Stuart's original) stands conspicuous, the wounded tiger, the avalanche, portraits of distinguished women, views of several of our popular steamboats, the rail road bridge near Philadelphia, and several views in the south. The †*"tout ensemble,"* is more like a moveable gallery of the fine arts, than like a train of rail road cars. The springs of the cars are of Philadelphia make, and bear evenly. The †"journals" are on a new plan, obviating all previous objections. The wheels are of cast iron, with patent rolled iron tire, well †annealed and wrought, being put on the cart wheel while hot. The cooling of the tire, and the contractions of the iron, render it impossible to deviate from its place. The whole is then turned in a steam lathe by machine tools, thus rendering the circle of the wheel perfect from its centre, which is a great †desideratum.

The cars were made in Troy by those famous coach builders, Gilbert, Veazie and Eaton[112], aided by Mr. Starbuck, a scientific machinist. Connected with the cars are two beautiful locomotives called the "Erie" and the "Champlain."

114

I don't think I ever saw a greater number of more beautiful girls

SAMUEL K. DAWSON

In September 1837, a West Point cadet from Pennsylvania, Samuel K. Dawson, wrote his friend Hogg to report on his visit to Saratoga Springs. Dawson was fascinated by the amusements offered by the village which were, with the increase of business following the opening of the railroad, becoming more varied. And, as befitted a 19-year-old whose visit was "for the purpose of distributing invitations" to a West Point ball, he noted the many beautiful young women there. Dawson was graduated and commissioned two years later, and served well as an army officer through the Mexican War and the Civil War, retiring from active service in 1866. He died at Orange, New Jersey, on 17 April 1889 aged 72.

"High Life at Saratoga 1837," *American Heritage* 18 (June 1967): 107. The manuscript was then in the collection of the Historical Society of Western Pennsylvania, which is unable to locate it. Biography is found in G.W. Cullum, *Biographical Register of the Officers and Graduates of the U.S. Military Academy at West Point,* 5 vols. (Boston: Houghton Mifflin, 1891–1910), 2: 13–14.

My Dear Hogg:

IT SO HAPPENED that I was able to get a leave of 5 days for the purpose of distributing invitations to our ball at Catskill, Hudson and Albany and Saratoga Springs.

At the latter place, I remained three days and the pleasures I enjoyed would have been doubly relished if I had had your company. As you have never been at Saratoga, probably a slight description of the place and the manner in which visitors amuse themselves may not be uninteresting.

The Village has but one street of any importance on which are situated the four large wooden Hotels of the place. At the one called

The Pavilion are fine walking grounds and a beautiful laid off garden. The nine pin alley and the Billiard rooms are also at this place, and on the whole the village presents rather a pretty appearance.

Its population is about five hundred. The routine of the pleasures of the day are as follows: breakfast at eight o'clock, and then all retire to the drawing room and the Ladies and Gentlemen for an hour or so promenade, then a party either takes a ride out to a very beautiful little Lake called Saratoga, situated 4 miles from the village, or go down to the nine pin ally and play until they get tired. I went down the second morning I was there with a party of Ladies who seemed to enjoy the Game very much indeed. I was considerably amused at the manner in which they rolled the balls.

They dine at two, promenade up and down the drawing room for an hour and then take an evening walk or go to the circular railway and ride round for a while. This circular railway is about a hundred yards around, the cars are very high and contain but two persons and is propelled by the Gentleman in the car turning a crank. It is beautifully situated amidst a grove of young oaks at the village.

Sup at six; promenade and then at eight the dancing commences and continues until twelve or one. They have three balls a week and three hops which are the same thing only the ladies do not dress as well. It is almost impossible to give you any idea of the high enjoyment a person may have there for two or three days. I don't think I ever saw a greater number of more beautiful girls. I would not have given much for your heart if you had been along with me.

The contest for the dishes is a perfect scramble

JAMES SILK BUCKINGHAM

One of England's great travel writers of the early Victorian period, James Silk Buckingham (1786–1855) went to sea in his tenth year and began accumulating a store of observations that he turned into a long series of books. In 1818, he started a newspaper at Calcutta, which he ran for four years until his criticism of the British colonial regime resulted in his expulsion. In the early 1820s, he traveled in the Near East and the present Iraq and Iran. His four-year tour of North America generated four separate works totaling nine volumes. His account of his visit to Saratoga starting 28 July 1838 is a long one; only his observations on the characteristics of the hotels and the strange mealtime customs are quoted here.

James Silk Buckingham, *America: Historical, Statistic and Descriptive* (London: Fisher, Son and Co., 1841), 2: 427–467 and 3: 182–183.

We arrived at Saratoga about one o'clock, and having previously engaged apartments at the Union Hall, we soon found ourselves amidst the bustle of a large party of more than 200 persons, promenading the drawing-rooms and piazzas of the hotel, waiting for the approaching hour of dinner, which was two o'clock; and taking our seats at the table, we were soon recognized by many whom we had met in different parts of the Union, and found ourselves more at home than we had anticipated.

Of these hotels the Congress Hall is frequented by the most fashionable classes, those who pride themselves on their birth, connexion, and breeding, rather than their wealth; and this is consequently the aristocratic or whig house, in which conservative doctrines in politics and religion are most current and most acceptable. The United States Hotel is more frequented by the rich mercantile classes, whose wealth makes their importance equal in degree, though differing in its source, to that of the more "ancient families;" and this is the democratic house. The Union Hall is frequented chiefly by the clergy, and religious families, by judges, professors, and grave and elderly people generally; and this is called the religious house. The Pavilion is more miscellaneous in its company, and is occupied more by persons who make a short stay, than by those who remain for any length of time; and this is called the travellers' house. The largest of these will accommodate 300 persons, and the smallest will accommodate 200; besides these, there are smaller hotels and private boarding-houses; and in the whole of them there was estimated to be at least 3,000 strangers, the village having at present more company than on any former occasion that can be remembered.

From day-light, therefore, until seven o'clock in the morning, the well or fountain, which is enclosed beneath a roof supported by a colonnade of fluted wooden pillars, is crowded with drinkers, and some are said to take the number of twenty tumblers of the water before breakfast. A circular railway, by which two persons can propel themselves round a circle of about one hundred yards' diameter, in an easy chair, is judiciously provided within the distance of a short walk from the spring, and the more active among the drinkers repair to it for exercise, to aid the effect of the waters. During the day, the more †chalybeate qualities of Hamilton and Flat Rock springs are taken; but the general impression here is, that every body drinks the waters to excess, and that quite as many persons are injured as benefited, from this misuse and misapplication of them.

Take the general routine of a day at the Springs, as an example. All rise between 6 and 7 o'clock; and at half past 7, the drawing-room of each of the larger hotels is filled with from 200 to 300 persons promenading till the folding doors are thrown open for admission to the dining-hall, when this large number seat themselves at breakfast. The meal is generally a substantial one, a variety of dishes being placed on the table; and few persons breakfasting without partaking of some description of animal food: but the rapidity with which it is despatched, is its most remarkable feature, the longest time taken by the slowest being never more than 15 minutes, some of the quickest getting through the meal in 5 minutes, and the average number occupying about 10.

In the busy cities, the reason assigned for this haste is the keen pursuit of business, and the eager desire to get to the counting-house or store; but here, with the entire day before them, and nothing whatever to do, they eat with just the same haste as at other places. The contest for the dishes is a perfect scramble; the noise and clatter of the waiters and their wares is absolutely deafening; no one gets precisely what he wants, though every one is searching after something. The quiet elegance of an English breakfast, is as great a contrast to the noisy rudeness of an American meal, as can well be conceived, even when both are taken in public hotels like these. Elegance of manners in such a scene as this is quite out of the question. People eat as if they were afraid that their plates were about to be snatched from them before they had done; mastication may be said to be almost entirely omitted; and in nine cases out of ten, persons do not remain in their chairs to finish the meal, short as it is, but rise with the last mouthful still unswallowed, and dispose of it gradually as they walk along.

The period between breakfast at 8 o'clock and dinner at 2, is occupied by the more active in excursions to the surrounding points of attraction, on horseback or in carriages: but the greater number remain at home; and the drawing-room is then the general lounge, where groups of the young are formed, who sit for hours engaged in the merest gossip of trifling talk, for it hardly deserves the name of conversation; and neither books, music, nor drawing occupy any portion of the time.

Dressing for dinner fills up a vacant hour; at one, and at half-past one, the drawing-room is again crowded with the promenading parties waiting for the opening of the folding doors to admit them to dinner. The hurry and bustle of the breakfast scene is again repeated, with little of table enjoyment, to reconcile the parties to the heat and noise of the room. The fare is what in England would be called coarse and bad—the dishes few in number, and wretchedly cooked, besides being lukewarm; and the miserable sprinkling of bad vegetables, being almost as cold as if they had been dressed on the preceding day—no covers for the dishes, or warm plates for the guests—no appointed carvers—an insufficiency of attendants—and altogether an ill-managed and an ill-enjoyed dinner. The escape from this is almost as rapid as from the breakfast, and 15 minutes may be regarded as the average time occupied in it; though a few may sit perhaps from 20 to 25 minutes, but none for half an hour.

The afternoon is literally whiled away between the drawing-room and the sleeping-room; or in the spacious and shady piazzas or verandahs, in one of which fronting the garden at the back of the house, the gentlemen retire to smoke their segars; and in the other, in front of the house, ladies and gentlemen, not otherwise occupied, mingle in the promenade. In all the great houses, everything is sacrificed to appearance. The piazzas are of splendid dimensions, 200 feet by 20, and 50 feet high, supported by lofty pillars, entwined with spiral wreaths of foliage—the dining halls capable of seating 400 persons—the drawing-rooms, especially that of the United States, of magnificent dimensions, and handsomely furnished: but the bed-rooms are generally exceedingly small, those of Congress Hall especially, scantily provided, and altogether inferior to what the scale and style of the house, in other respects, would warrant the visitor to expect.

The third meal, of tea, is taken at seven o'clock, and is, in short, a supper, as meats of various kinds are placed on the table, which is covered with a tablecloth, as at dinner, and at which the 200 or 300 visitors seat themselves in the same way. This is got through with the same rapidity as the two preceding ones; no fatigue during the day, or other consideration, inducing persons to relax in the least from the hurry with which everything is done in this country.

The evenings are more varied than the day, as there is sometimes a ball, and sometimes a "hop," as it is termed here, the difference being, that at the former a full-dress is expected, at the latter the ordinary dinner-dress will suffice; occasionally there is a concert, sometimes a display of ventriloquism, now and then a farce by a company of strolling players, and this again varied by a conjuror with tricks of legerdemain.

"Me don't want bad water"
ROBERT FRANCIS WITHERS ALSTON

For two centuries, the South Atlantic coast was an important rice-growing region; in the generation prior to the Civil War, the Georgetown District of South Carolina produced a third or more of the entire United States crop. One of the leaders of rice culture was Robert F. W. Allston (1801–1864), owner of many large plantations in the Georgetown District. A West Point graduate, he served as surveyor-general of his home state, became an advocate of state's rights, served in the state legislature and state senate, and as governor in 1856–58. In 1838, he took his family, consisting of his wife Adelle and several children, to Saratoga Springs. His letter to his aunt, Elizabeth Frances Blyth, with the usual budget of observations on the waters, is at its best as a description of a young family enjoying their Northern sojourn.

Robert F. W. Alston, letter to Elizabeth Frances Blyth, 11 July 1838. Allston Family Papers, South Carolina Historical Society, Charleston, S.C. It was published in Harold Easterby, *The South Carolina Rice Plantation* (Chicago: University of Chicago Press, 1945), 77. Biography is found in Easterby, 11–19.

Saratoga 11th July 1838

MY DEAR AUNT, I[t] gave both Adelle and myself the sincerest pleasure to receive your letter of the 29th June at this place. We were glad that you had reach'd the Sea shore in safety and trust that you will pass the summer in comfort.

We are drinking the waters of Congress Spring with some effect now, 'tho for several days Adelle did not take to it kindly and Rob to this day will not take more than one mouthful, puts down the tumbler and turns his back upon it saying "me don't—want—bad—water." I gave him a ride this morning on a little circular pleasure Rail-Road that is on the hill just above the Spring (ride three times

Columbian and Congress springs. Cabinet photograph, *circa* 1865. Skidmore College.

round for seven-pence a piece) and he has promised in consequence to drink a full tumbler tomorrow. He is not well this day or two and I am the more anxious that he should drink the waters. Ben[113] drinks it very readily. He takes one tumbler, A[delle] takes 5 and I 4, sometimes 6 before breakfast beginning at 6 O'clock the rides about the village are pleasant but horse-hire is so high that we do not go about much, there is a fine court-yard attach'd to the house (Congress-Hall) at which we stay, where the children are enabled to run about and play in the shade all day, they have a swing among the trees and there are several other children of several nations and they are very happy. Little Sis. is as fat and lively as she well can be, not a tooth has yet made its appearance, she is very strong and is improving much. I thought at first that the waters did not agree with my wife, her nerves and muscular system are still very unstrung, the day we came up the Hudson the day was hot, and the boat somewhat crowded, she was so much fatigued that I was induced to stop a day at Albany to rest. I am in hopes now tho' that if she will continue to take it regularly it will prove beneficial, with this view I think of remaining a week longer. If A[delle] is then strong enough we will go to the Falls of Niagara. There are a number of persons here but the houses are not at all crowded yet. People come here from all and every region of the country and of every description of character, a family from Philadelphia named McCauley have been very polite in giving us their card and requesting to be informed "when we reach that City." We will not be there till October, when on my way home.

The U. S. is full, cannot take another
MILO LINUS NORTH

Dr. Milo Linus North (1789–1856) left a remarkable record of everyday life. A graduate of Yale, he had practiced medicine in Sharon, Ellington, and Hartford, Connecticut, but in 1838 he moved to Saratoga Springs because of poor health. He had visited at least once a decade earlier, writing in his journal that he "left after a week worse," but this time he moved wife and two sons to the spa, where he apparently took over Dr. John H. Steel's practice, which numbered among its patients many of the summer visitors. In 1840, North published Saratoga Waters; or, The Invalid at Saratoga, *which went through many editions. His journal noted the renovation of his house, the schooling and apprenticeships of his sons, and several attempts after they were grown to "give up housekeeping."*

Milo Linus North, journal. Malloch Collection, New York Academy of Medicine. Transcribed by Field Horne. Biography is found in Franklin B. Dexter, *Biographical Sketches of the Graduates of Yale College,* 6 vols. (New York: Henry Holt, 1885–1912), 6: 591–592.

[1838] 6/1 Entered S[aratoga] at noon. cars, via Schenectady. Fare from Albany 1.75. Stopped at Mr. Root's Washington Hall. Board $5. Hired offices & furniture of late Dr. Steel $75 pr annum.

Friday June 15. Commenced board at Mr. Abel Hendrick's, 3 Dolls.

July 17. offered $1650 for dwelling house, store & barn.[114]

Friday 28th reached Hartford, morning, *Cleopatra,* boarded with G. Sanford, sold goods at auction 79.99, disct 10 prcent. Add private sale 110 Dolls. Boxed furniture for Saratoga, 17 boxes, 29 bundles, chairs, bedsteads, &c. Freight $23.77 to Albany. Thence to Saratoga in 2 cars 10 Dolls. They reached Saratoga in exactly 4 wks from the day we shipped them on board schooner *Brace*, Capt. Ransom, badly damaged; no delay at Albany.

Family Journal May 1, 1839 Thomas M. North. This dear son of ours left us this morning to take post in G.M. Davison's[115] Bookstore & Reading Room. Mr. D. prefers to board him. He will stay 2½ years if all things permit. I have many hopes of Thomas. He seems to love the Bible, the Sabbath, prayer; and is active in a small praying circle of boys.

May 3. 1839. Friday. Mr. Hodges made our garden, planted beans, beats, squashes, tomatoes, cucumbers, & radishes.

Altering House. This was concluded May 20. Done by Enos W. Cole. Contract 123.17. Overplus & contract 133.91. Adams's paint 11.84. making wall in s.e. part of garden say 7 Chestney's bill. In all say $160. add for the cistern, finished May 16 by John Sales 23.17 appurtenances to cistern added $25.

Eddy commenced attending school this day 25th [June] at the Universalist Church, under Miss Woodworth. scarcely knows a letter: and cannot count 3. Yet Mr. G.M. Davison thinks him the most intelligent child of his age he ever knew! Was reluctant to go this P.M.

The Springs July 19. The U.S. is full. cannot take another. So at Union. The U.S. have say 275 boarders. Their table full. Price 12 Dolls. wk. Wine & separate parlor, extra. Union have 208.

Pavillion Spring. Apl 25. [1840] Mr. McLaren has this day finished filling the cavity made for this fountain. It was sunk 33 feet the enclosure being 12 or 15 feet square, made of logs. The forcing pumps were in constant requisition to keep the hole clear of water. The gas was so abundant that it was requisite to keep a fire burning continually near the bottom.

July 4. Twenty seven cars, decorated with oak boughs, flags, &c. with 2 locomotives conducted the Saratoga & Ballston Sabbath Schools from S to B at ½ past 1 PM.

My business has not been as great as if other physicians had not come in. Yet have laid up something for family although my absence last winter was expensive.

[1841] Mr. Hudson executed [my daguerrotype] 10th Sept. & expects to take Mrs. North's & Eddy's to morrow. Thomas's was taken by a Mr. Flemming.[116]

[1842] Thomas on a farm. T. entered the family of Mr. Zalmon Olmstead on the banks of the Hudson Moreau June 20th.[117]

New Presbyterian Church[118] dedicated. 11 AM Thursday June 30th 1842 Rev. Dr. Sprague of Albany preached one hour & Rev. Dr. Milldollar, Msrs. Wayland & the pastor Rev. A.T. Chester made the prayers.

Thomas commenced his own school for lads in 2d story of Clark's house June 7, 1843.

Saratoga Springs, Aug. 7. Rev. Sylvester Homes says he walked 2 hr. Saturday 5th to find a lodging. Everything is full.

at 4 A. M. October 11th the flames burst out of the roof of the Pavilion, near the center of main building. It spread under the roof quite to the East end of the south wing the whole pile was consumed in little over 2 hours. No other buildings burned. The air was perfectly still. Considerable furniture saved.

February 16th. [1844] a pleasant scene. at 1 PM there sits a boy nearly 9 years old on a load of wood in front of our home with a bundle of *Youths' Temperance Advocates* in his hand reading to Mr. Perry of Wilton and urging him to sign the teetotal pledge.

A fire broke out in a drug shop opposite G.M. Davison's, Broadway 2½ AM Nov 22. It destroyed several buildings north & south.

[1846] Edward entered M.M. Berry's Book store as a clerk June 1.

Fire. June 8. at 3¼ A.M. *Sentinel* office on fire. In 2 hours the fire was arrested at the Center House, having destroyed some 6 or 7 stores. Damage 30.000?

Edward is not only a clerk for M.M. Berry on wages but is an assistant to Mr. Makepeace in the Telegraph Office and is carrying messages daily & almost hourly. He rises regularly soon after 5 A.M. & opens the store.

Dec 1 '46 Aquaduct The aqt. corporation introduced the water from several springs 2 or 2½ miles west in Nov. Several hydrants are erected from Judge Warren's to Union Hall. The village to be supplied next season.[119]

1847 Thomas left for Wms. College Wednes, Jan. 27. Health excellent. Has been to Robertsons (near Iodine[120]) Spring every morning before breakfast for 7 weeks, without fail.

Saratoga Telegraph. Commenced July 23. [1849]

Renting House.[121] Peter Thompson took possession Monday July 30. Boarding out. Mrs. N. & myself commenced board, merely food at Columbian Hotel tuesday July 31 at $2.25 each. Boarded till Sept. 20th.[122]

Giving up Housekeeping. This morning Mrs. McClelland took possession of the house, the rent to be 150 dolls. pr. an. including the back office, except 4 months. Mrs. N. & myself commenced boarding this morning. For our meals & washing & a right in the parlor, $5 pr. week. P.S. Mrs. M'C found she had miscalculated & reduced herself to her former position, with our hearty consent after exactly one week of trial.

Oct. 31 '49 sold my House in H[artford].

Greenfield Water brought into my cellar May 30 1850 at $6. a year. The lead pipe, labour & all cost $20 nearly.

I performed many hard days' labor
SOLOMON NORTHUP

The earliest African American voice of Saratoga Springs is that of Solomon Northup (b 1808) in his best-selling book, Twelve Years a Slave. *Born at Minerva, Essex County, the son of a Rhode Island-born freedman, Northup moved to Saratoga Springs from Fort Edward in 1834. In 1841, two men tricked him into accompanying them to Washington, D.C., where he was sold as a slave and taken to the Bayou Boeuf in Louisiana. Nearly 12 years later, a Yankee schoolmaster there agreed to mail a letter for him to friends in Saratoga Springs, who alerted Henry Northup, whose father had freed Solomon's father. Henry went to Louisiana, found Solomon, and demanded his freedom. Three months after Solomon returned to Glens Falls, his book was published; 30,000 copies were printed within a decade. Solomon was in demand as a speaker, but within a few years all trace of him disappears from the records. His book outlived him to endure as one of the most articulate and compelling slave narratives. The passage quoted here describes his life and labor around the spa.*

Solomon Northup, *Twelve Years a Slave* (Auburn, N.Y.: Derby and Miller, 1853). Sue Eakin and Joseph Logsdon, *Twelve Years a Slave* (Baton Rouge, La.: Louisiana State University Press, 1970) is the standard modern edition, in which the section reproduced below is at 9–11. Biography is found in its introduction.

IN MARCH, 1834, we removed to Saratoga Springs. We occupied a house belonging to Daniel O'Brien, on the north side of Washington street.[123] At that time Isaac Taylor kept a large boarding house,

Solomon Northup in his plantation suit. *Twelve Years a Slave* (1853).

known as Washington Hall, at the north end of Broadway. He employed me to drive a hack, in which capacity I worked for him two years. After this time I was generally employed through the visiting season, as also was Anne, in the United States Hotel, and other public houses of the place. In winter seasons I relied upon my violin, though during the construction of the Troy and Saratoga railroad[124], I performed many hard days' labor upon it.

I was in the habit, at Saratoga, of purchasing articles necessary for my family at the stores of Mr. Cephas Parker and Mr. William Perry[125], gentlemen towards whom, for many acts of kindness, I entertained feelings of strong regard. It was for this reason that, twelve years afterwards, I caused to be directed to them the letter, which is hereinafter inserted, and which was the means, in the hands of Mr. Northup, of my fortunate deliverance.

While living at the United States Hotel, I frequently met with slaves, who had accompanied their masters from the South. They were always well dressed and well provided for, leading apparently an easy life, with but few of its ordinary troubles to perplex them. Many times they entered into conversation with me on the subject of Slavery. Almost uniformly I found they cherished a secret desire for liberty. Some of them expressed the most ardent anxiety to escape, and consulted me on the best method of effecting it. The fear of punishment, however, which they knew was certain to attend their re-capture and return, in all cases proved sufficient to deter them from the experiment. Having all my life breathed the free air of the North, and conscious that I possessed the same feelings and affections that find a place in the white man's breast; conscious, moreover, of an intelligence equal to that of some men, at least, with a fairer skin, I was too ignorant, perhaps too independent, to conceive how any one could be content to live in the abject condition of a slave. I could not comprehend the justice of that law, or that religion, which upholds or recognizes the principle of Slavery; and never once, I am proud to say, did I fail to counsel any one who came to me, to watch his opportunity, and strike for freedom.

I continued to reside at Saratoga until the spring of 1841. The flattering anticipations which, seven years before, had seduced us from the quiet farm-house, on the east side of the Hudson, had not been realized. Though always in comfortable circumstances, we had not prospered. The society and associations at that world-renowned watering place, were not calculated to preserve the simple habits of industry and economy to which I had been accustomed, but, on the contrary, to substitute others in their stead, tending to shiftlessness and extravagance.

At this time we were the parents of three children—Elizabeth, Margaret, and Alonzo. Elizabeth, the eldest, was in her tenth year; Margaret was two years younger, and little Alonzo had just passed his fifth birth-day. They filled our house with gladness. Their young voices were music in our ears. Many an airy castle did their mother and myself build for the little innocents. When not at labor I was always walking with them, clad in their best attire, through the streets and groves of Saratoga. Their presence was my delight; and I clasped them to my bosom with as warm and tender love as if their clouded skins had been as white as snow.[126]

Thus far the history of my life presents nothing whatever unusual—nothing but the common hopes, and loves, and labors of an obscure colored man, making his humble progress in the world. But now I had reached a turning point in my existence—reached the threshold of unutterable wrong, and sorrow, and despair. Now had I approached within the shadow of the cloud, into the thick darkness whereof I was soon to disappear, thenceforward to be hidden from the eyes of all my kindred, and shut out from the sweet light of liberty, for many a weary year.

All the world is here

PHILIP HONE

Saratogians and their summer visitors took their politics seriously. We have no better witness to this than Philip Hone (1780–1851), one of the greatest American diarists of the 19th century. Born into a working-class family, Hone harbored a desire to rise in society. He went to work in his brother's auction house, helped make it a great success, and retired at 40 with a fortune of half a million dollars. Cultivated and agreeable, he believed in the importance of public service, and was elected mayor of New York City for a one-year term in 1825. Later, in keeping with his essentially conservative beliefs, he became a supporter of the Whig party. From 1828 until his death, he recorded his experiences, thoughts, and observations in a brilliant diary. He was present at Saratoga Springs in 1839 at the same time as President Van Buren and Henry Clay, and was in the thick of the political observances. Though he was a Clay supporter, he was measured and urbane, and his account of the two men at Saratoga is a far more believable one than our chief source, the partisan press.

Philip Hone, diaries. The New-York Historical Society. His 1839 visit appears at 15: 437–450. Extensive extracts have been twice published: Bayard Tuckerman, ed., *The Diary of Philip Hone* (New York: Dodd, Mead, 1889), and Allan Nevins, ed., *The Diary of Philip Hone* (New York: Dodd, Mead, 1927). The first paragraph of the 5 August passage was not included in the edited versions and was transcribed by Field Horne from the manuscript.

SARATOGA SPRINGS, Tuesday, July 16.—We are here located (as we Yankees have it) at the United States Hotel, and no watering-place in this or any other country can boast of a pleasanter establishment, or one better conducted. We have a suite of two parlors and four bedrooms in the delightful south wing. Several additional buildings have been erected since the last season, and the ground laid out in a well-rolled and well-mowed lawn, and clean gravel walks. A large clubhouse and two cottages, in an exceedingly pretty style of architecture, add to the beauty of the grounds and the comfort of the visitors. On the whole, there has never been accommodation so good at Saratoga.

Friday, July 19.—A ball this evening, but I do not think it was as pleasant as the hop on Wednesday evening. I officiated as manager, with Col. McAllister, Messrs. Wilson, Stockton, Tevis, etc. The balls are understood to require more dressing, and a greater degree of etiquette prevails, so that the young ladies do not engage in them with so great avidity as in the hops; but, on the other hand, there are champagne, and ice-cream, and †blanc-mange, whose agreeable presence is confined to the most dignified of these amusements.

Saturday, July 20.—Gov. Seward came here to-day. The Governor is plain and unostentatious (perhaps a little too much so), but his intelligence and sociability seem to have made him many friends here. He has one of the poorest rooms in the hotel, so small and inconvenient that he was forced to come into our parlor to write a letter; of all this he makes no complaint, but takes things as they come. The Governor, Mr. C. L. Livingston, Col. McAllister, and I were invited by the managers of a hop at Congress Hall to a supper this evening, and a nicer supper I never saw. We had four trout weighing I should think three pounds each, and six dishes of woodcock of four each in capital order and cooked to perfection, with champagne, etc., etc.

Wednesday, July 24.—Every house is well filled; it is computed that there are 2,000 visitors at this place at the present time. At Congress Hall and this house there are many distinguished men and fine women; antiquated belles of a bygone generation, enjoying with gayety and cheerfulness the scenes of their former triumphs; fine married women and lovely girls, the ornaments of the present and the hopes of the future; and men uniting as in one brilliant focus the talent, intelligence, and civic virtues of the various parts of the country.

Monday, August 5.—Margaret Philip and I left our pleasant but solitary home in New York on Saturday afternoon in the *Rochester*. Slept uncomfortably on board, transshipped yesterday morning at five oclock, went to Troy where we breakfasted at the Troy house. Started on the rail-road and arrived here before ten o Clock, where we found every hole and corner occupied; our apartments are well enough but the Table is to full. That the brief space of time allotted to the meals is a sort of ring fight to secure enough to eat. Noise, confusion, elbowing, disputing for places.

In the number of arrivals during my absence is the President of the United States and Mr. Secretary Forsyth, with Mr. Edward P. Livingston and a few others of the faithful.

"The Cut Direct." An early political cartoon, it depicts the snubbing of Martin Van Buren by the widow of DeWitt Clinton in 1839, described by Philip Hone in his diary.

The President came here Thursday last. He was met some distance from the village by a cavalcade, and followed to his quarters in the United States Hotel (our house) by a motley group. The Whigs say it was a slim concern, and the Locos[127] say otherwise. But here he is, conducting himself with his usual politeness, and making the best of everything, as he is wont to do. I called upon him yesterday immediately after my arrival, and was most graciously received. He hoped I would pass an occasional spare half-hour in his apartment. He has been civil to my wife, and sends his bottle to her and me to drink with him at dinner. I have studied to treat him with all the respect due to his high station and the regard I feel for an old friend, and I acknowledge the kindness with which my advances have been received. This conduct has been pursued by most of the gentlemen, political opponents as well as political adherents; but there has been one exception, on the part of a lady, which in my judgment was equally at variance with good taste and proper feeling. The evening of the President's arrival, whilst he was engaged in playing the gallant to the ladies in the great saloon, he espied Mrs. DeWitt Clinton, and crossing the floor, extended his hand to her. This lady, who gives herself a great many airs, has been boasting of her intention to insult him, and on his friendly approach, in the view of the whole company, she folded her arms, gave him a scornful look, and turned off. Mr. Van Buren has too much tact to be disconcerted by such a piece of rudeness, and Mrs. Clinton's conduct has not been justified by any person whom I have heard speak of it.

Tuesday, Aug. 6—The President takes the head of one of the tables, and the *modest* Mr. Bennett[128] of the *Herald* the other. The President cannot help this, to be sure, and the juxtaposition is somewhat awkward. Bennett will make a great thing of this with those who are not aware that any person may take his seat who has impudence enough, and that it would require a pretty smart rifle to carry a ball from one end of the table to the other. I wish the President would leave his seat and give the *Herald* man all the honors of the table.

Wednesday, Aug. 7—The village is alive with preparations for Mr. Clay's[129] reception. I received a letter from him dated Montreal, 4th instant, and another by a messenger who was sent from hence to confer with him, dated on his voyage to Burlington, 6th instant. He is to lodge at Lake George to-morrow night and will come to Saratoga on Friday afternoon, where apartments are provided for him at the United States Hotel. A program is published of his reception, signed by a committee of more than 100 Whigs. We wished to repress this public demonstration, but it could not be; the movement is spontaneous, and the people seem determined to out-glorify the other party.

The Whig visitors at Congress Hall have been in a ferment about the impropriety of bringing Mr. Clay in contact with his great rival at the United States, conferences have been had and disputes held on the subject; but the difficulty is removed by the President's determination to leave Saratoga on Friday. He is to dine with the young Locofocos at Ballston, and go to Troy to be received there by his friends on the same evening, and will not return until the first of next week. This may be *accidental*, but it is a happy coincidence for us, and I am mistaken if we do not model something handsome out of this *Clay*.

Thursday, Aug. 8.—The number of visitors increases by the arrival of every train of cars. Gen. Scott, the rising sun, shone among us today. We have Secretaries Forsyth and Poinsett, Senator Tallmadge, members of Congress from all parts, and more State officers than can find "where to lay their heads." The record of the United States Hotel has been for several days blocked up by the inhospitable word *full*, but the cry is "still they come."

Friday, Aug. 9.—The day was ushered in by cloud and rain, thunder and lightning; but all passed away, and the glorious sun shone out by eight o'clock and dispersed the vapors from the natural as we trust the man who comes among us will those from the political horizon. Secretary Forsyth took away his discontented countenance last evening, and Secretary Poinsett went this morning to Cattaraugus on business relating to the Indian treaty. The President also went to Ballston and thence to Troy to receive the homage of his lieges; leaving their several vacancies to be filled by Clay.

Arrangements having been made for a number of the visitors to meet Mr. Clay on his approach to Saratoga, a large number on horseback and in carriages left the village at eleven o'clock, and went to Emmerson's Tavern[130], nine miles on the Glenn's Falls road. In less than half an hour he arrived, accompanied by committees from Caldwell and Glenn's Falls, and after our salutation we sat down to a collation, prepared under the direction of Col. Westcott, and served up in a rather homely but hearty style. Provisions had been sent out in the morning from Saratoga, and champagne was taken by the gentlemen. The company, which consisted of seventy or eighty, comprised many bright spirits and distinguished men. I had the honor of presiding at the feast, and it is certain that we made the most of the time allowed us.

At three o'clock we left Emmerson's and came to a place two miles in advance of the Springs, where the carriages, wagons, horsemen, and pedestrians who were to form the procession were collected to receive us. Mr. Clay was placed in a new †barouche, drawn by Gerald Coster's four gray horses; the other seats occupied by Judge Walton and two other gentlemen of the Saratoga committee on arrangements. The line of march was then taken up, preceded by Frank Johnson's band[131] of music; and such a cavalcade was never seen before in the county of Saratoga. It formed a compact line a mile and a half long. I rode in a †barouche with Dr. Duncan of Mississippi, Mr. Green of Louisiana, and Reverdy Johnson of Baltimore. Our approach was announced by the discharge of artillery from the hills, and the line of march preserved until we came to the United States Hotel, where quarters were prepared for "the man whom the people delight to honor." Here the avenues to the hotel were blocked up with the expecting crowds, who made the village ring with shouts of welcome. The large piazza in front of the hotel was filled with ladies, for whose exclusive use it had been reserved. It had been arranged that the address should be made, and the reply received, from the

132

steps of the hotel, but this was rendered impracticable by the crowd, and the horses were taken out and the †barouche dragged around in front. Here Mr. Clay was addressed by Mr. John W. Taylor[132], formerly Speaker of the House of Representatives, and replied in a speech to the assembled multitude of more than an hour; too long, I thought, for the occasion, and entering too much into political detail, but I suppose it was unavoidable. The townspeople had the regulation of this part of the ceremony, and they were not disposed to let the opportunity be lost to the people of hearing a "holy descent"[133] upon the misdeeds of their rulers from the lips of the oracle of the day. After the address Mr. Clay was conducted, amid the shouts of the men, and the waving of the women's handkerchiefs, to his apartments, fatigued with travel and exhausted with excitement.

But the affair did not end here. The great dining room of the United States Hotel had been fitted up during the day with bouquets of flowers and festoons of evergreens, and in the evening the most splendid ball was given that was ever witnessed here. Eight hundred persons were present, comprising a greater number of distinguished men and fine women than have probably ever been collected in this country.

I was the senior manager, and by previous arrangement, after the first set of †cotillions, Mr. Clay and his son were led into the room by me and Mr. Meredith, the band playing "Hail Columbia," and the company opening to the right and left to afford us a passage to the upper end of the room. It has been a day of prodigious excitement, and everything went off well.

An incident occurred at Emmerson's which set off to advantage Mr. Clay's readiness at repartee. There was an old gentleman there, a farmer named Col. Berry, who although he acknowledged himself a Loco-foco, professed to be an admirer of our distinguished guest, and joined in our hurrahs for Clay as loudly as the best Whig in the company. This old gentleman, partaking of the general enthusiasm, came up to me at the head of the table, and laying his hand upon my shoulder, exclaimed: "Almost thou persuadest me to be a Whig." Mr. Clay, alluding to the circumstance in a brief speech which he made on my proposing his health, said that as his old friend quoted Scripture he also would apply a quotation to him. "There is joy," he said, "on earth, as well as in Heaven, over one sinner that repenteth."

Monday, Aug. 12.—This is the meridian of the Saratoga season. All the world is here; politicians and dandies; cabinet ministers and ministers of the gospel; officeholders and officeseekers; humbuggers and humbugged; fortune-hunters and hunters of woodcock; anxious mothers and lovely daughters; the ruddy cheek mantling with saucy health, and the flickering lamp almost extinguished beneath the rude breath of dissipation. In a few days this brilliant company will be scattered over the face of the land, and who can tell of how many of them this will be the last season? My daughter Catharine, now on her first visit, at a time of life when everything is †*couleur du rose*, admired as I think she deserves to be, enjoys the passing moments to the top of her †bent. Mary, too, delicate as is her health, is a favorite with all, and has a share of pleasure great as her strength will admit of.

I like Saratoga as well as Milford, if not a little better

LUCY LOUISA COOKE

A schoolgirl has left us another view of politics between Whig and Democrat but, more significantly, of the experiences of a little girl from a country village sent to boarding school. Lucy Louisa Cooke (1828–1921) was the daughter of Timothy and Elizabeth (Westcott) Cooke of Milford, Otsego County. Her mother was a Saratoga native and had brothers and sisters there so, in 1839, Lucy came to attend the Misses Wayland's School on the southwest corner of Broadway and Washington Street. Her letters to her mother and sister are somewhat formulaic but full, nevertheless, of the wonder of a child from a tiny farming community who found herself in an urbane setting. In 1849, Lucy married Charles Smith Lester; some of her letters from that period of her life are reproduced further on.

Lucy Louisa Cooke, letters. Collection of Saratoga Springs City Historian, gift of Milford D. Lester. Transcribed by Field Horne with punctuation added. An obituary, "Mrs Lester First Pres[iden]t. of Hospital," appeared in the *Saratogian*, 3 November 1921. A brief discussion of the Misses Wayland's School is in Sylvester, 183. The 3 July 1842 letter is given *literatim*; the others are brief extracts.

October 21, 1839 to "Ma"

SARATOGA is a beautiful place, and I have taken many pleasant walks with the little girls. My teachers are beautiful ladies, and I love them because they are so very kind to me; I have visited the little girls at their house quite often, and they were so kind as to take me to ride one afternoon—I rode with Miss Wayland in a beautiful carriage, and we went to the lake, and after takeing a pleasant sail we came home. There was company here last night, and we had some very fine music. Mr. Watts played with the piano, on his flute. I have been introduced to most all the ladies, and like to be in company very much. I was a little homesick the first day, but have not been atall since then, and am very glad that I am to stay at Saratoga. I like Saratoga as well as Milford, if not a little better.

April 8, 1840 to "Mother"
I hope Joseph and Libby are learning very fast. It seems to me now, a great ways that they have to walk to school. I have only a short distance up Washington Street. I suppose you have apples at Milford but it is very difficult to procure them here. We take Oranges and lemons instead of apples. I go to the spring very often but cannot say that I am fond of it but I like it much better than when I first tasted it. There has been much excitement this last week in the erection of a log cabin dedicated to Gen. Harrison[134], built by the Whigs. The opposite party are not much pleased. On Thursday theire were 15 teems with the logs and by Saturday it was completed. Cousin Mary sends Uncle J a paper with the description of it, and also containing a speach delivered in it by Mr. Ellsworth. I am waiting patiently for Summer to come when I expect to see the large Hotels opened, and a vast many of people who come from all around to drink Spring Water and to partake of the innumerable pleasures that this delightful place affords.

April 8, 1840 to "Sister M—"
The boys in this village have commenced their favorite plays, there is at all hours of the day ball playing in the street. As soon as it is summer I am going to the Pavilion garden, Louisa informs me that it is a beautiful place, and she says it contains some flying Horses[135] and a delightful little pond with many fishes in it. and It also contains a swing which is very high and made of large iron rods attached to a beautiful boat with seats in it. It will swing very high and I should think it would be very delightfull. There is also the circular railway which was closed when I came here but has not been opened yet but I hope will be soon for the little cars are so beautiful. I should like to

discribe all the couriosities and amusements that this pleasant place is filled with but I have not time. When I see you I shall have much to tell you.

July 3rd 1842
Dear Mother—
I have been intending to write to you a long time but I think in future I shall be more punctual in answering your letters. Uncle James thinks of going to Milford Friday, and I took the opportunity to write you. I anticipate much pleasure on the fourth of July. Yesterday they put up a †liberty pole; Cousin Mary and I were upon the top of the house and saw them put it up. after they had raised it a man climbed to the top of the pole and cut off the ropes that they raised it with and slid down. Tomorrow morning I shall not sleep much after sunrise. they are going to ring the bells and fire the cannon every half hour.

The sunday schools are going to have a picknick in Beekman's woods[136] in the afternoon and the temperance people of this county are going to march through the streets.

I hope you will enjoy yourselves very much too. I suppose Uncle Joseph will have a ball in his new ball-room. I should like to be home so as to enjoy myself with you. Examination comes in about four weeks. I hate to have it come so soon but I hope I shall be prepared for it when it does come. This term I study Botany, Arithmetic, Ancient Geography, Grammar, and Parker Exercises[137], besides Reading, Reciting, Poetry, and drawing maps. It takes me most of the time to get my lessons. The school is out at three o'clock and I study until five or six. I have to go to Botany at eight o'clock in the morning and I stay in school four hours and a half before I come home. I think I stand very well in all my classes. I am no lower than number two in all my classes but Botany. in that I must be excused for being number five because there are so many large girls in the class that were put above me when the class began and I have not been able to get above them.

There is not so much company in the village as there was last summer about this time but there is a great deal now.

They have been fixing the Congress spring this summer. they dug out a great deal of dirt that had been collected in the bottom of the spring and it is delicious now: everybody goes to the Congress. A gentleman named Mr. Miller[138] has been preaching here and he says the world will come to an end in eighteen hundred and forty three or in eighteen hundred and forty seven. I went to hear him two or three times. He is quite old and he has had the palsey and he shakes very badly. He created a great sensation here and some of the farmers near here have believed him so truly that they have not planted nor will work this summer for they say they have enough to last them until eighteen hundred and forty three. I think it is very foolish in them for I do not believe that the world will be burned up quite so soon as that.

I had a delightful ride to the lake about three weeks ago we enjoyed ourselves very much: after we got there we went into the fields to get some flowers and found some very pretty ones then we went down to the lake and walked along the shore and then went out on the lake. I enjoyed a fine sail. It was about seven o'clock when we got home.

If I had not been so much engaged with my school I should have come out with Cousin Mary but I could not leave as I must stand well in my classes for examination which is the first three days of August. I shall probably see you this fall and anticipate much pleasure.

I have stayed home this afternoon to write to you. All the family have gone out to tea, and Louisa has sent for me to come and see her this evening, and as it is almost dark I must close with love to all.

from your affectionate
Lucy

McLaren would reccommend it as a delicious perfume
Edmund James Huling

Edmund Huling, whom we met through his late-life memoir about his 1831 move to town, began a daily diary on 1 August 1840 and kept it at least until early 1842. In it he gives us yet another perspective on the "Log Cabin" election of the fall of 1840, comments on the practice of "horning" (serenading a couple on their wedding night), and makes contemptuous remarks about camp meetings and other activities of people of faith – though, oddly, he chose to attend their meetings with some frequency. He was a clerk in a bookstore at the time and, in October, the 20-year-old was sent to New York to buy stock, a trip he recounts in some detail. The following extracts from the first five months of the diary were selected to provide a sense of village life in that era.

"Edmund J. Huling's Diary / Commenced Saratoga Springs, August 1, 1840." Saratoga Room, Saratoga Springs Public Library. Transcribed by Field Horne.

SUNDAY, AUG. 2—Had some conversation with Dr. Troutbeck & Mr. Winston about the virtues of the Pavilion Spring[139]—Come to the conclusion that McLaren would reccommend it next as a delicious perfume, that will supersede Lavender & Cologne.

Tuesday, Aug. 4—Went down to the Union Hall and heard Music murdered by Mr. Colman, & then went over to the Congress Hall and saw the Russian Minister and his young wife, and the Hon. Luther Bradish.

Thursday, Aug. 6—Great preparations being made on Congress Hill for holiday political meetings; the Loco Focos having joined with the Whigs in fixing and clearing the ground. Corey is in his glory ordering the men.

Saturday, Aug. 8—Tippecanoe meeting on Congress Hill in the afternoon and in the Log Cabin[140] in the evening. About 3000 present in the Grove. Addressed by Stanley of N.C., Barnard of N.Y., and others; couldn't go as I had to stay in the store.

Sunday, Aug. 9—Went to church this afternoon and got asleep as usual. Mr. Gage Preched—Had some capital singing.

Friday, Aug. 14—Saw Gen. Scott to-day. Six men belonging to the band of the 71st Highlander arrived in town from Canada to-day.

Wednesday, Aug. 19—This has been a great day for the Whigs, as there has been one of the greatest meetings that have been held in the state of New York. It was addressed by the Hon. Daniel Webster for more than three hours, with great eloquence. Saw the Governor to-day.

Monday, Aug. 31—Been engaged in warning men to Training, &c. to-day. Camp meeting commenced on Mr. Hart's farm two miles from the village.

Tuesday, Sept. 1—There was a great meeting at Glens Falls to-day numbers from here attended.

Wednesday, Sept. 2—Been down to Camp Meeting to-day & of all the fanatics, this beats the whole.

Sunday, Sept. 13—Heard of a great Protracted Meeting which has been in progress in Ballston Spa for about two weeks, Mr Knapp conducts it, He is one of the greatest fanatics in the world.

Tuesday, Sept. 23.—I went out to the farm to-day. The neighbors are getting up a squirrel hunt to kill off the squirrels which are very thick and are destroying chestnuts and com in great quantities.

Pavilion Fountain House. Drawn by August Köllner. *Views of the United States* (1848–51).

Saturday, Sept. 26—Miss Waylands commenced their school yesterday, and the scholars have been running around to get their books together for next week.

Saturday, Oct. 3—Eat to many chestnuts to-day, unhealthy.

Sunday, Oct. 4—Sick all day.—Did'nt get up 'till ½ past 9, and eat nothing but a bit of toast.

Monday, Oct. 5—Been quite pleasant to-day. Got a new coat, very good fit, Clement is a good Tailor. School Meeting to-night.

Wednesday, Oct. 7—This has been a beautiful day. I went up to the new Spring, above the Iodine, for the first time to-day—very good Spring, nothing extra.

Tuesday, Oct. 13 – Started for New York to-day, at ½ past 7 AM. Went down the river in the *Swallow,* Capt. McLean. A cold night.

Wednesday, Oct. 14—Arrived in New York this Morning about ½ past 3. A.M. making the passage from Saratoga in about 20 hours including stoppages in Troy, Albany, and other places down the river. Been engaged all day in purchasing books, very busy.

Thursday, Oct. 15—Engaged yet in purchasing books, &c. Saw

Greeley, the editor of the *New Yorker*, and Park Benjamin of the *New World*,[141] and for as smart writers as they are, they appear to be very inferior looking men.

Friday, Oct. 16—Went to the fair of the American Institute[142] to-day. Saw a large assortment of finery with a great deal of useful machinery. Among the useful may be mentioned a Life Boat, a great many kinds of cooking stoves, a machine for reeling silk, a machine for planeing and dressing barrell staves, by which a piece of timber was by one operation planed on both sides & the edges chamfered off at both ends, corn shellers, straw cutters, &c., &c., &c. Started for home to-night in the *Swallow*.

Wednesday, Oct. 28—There was an abolition meeting at the Baptist meeting house to-night, which was addressed by a Mr. Glenn.

Saturday, Oct. 31—A great Whig Meeting was called to-night at the Log-Cabin, but as that would not contain the multitude it was adjourned to Soper's Bowling Alleys. The meeting was addressed by J. K. Porter, Esq. of Waterford. He instituted comparisons between Van Buren and Harrison, which were rather more unfavorable to the former than I can agree with him.

Sunday, Nov. 1—Went to Methodist meeting this forenoon, Rev. Mr. Goss preached. Sermon very good for a Methodist, not quite so much rant as there was at the Camp Meeting.

Monday, Nov. 9—There is a party next door to welcome G. Peck's Bride to Saratoga—wonder when they will make a party to welcome my bride here—sometime I think.

Saturday, Nov. 14—There was a great robbery committed in this place last night, Mr. Clement's Tailor Shop being broken open & about $150.– worth of Clothing taken away. No trace of the thieves has yet been discovered.

Friday, Nov. 20—Went to Schenectada to-day to get Powder &c., for the Whigs to celebrate with and of all places for dullness of looks, and old style of the buildings that place beats, every thing seems going to ruin there and there is no building going on there, that I could see.

Friday, Nov. 27—The folks who were married yesterday have been †keeping wedding all day to-day rather a foolish practice.

Sunday, Nov. 29—Aunt Betsy is very sick and contrary to the advice of regular physicians she follows the prescriptions of an old woman of a quack doctress.

Wednesday, Dec. 2—Had some thoughts to-night to call the

"Club" together soon if we don't have dancing school to pass these long Winter evenings, for if I read all the evening my eyes feel weak.

Monday, Dec. 7—The snow that fell yesterday makes very good sleighing and people have begun to draw wood a little, yet the sleighing is not good enough for me to commence drawing our yearly supply, as I intended to do this winter myself.

Saturday, Dec. 12—I wrote to Dr. Taylor to-day, and among other things I spoke about getting a certificate of the efficacy of his Balsam of Liverwort[143]—hope he won't manufacture it as he did one last spring. These Quacks have not much conscience.

Friday, Dec. 18—To-day I am twenty years of age. How fast time flies, it seems but yesterday that I was a little boy †trundling a hoop or riding down hill, and now I am almost a man.

Sunday, Dec. 20—Been sitting in the house all day reading and talking. Been talking about going to Washington to [see] Harrison take his oath of office—I keep talking about it until finally I may get my father's consent to go.

Tuesday, Dec. 22—They butchered the hogs on the farm to-day and I had to stay in the store all day.

Thursday, Dec. 24—The same old story of every Christmas Eve, Church trimmed and a ball to-night.[144]

Monday, Dec. 28—Went to a ball to-night and danced until ½ past four O'clock in the morning, all for the benefit of the church as the profits went to the Episcopal Church.

Tuesday, Dec. 29—After dancing all last night I walked out to Milton, six miles, to-day.

Wednesday, Dec. 30—Commenced drawing wood from the "Range" to-day. Sleighing rather poor yet as the snow is so light that it does not pack.

Thursday, Dec. 31.—This is the last day of the year. How many things have been done during this year which the authors of them would like to recall, and how many good actions which might have been done have been neglected, yet every thing goes on in the same old routine.

He has been quacking himself
MORLEIGH

We unfortunately do not know the identity of the author who styled himself "Morleigh in Search of an Estate" but his book provides wonderful images of Saratoga boarding-house life and of swimming at Saratoga Lake, immensely enriched by his lively prose and filled with acute dialogue. His visit took place before the start of the season, in June of 1842.

Morleigh, *Life in the West: Back-Wood Leaves and Prairie Flowers* (London: Saunders and Otley, 1842), 132–143.

THE SEASON had just begun—that is to say, the hotels and boarding-houses were airing, repairing, painting, and glazing, for the reception of visitors at Saratoga Springs when I arrived at this far-famed watering place.

"You will find it rather dull just now," said a railroad companion, "Congress Hall and the Pavilion empty."

"Try my private boarding-house, sir," said a respectable looking old man, touching his hat.

"I don't care if I do," said I; and followed my leader to the outskirts of the town, to the white stoops and unpretending front of his boarding-house, with its little martin-house perched over the rose-embowered windows.

"You may please yourself, and choose any room you like," said my host, as he led me through the house; "we have very few boarders just now."

I soon fixed upon a quiet little chamber, opening on the veranda or stoop, and made myself quite at home. We dined at two o'clock—a plain and homely meal, of which the host and about a dozen boarders partook, while four nice girls, his daughters, waited at table; judging from the appearance of the boarders that they were invalids, I inquired of an austere-looking man who sat next me how the waters agreed with him; he answered with some embarrassment, and took his departure without satisfying me on that head. This man I afterwards discovered to be a carpenter, particularly sensitive as to his position in society; being originally intended for the church, and not having the gift of gab, he was what the Scotch call a sticked minister, and now honourably supported himself as a journeyman carpenter.

A lawyer's lady, and her sister and daughter, from Albany, acknowledged they had received much benefit from the Iodine.

"Give me the Highrock," said a dark-complexioned youth, the wag of the party, a young barrister, who sat at the foot of the table; "try the Highrock spring, sir; it is famous for sharpening one's appetite."

Took a delightful stroll through the pine-groves at the back of our house; there is something exhilarating in the air wafted through a pine grove. Returning to the house, I overtook one of our boarders, a tall, good-looking man, in the everlasting black coat and continuations, and attempted to enter into conversation with him. He seemed in †rude health, but fancied he was very ill indeed, and drank prodigious quantities of water. He was from Massachusetts, and was one of the most reserved men I have ever met with. One day, I found him fainting on a sofa in the parlour, and one of our kind-hearted ladies fanning him and supporting his head. I proposed that he should be carried to bed, and a doctor sent for; but, opening his great black eyes, he protested against receiving any assistance with great vehemence, begged that a basin might be set beside him, and that he might be left alone. But the ladies having gathered about him, I lingered at the window, while our venerable hostess kindly inquired into his ailments.

"I have been drinking five tumblers at the Congress, two at the Pavilion, and one at the Iodine," murmured the patient. "Oh! Those waters will be the death of me!" he groaned; "instead of soothing my tortured stomach, those sharp and chilling waters have scourged my entrails."

"Oh! Mr.—— ! my! Mr.—— !" "Oh!" and "my!" ejaculated the ladies, as they retreated, and left the victim of the spas to the care of the old hostess and myself. He became so ill that we had to put him to bed, and send for a doctor after all.

"He has been quacking himself," said the doctor, as he descended from the invalid's chamber; "he has been drinking the waters without medical advice—wrong, wrong, very wrong, to drink the waters without first consulting a medical man."

Sallied out before breakfast with the barrister, took a sip at every one of the springs from the Congress to the Highrock, clambered up the ricketty wooden steps at the last, and retraced our steps through the shabby wooden houses occupied by the renegade Canadian French[145], to the upper end of Broadway, and sat down to breakfast as voracious as hungry wolves.

Rode to Saratoga Lake with the barrister, put up our horse and buggy at the hotel, and descended to the lake in quest of a boat—found one stuck in the mud, which we could not launch, and espying another south side of the lake, we looked about for its owner, but finding none, took the liberty of rowing up the lake in it. Presently a man began hallooing after us; but, as my learned friend observed, the fellow was on the opposite side of the lake from that which we had taken the boat, and ergo, the boat did not belong to him. Resting on our oars, however, we heard his voice denouncing us loud and clear, for having presumed to take the ferry-boat. My learned friend rose up in the boat and responded, giving his opinion, gratis, that the appellant might terminate his doleful days with a rope, *felo-da-lac* or *felo-da-se* [146], before he would get the boat from us; and by the way of shewing a *non sequitur*, we resumed the oars, and pulled vigorously up the lake. Shoals of little fishes played round us; and we admired the wooded banks of the lake, a round wooded hill especially. The flies soon became very troublesome, and we returned slowly towards the spot from whence we had taken the boat; but the man who had hailed us from the shore, now made his appearance in another boat, which he pulled towards us with great speed; we pulled our oars and arrived at the landing-place before him. "Now let us make a strait coat tail for the buggy!" said my legal friend. I was not disposed to run, and advised a parley. Meantime the ferry-man approached us, and reproached us with having made away with his boat, and finally demanded half a dollar damages.

"Half a dollar!—half a dollar, indeed!" exclaimed my friend, slapping his brow—"who ever heard of such an extravagant demand?—well, after that I find you are deaf to reason. I'll not argue with you." And my friend marched off into the bush, and deliberately took off his clothes, entered the lake, and began to swim about.

"Well, stranger," said the angry boatman, turning to me, "I guess you must pay me for the boat."

"Extortion!" bawled the barrister, as he sputtered along through the water.

"You'd best be civil, my chap," said the boatman; "if it wasn't for your darn'd imperence [*sic*] to me when you took the boat I'd not have looked for a cent."

"Don't mind him, sir," bawled the barrister; "let him take an action and recover by law. If he recovers at the court of Saratoga, we can appeal, and take our position in the higher courts at Albany, and laugh at his beard. Hurrah! If you had known how warm and pleasant the water feels, you might have joined me, and we could have swam round the lake, without tugging his heavy old boat along."

"I'm not going to argue law with you now," said the ferryman, walking into the bush; "and as you took possession of my boat without asking, I'll take possession of your clothes until I'm paid."

This †*coup de main* swamped the barrister. How could he return to Saratoga in a state of nudity; but to be outwitted by a clown was most inglorious. He protested and exclaimed against the barbarian in vain, and finally I was obliged to pay him and send him about his business, grumbling against the barrister for his *tarnation tongue.*

Sung last night to a hall full of seats
THE HUTCHINSON FAMILY

Of all the stage performers of nineteenth-century America, perhaps none represented old New England better than the Hutchinson Family, Judson, John, Asa, and Abby. Four of the 13 children of a Milford, N.H., farmer, they had begun performing late in 1840 in their home town. In June of 1842 they set out on a career that was to take them through 12,000 concerts in America and Europe, nearly until the century's end. Alone among performers of stature, they left a detailed record of their business in journals kept collectively. Their short and not-very-successful appearance in Saratoga Springs that first August is chronicled in wonderfully droll prose that, but for differences in language, sounds remarkably like that of a modern American with a sense of humor. Twenty years later John Hutchinson wrote a song that, for many Victorians, expressed well the spa experience:

They eat, they drink, and they sleep,
They talk, they walk, and they woo,
They sigh, they laugh, and they weep,
They read, they ride, and they dance,
With other unspeakable things,
And they pray, and they play, and they pay,
And that's what they do at the springs.

Dale Cockrell, ed., *Excelsior: Journals of the Hutchinson Family Singers, 1842–1846* (Hillsdale, N.Y.: Pendragon Press, 1989), 37–41.

Saratoga Springs
Tuesday P.M. Aug 2d [by John]

JUDSON, John, Abigail and three Strangers in this our sitting room. They are playing *domino*. Count up. O! Me—
We gave a Concert at the Pavilion Fountain House last night. Took150.00[147]
D. McLaren made a bargain with us to Board us and keep our horses and give us ⅓ of the proceeds. Pretty Lively times in this place, the rides, the *Balls* and other entertainments, how amusing. Went up to the U[nited] S[tates Hotel] after our Concert. They had a *cotilion* party at that place. At the Congress Hall they had a ball—at which place Frank Johnson's band presides—

[by Judson]

14 Different Springs here. The most curious of which is High Rock Spring, which comes up through an orifice in a solid rock 5 feet [high] as large as a man's hat. Congress is the most popular although no better than others. Came here Monday. Bought nothing and paid in nothing. Sung last night to a hall full of seats. (Oh brimstone). Going to Bolston to day. Hope for better luck soon or we shall squash. The spring water does not suit me. The road from Glens falls to Saratoga springs is one continued bed of sand. Oh popcock and hoboken. The poor ye have always with you but me, ye have not always. I wish I was in Mass. I am of the opinion that I shall make a noise in the world yet. But when I think of the future my eyes become dull and I am going to sleep. I am asleep now when I write. Mr. Williams keeps the bath house here. He is a fine man. And he says they are trying to run him out and can they is the question. A great deal of oposition here. Great many things in this world Capt. Dickerson.

Aug 3/42 [by John]

J.W.H.—Well here we are Judson, Abigail & John at the Springs a trying to enjoy our selves. But I think that I've Scene an end of what they call perfection here below. O! The changing scenes of life. This world is all a fleeting show so it is.

[by John]

J. H.—We have been here 2 days. Given two concerts at the Pavilion Fountain house. Met with poor encouragement. Think we shall not try it another night. Brother Asa has gone to Ballston to make engagements for tonight. Hope he will succeed in his undertakings. Think that he will. I am myself rather non Compass Mentass today. Wish that I was in Mass. Lynn. Would like to see [Tryphena]. Since we have been in this state we have not paid our expenses. The last fortnight we have lost $15. It is rather *Dis*[?couraging]. Hope to do better business *soon.* Saw today a gentleman Friend from Peterborough N.H. Also a Minister of his acquaintance. Went this morning to Congress Springs to hear F. Jonson's Band perform. This band composed of 10 Black Men from the south. They play very well but no equall to Kendles Brass Band of Boston.

Nothing more to write now. Leave this afternoon for Balstown 7 miles from this place, then we go to Albany, Ny. All well. *God is good.* Amen.

A little room of about the size and temperature of an ordinary oven

JOHN ROBERT GODLEY

John R. Godley (1814–1861) was an Anglo-Irishman from Killegar, county Leitrim. Educated at Harrow and Oxford, he was admitted to the bar, but practiced little if at all. His first book, a two-volume work, recounted his visit to America in 1842. Later, he became interested in colonization schemes and planned Canterbury, New Zealand; when his health became poor in 1849 he left England and took up his residence at Canterbury, but returned to England three years later and held several government positions before his death in London at a young age.

John Robert Godley, *Letters from America* (London: John Murray, 1844), 1: 42–48.

SARATOGA, as every one knows, is the Cheltenham or Baden of America: it is now the height of the season; and though they say it is not so full as usual, in consequence of the commercial distress and scarcity of money, it is very unpleasantly crowded nevertheless. I am in a little room, of about the size and temperature of an ordinary oven, in a lodging-house appendant to the Congress Hall Hotel. I cannot say that I enjoy Saratoga. Watering-places at all times and every where are †*ennuyant* enough; but this, I think, beats in stupidity most that I have seen. The fact is, that neither the Americans nor the English are fitted for a watering-place life. They are too fond of politics, of business, of excitement, and soon weary of the simple routine which a watering-place affords of †*vie en plein air*—early hours and gossipping familiarity—and which the easy, sociable habits and manners of the continental nations, particularly the Germans, qualify them to enjoy so thoroughly. I never saw an Englishman at a foreign watering-place whose chief resource did not consist in looking out for the English mail, and reading the English papers; and then we are so jealous, so distant, so afraid of foreigners and of each other, that I never can help feeling that an Englishman makes the worst and most ungraceful lounger in the world, except an American. Here we are all making believe to be exceedingly gay, and looking as if we thought it the greatest bore in the world. There is none of the †*laisser-aller* and †*déshabille*, which is the redeeming point about a German bath. One is obliged to dress, with the thermometer at 90°, as though one were in London or Paris (not that I do, but I ought), or indeed more so, for I do not think I ever saw so large a proportion of highly-dressed men and women. The Parisian fashions of the day are carried out to their extreme, detestably ugly as they are. Really the modern European (and American) costume gives a woman the appearance of something between a trussed fowl and an hour-glass; her elbows are pinioned to her sides by what are facetiously called *shoulder*-straps, while she is compressed in the waist, and puffed out above and below it, to such an extent that one expects her to break off in the middle at the slightest touch.

Heaven help me for coming here for aristocracy

HENRY MCCALL JR.

"Harry" McCall (b 1821) was Louisiana-born, son of a wealthy planter originally from Philadelphia. When his mother died in 1825, he was sent there to live with three maiden aunts, was educated there and became, as he put it, "a humble practitioner of the Law." In a letter to a relative during his Saratoga sojourn in 1843, he provided the usual synopsis of the social scene with an emphasis on upper-class Philadelphians, but expressed dismay at the diversity of the visitors.

1843 HENRY McCALL JR.

Henry McCall, Jr., letter to Peter McCall, 13 August 1843. Cadwalader Papers, Historical Society of Pennsylvania. Transcribed by Field Horne. No biography of McCall has been located, but he wrote "Chronicles of the McCall Family" (1845) which, along with a "McCall Family Chart" (1882) by George A. McCall, provide the basic facts.

148

HEAVEN HELP me for coming here for Aristocracy For such a collection of Swells and Rowdies it has rarely been my chance to lay my eyes upon. Not a Soul here from Philadelphia I knew, but Mrs. Butler and Miss Randolph. Some few Baltimoreans—The Schleys and Ridgely's but none of our set—As for the New Yorkers they are of all sorts and sizes from Van Buren down. Here and there one or two passable people But no fashion and little beauty. All exclaim against the dullness of the Season and yet we are crowded to death—And as the Season is just finishing there is no chance of our getting anything better. Emma Meredith is here—Miss Granger—the Duncans of Linton—the O'Donnells— †*Voila tout* that is known to Fame.

We paid our bills—as a good many do not who visit the springs

ISAAC MICKLE

Though a youth of 21 and just finished with the study of law, Isaac Mickle (1822–1855) was already a man to be reckoned with when he stayed at Congress Hall for a few days in the summer of 1844. Born into a wealthy land-owning family in Camden County, New Jersey, he had become the editor of the Camden Eagle *the previous January and, as such, was a minor force in politics, a world that fascinated him. His journey was for reasons of health, and he duly noted that the mineral waters were efficacious; but his health gradually failed in the years that followed, and he was only 32 when he died of tuberculosis.*

Philip English Mackey, *A Gentleman of Much Promise: The Diary of Isaac Mickle 1837–1845* (Philadelphia: University of Pennsylvania Press, 1977), 2: 464–466. Biography is found in the introduction, 1: xiii–xix. The manuscript is in the collection of the Camden County Historical Society.

13 August, Tuesday. Saratoga.

We came hither this morning by rail-road. The United States being full we quartered at the old Congress Hall, once the leading house but now number three in the scale of popularity. I met with none whom I knew except ex-President Van Buren. He is at the States. We called on him this evening and had a short interview. He looks well, and says that political affairs in New York look ditto.

14 August, Wednesday.

I have made a few acquaintances here, and among the rest one with Charles Secor, a New York democrat, and one of those who were going to throw Hineline overboard on our way to Baltimore for opposing Mr. Van Buren. I find him to be a very clever fellow.

There is but little beauty here, but of course a great deal of folly. The most distinguished flirts at all the houses are as ugly as the devil.

The water here improves with use. When I first drank it, it went down like medicine. Now I can drink five or six tumblers with ease. It has had a considerable effect in opening my bowels.

I called to-day on the two democratic editors here.

15 August, Thursday.

Carman's girls arrived here to-day from the north. Being the only ladies I know of course I do the gallant to them, though the elder one is horridly ugly. I have made several other acquaintances among the gentlemen, among them with Josiah Randall, Esq. of our bar.

16 August, Friday. Utica.

Jeffers and I held a consultation to-day and resolved to go to Niagara. Accordingly we paid all our bills—as a good many do not who visit the Springs—and started at noon, via Schenectady, for this place.

Aunt Hannah would think this was worse than Sodom and Gomorrah

Henry Lillie Pierce

Henry L. Pierce (1825–1896) was not quite 19 when he visited the spa, but he was already a health seeker, as his letters home make very clear. His abolitionist sympathies led him into the Free-Soil Party campaign in 1848; the fol-

lowing year he entered his uncle's Dorchester cocoa factory, which he took over in 1854. He built it into America's dominant cocoa firm. After the Civil War, he became active in politics, serving two years as mayor of Boston and two terms in Congress. His first letter was to his younger brother Edward, later to become Charles Sumner's biographer; the second was sent to his father and was addressed to the family.

Henry L. Pierce, letters to Edward L. Pierce, 5 July 1844, and to Jesse Pierce, 10 August 1844. Pierce Family Letters, Massachusetts Historical Society. Transcribed by Field Horne.

Congress Spring House[148]
Saratoga Sprins [*sic*] July 5th [1844]

Edward,

I RECEIVED your letter today noon and I was much gratified at the occurrence. I gave an account of my journey here and will say nothing about it now. I suppose you would like to have me give you an account of all that is passing but that will be too tedious. I will however give you the [?general] items. There have been and are here several people with whom my Father is acquainted. Among them the Hon Frederick Robinson Warden of our State Prison. He is a very pleasant man. We discussed the whole subject of Massachusetts politics. Gen Whitney of Milton & Lady are here and a young Lawyer from Andover. Rev Mr Lanfare of Medway is also here & Mr Cozzens of Milton was here the first day or two. Gov Briggs is also here. On Wednesday last the Massachusetts people paid him a visit your humble servant among the number. He shook hands with us all and made a speech. As to the effect of the water upon me I cannot well judge. They do not prove so cathartic as I desired. I shall be able to decide in one week more. I eat more than when I was at home and I think it does not distress me so much. Father thinks they have helped him considerably and will remain untill sometime next week. My toes have annoyed me confoundedly and have detracted a good deal from my enjoyment. The day after I arrived the nail on my well foot began to grow in and become very sore. I was obliged to go and buy a pair of slippers. Cut an airhole for my great toes and stamp it about in this Emporium of fashion in the manner described. I have not worn a boot since I came here and probably shall not. If they do not get better I shall return with father. In other respects I have not felt more comfortable this great while. I am going to rest a little while and get a glass of Congress Water.

I have just returned from the Spring and will now proceed with my letter. This week and next will be the most fashionable weeks this Season. The United States Hotel and Union Hall are now full and have to Lodge some of their boarders out. Aunt Hannah would think this was worse than Sodom and Gomorrah. Eating, Drinking water and Sometimes a little [ ] in it, Balls, parties, Rolling ninepins, Gambling and Such like are the order of the days. I have just been to see them roll nine pins and while I was there Tisdale Drake came in. He arrived this forenoon and stops at Union Hall. So you see we have plenty of acquaintances. We have people boarding with us from every Section of the country.

I wish you would send me our *Statesman* which comes on Saturday next as I have not seen a Boston paper since I came here. Read it and mail it on Sunday at Easton. I shall then get it on Tuesday. I consulted Dr North & he directed me to proceed as follows; Drink two tumblers before each meal and before going to bed, Take a warm Sulpher bath, heat to 104° every other day, Eat meat and use mus[tard] cayenne peper and black peper freely. He says I ou[ght] to eat two spoonfuls of ground mustard every day. He said if the water taken as he directed did not prove cathartic I must increase the quantity. So I take 6 or 8 tumblers before breakfast. When I told him how Dr Bigelow directed me to live he laughed right out and said every one had some hobby.

I am tired and cannot write more so

Goodbye
Henry

I have not written to the *Democrat* and do not know as I shall. H.
[Addressed:] Edward L. Pierce / Stoughton / Ms.

Congress Spring House
Saratoga Springs Aug 10 44

Dear Friends,

When I wrote you last I gave you to understand that I should be at home this week, but I have since changed my mind and shall stay another week at least. My toes are convalescent although they get along slowly. I have not as yet been able to wear my boots, but wore fathers shoes to meeting yesterday and also some today. The water does not effect me so favorably as I could wish. It does not operate as a cathartic and has not since I came here but acts powerfully as a diurretic. I have had nothing pass my bowels since I came here except through the influence of medicine. A gentleman who lives here in perfect health tells me that he is never troubled with costiveness except when he takes the water. With most people who are here however it is powerfully cathartic and 6 tumblers is equal to a portion of salts. I drink 8 tumblers before breakfast and two before each meal and before going to bed.

Notwithstanding the drawbacks of my toes and the unfavorable operation of the water I am full as well as when I left home, feel stronger, *am in good spirits* and enjoy myself very well.

This is the most fashionable week of the season. The Public houses are full all the time. The cars go and come full twice every day so you see we have bustle enough. It commenced raining on Saturday about noon and continued through the day yesterday. It is very hazy today and portends rain. It was very cool this morning and not much fun in drinking the water. I would write more but the bell is on the point of ringing for dinner and I must carry this to the Post Office as soon as I have done or it will not go untill tomorrow. Father thinks the water helps him and he is [?]

Love to all, Henry

P.S. Tell Aunt Hannah and Uncle Lem we have one Slave boarding here who came to wait on her master. The waiter a black fellow told me he offered to get a coach and carry her to Canada but she said she would not leave her Master for nothing in the world.
[Addressed:] Jesse Pierce, Esq / Stoughton / Ms

Drinking the very nasty but very valuable waters

GEORGE DROUGHT WARBURTON

George Warburton (1816–1857), another Anglo-Irishman, was educated at the Royal Military College at Woolwich and served in the artillery. In 1844, he sailed for Canada and began accumulating the material for his first book, published anonymously in 1846. It detailed his travels in the United States, including a visit to Saratoga. Although he made pointed comments on the manners of the Americans, Warburton comes across as a Briton who was moderately charmed by those he met; but his biographer, in the Dictionary of

National Biography, *called him "scarcely more complimentary to the manners of the republicans than . . . Mrs. Trollope."*

[George D. Warburton], *Hochelaga; or, England in the New World* (New York: Wiley and Putnam, 1846), 2: 11–14.

ABOUT MID-DAY, we arrived at an immense hotel at Saratoga; my Georgian friend introduced me to the proprietor, who shook hands with me and hoped I might enjoy my visit; in short his reception was such as if he had invited me to pass some time with him, and he was in reality as kind and attentive as if I had been an invited guest. There were I think four hundred people staying in the hotel; all the rooms were full, but our host provided me a very nice lodging in a house close by, and I lived at the hotel table. My bed-room had folding doors opening into the sitting-room of the family. Unfortunately for me, within there was a piano, and the young lady of the house was learning the "Battle of Prague."[149] The next morning, returning sooner than was expected after breakfast, I disturbed her in sweeping my bed-chamber; not to lose time, she laid aside her brush and ran over a few of the most difficult passages, till I left the room clear for her to resume her more homely occupation. I do not give this little sketch with a sneer—far from it: I tell it with pleasure and admiration. Would to Heaven that some of our poor household drudges had such innocent pleasures! I would rather hear one of them play the "Battle of Prague" than listen to Listz [*sic*] for a week.

I was very much amused and interested at Saratoga; there cannot be a better opportunity for acquiring a general idea of the national character in a short time, than a stay there in the autumn offers. I was introduced to hundreds of people, all shook hands, as part of the ceremony, though the weather was so very hot; there were Southerners and Northerners, Downeasters and Westerns, New-Yorkers and Bostonians, all different from each other in detail, and very different from Europeans. Though many of the young gentlemen adopted the newest Parisian style of dress and wearing the hair, I could have sworn to them anywhere; there was something Transatlantic about them which could not be mistaken. Some few of the elder men, who had travelled and seen the world, were in their appearance and conversation free from any peculiarity. I could readily have supposed them fellow countrymen; it is never an unwelcome thing to an American to be mistaken for an Englishman, no matter how much he may disapprove of our country and institutions.

There were several families of the higher classes of society, people who would be admired and sought after anywhere; but there was of course a very large alloy of the ill-bred and obscure, who, perhaps by some lucky turn of trade, had got together a sufficient number of dollars for their summer amusement without ever before having had the leisure or the means to play gentility. Opposite to me at dinner, on the first day, sat a party of this latter class, whose conversation I enjoyed even as much as the very good fare on the table. A gentleman addressed the lady next him, "Ma'am, are you going to Bosting (Boston) right off?" She answered, "No, Sir, I reckon I'll made considerable of an circumlocution first," and in this style they continued.

In the evening there was a "hop" as they called it, graced by many very pretty faces. A young English officer, waltzing away at a great pace with the possessor of one of the prettiest of them, was tripped up by a nail in the floor, and fell, his partner sharing his misfortune. The young lady's mother, highly indignant, rushed forward to pick her up, saying to the unhappy delinquent "I tell you, Sir, I'll have none of your British tricks with my daughter." I suppose the old lady's wrath was as easily soothed as roused, for I saw the young couple spinning away again in a few minutes as if nothing had happened. The higher class of visitors did not mix much in these general amusements, seldom appearing but at meals, and sometimes not even then.

Riding, driving, playing at bowls, and drinking the very nasty, but, I believe, very valuable waters, were the pastimes of the day. Dinner was at half-past three, in an enormous room, or rather two rooms thrown into one, at right angles to each other; upwards of five hundred people sat down each day, some of the ladies dressed splendidly for the occasion, as if for a ball; they looked rather odd I thought afterwards, walking about in these gay costumes under the verandahs, or in the large and well kept gardens; but there was much beauty and grace to carry it off, the shape of the head and neck is universally very good, eyes brilliant, features regular; the failing is in the complexion and the outline of the figure; many of them dressed again for tea, and, twice a week, on the nights of a ball, they dressed again for that.

After dinner the gentlemen lounged about or sat outside the barroom reading the papers, some of them in the extraordinary attitudes we have so often heard of, while they "cigared it," "mintjuleped it," or "sherry-cobblered it," as their different tastes suggested. There were billiard-tables and shooting-galleries, where gentlemen with frightful beards and moustaches abounded.

Nor is there any lack of opportunity for indulging the taste for literary pursuits; little boys are perpetually going about tempting you with sixpenny worth of Scott, Bulwer, D'Israeli, and indeed all popular authors, with coarse and clumsy translations of French works, from the filthy wit of Rabelais, to the refined and insidious immoralities of George Sand.

The morning I left Saratoga was made remarkable to me by almost the only instance of rudeness, or indeed of the absence of active kindness, which I met with in America. As I was walking in front of the hotel, a button came off the strap on the instep of my shoe. Seeing a shoemaker's shop close by, I stepped in, and in very civil terms asked the man to sew it on for me; he told me to sit down on a box and give him the shoe, which I did. He turned it round, looked at it, and then at me, and "guessed I was a Britisher." I owned "the soft impeachment." He then put the shoe on the counter, and took no further notice of me. After about ten minutes, I meekly observed that as I was going by the twelve o'clock cars, I should be much obliged if he could sew it on at once. He "guessed" that he had not time then, but that, if I called in a quarter of an hour, perhaps "he'd fix it." I hopped over for my shoe, and, curious to see how the affair would end, returned in about twenty minutes, and again urged my request. "Sit down and wait," was the stern reply. Another quarter of an hour passed, and though my patience was not in the least exhausted, I was afraid of missing the train by indulging my curiosity as to his intentions, so I again alluded to my button, and to my time being limited. He then called to a person in an inner room, "Fix this button for that man on the box if you have nothing else to do." A minute sufficed. I laid a dollar on the table, asking what I owed him, and at the same time thanking him as quietly for the job as if he had been all kindness. He threw me the change, deducting a shilling for the button, and as I left the shop said, "Well, I guess you're late now." His guess was, however, a bad one, for I was just in time.

I confess my anger rose a little, a very little, but I drove it down, and determined, above all, that I would not let the rude act of one unchristian churl give me even for a moment a false impression of a great and generous people.

The hall looked somewhat like the deck of a ship after action

ALEXANDER MACKAY

The Scot, Alexander Mackay (1808–1852), who had been a young newspaperman working in Canada, returned to Britain to work for a London paper. It then sent him to the United States to report on the 1846 congressional debates on Oregon. When he again returned to Britain, he published a record of his travels, including a description of a Saratoga sojourn, commenting on the shift from "genteel" to "vulgar" then taking place. In 1851, he went to India to study agricultural economics and, while en route home, he died at sea.

Alexander Mackay, *The Western World; or, Travels in the United States in 1846–7* (Philadelphia: Lea and Blanchard, 1849), 1: 197–202.

SARATOGA has lately been losing cast, but it is still, to a considerable extent, a place of fashionable resort. For a time the "select" had it all to themselves, but by-and-by "everybody" began to resort to it, and on "everybody" making his appearance the "select" began to drop off, and what was once very genteel is now running the risk of becoming exceedingly vulgar. The waters are held in considerable repute as medicinal; but of the vast crowds who flock annually to Saratoga, but a small proportion are invalids. The town is very elegant, the main street being enormously wide, and shaded by trees. The hotels are on a very great scale, and so are their charges. At this, however, one cannot †repine, seeing that it is everybody's business to make hay when the sun shines. It scarcely shines for three months for the hotel-keepers of Saratoga, the crowds of flying visitors going as rapidly as they come with the season. For nine months of the year Saratoga is dull to a degree—Suddenly the doors are opened—the shutters are flung back from the windows—curling wreaths of smoke rise from the long smokeless chimneys—and the hotels seem suddenly to break the spell that bound them to a protracted torpidity. A day or two afterwards, a few visitors arrive, like the first summer birds. But long ere this, from the most distant parts of the Union people have been in motion for "the Springs," and scarcely a week elapses ere the long-deserted town is full of bustle and animation, and ringing with gaiety. A better spot can scarcely be selected for witnessing the different races and castes which constitute the heterogeneous population of the Union, and the different styles of beauty which its different latitudes produce. I stayed several days and enjoyed myself exceedingly, and seldom have I seen together so many beautiful faces and light graceful forms as I have witnessed on an August afternoon upon the broad and lengthy colonnade of the principal hotel.

I was so fortunate as to meet at Saratoga with a Canadian friend, who had been my fellow-voyager across the Atlantic. The gaiety of the place is infectious, and we soon entered into it with the same eagerness as those around us. Saratoga society is not encumbered with conventionalities. To society around it, in its general acceptation, it is what the undress boxes are to the more formal circle beneath. You make acquaintances there whom you do not necessarily know, or who do not know you elsewhere. The huge pile constituting the hotel covered three sides of a large quadrangle, the fourth side being formed by a high wall. The whole enclosed a fine green, on a portion of which bowls could very well be played. The three sides occupied by the building were shaded by a colonnade, to protect the guests from the hot sun. This part of the establishment was generally appropriated by them, where they lounged on benches and rocking chairs, and smoked and drank both before and after dinner. The meal just mentioned was the †"grand climacteric" in the events of each day. A few families who visit Saratoga dine in their private apartments, but the vast majority dine in public; and they get but a partial view of Saratoga life, who do not scramble for a seat at the †*table d'hôte.*

In the chief hotel the dining-room is of prodigious dimensions. It is, in fact, two enormous rooms thrown into one, in the form of an L. Three rows of tables take the sweep of it from end to end. It can thus accommodate at least 600 guests. The windows of both sections of the dining-room looked into the quadrangle, and my friend and I observed that several of the loungers in the colonnade every now and then cast anxious glances within as the tables were being laid for dinner. It soon occurred to us that there might be some difficulty in getting seats, a point on which we sought to set our minds at rest, so that we might be prepared, if necessary, for the crush. But we could effect no entrance into the dining-room to make inquiry, every approach to it being locked. At last, however, we caught in the colonnade a tall black waiter, dressed from top to toe in snow-white livery.

"Will there by any crush, when the bell rings?" I demanded of him.

"Bit of a squeeze, that's all," he replied. "But you needn't mind," he continued, regarding me, "the fat uns get the worst on't."

"Then you can't tell us where we are to sit?" said I.

"Jist where you happen to turn up, gemmen," he responded, grinning and showing his ivory.

"But surely," interposed my friend, "you can secure a couple of chairs for us?"

"It's jist within de power of possibles, gemmen," said he, grinning again, but with more significance than before. My friend slipped a quarter of a dollar into his hand. Oh! the power of money. That which was barely possible before, became not only practicable but certain in a twinkling. He immediately left us to fulfil our wishes, telling us to look in at the window and see where he secured chairs for us. The doors were still locked, but by-and-by we perceived parties of ladies and gentlemen entering the dining-room by those connecting it with the private apartments, and taking their seats at table. The †*ignoble vulgus,* in the interior colonnade, were kept out until the ladies and those accompanying them were all seated. Then came the noisy jingle of the long wished-for bell. Back flew every door, and in rushed, helter skelter, the eager crowd. We took our post at the door nearest the chairs set apart for us, on which we pounced as soon as we were pushed in, and were thus secure in the possession of places from which we could command a look of both arms of the dining room. It was some time ere all were seated; and in the *hurry scurry* of entering it actually seemed as if some were leaping in at the windows. It was not because they were famished that they thus pressed upon each other, but because each of them wished to secure the best available seat. It was amusing to witness, as they got in, the anxious glances which they cast round the room, and then darted off in dozens for the nearest vacant chairs. At length all were seated, and the confusion subsided, but only to give rise to a new hubbub. No sooner was the signal made for a general assault upon the edibles, which were plentifully served, than such a clatter of dishes and a noise of knives and forks arose, mingled with a chorus of human voices, some commanding, others supplicating the waiters, as I had never heard before. In one room were nearly 600 people eating at once, and most of them talking at the same time. The numerous waiters were flitting to and fro like rockets, sometimes tumbling over each other, and frequently coming in very awkward collision. Every now and then a discord would be thrown into the harmony by way of a smash of crockery or crystal. The din and confusion were so terrific as utterly to indispose me to dine. I could thus devote the greater portion of my time to looking around me. The scene was truly a curious one. There were many ladies present, but the great bulk of the company consisted of the other sex. The ladies were in full dress, the †*table d'hôte* at Saratoga being on a totally different footing from that at other hotels. In about twenty minutes the hall looked somewhat like the deck of a ship after action. The survivors of the dinner still remained at table, either sipping wine or talking together, but the rest had disappeared as if they had been carried out wounded or dead. Their fate was soon revealed to us; for, on emerging shortly afterwards into the interior colonnade, we found them almost to a man seated in arm-chairs or rocking-chairs, some chewing, but the great bulk smoking. Before dinner they risked their necks to secure seats at table; after it their anxiety was to secure them on the colonnade. Hence their sudden disappearance from table.

The place was crowded all day with country people

ALEXANDER PRENTICE

Another Scottish journalist, Alexander Prentice, spent a week at the spa in the summer of 1848. After 25 years as a newspaper editor and publisher, he had, the year before, sold his interest in the Manchester Times. *A champion of labor against the factory interests, he was regarded as a radical in his day. His travel narrative was published cheaply in order to appeal to potential immigrants. Perhaps this purpose explains his favorable disposition towards the spa, a perspective relatively uncommon among British visitors.*

Archibald Prentice, *A Tour in the United States* (London: Charles Gilpin, 1848), 92–93.

Saratoga Springs, July 8th, 1848.

ON TUESDAY was celebrated here, as at every town in the states, the anniversary of the Declaration of Independence. The place was crowded all day with country people, who came in the Jersey waggons[150] of which every farm furnishes one, with a couple of exceedingly active wiry horses, that pull those light vehicles at a trot of twelve or fifteen miles an hour. The waggon is a box about seven feet long, three feet and a half wide, and from nine inches to a foot deep, placed upon four light wheels of rather large diameter. With two light spirited horses put to this vehicle, farm produce is conveyed to market at a great speed. On visiting or gala days, one, two, or three seats, each to hold two persons, and each with †grasshopper springs, are placed across the box, and then the farmer drives along his wife and his daughters in as good style, bating the glare and glitter, as can be assumed by any nobleman in our land.

The procession was no great thing, but a great number of persons gathered in the open air to hear the declaration read and the oration delivered. The declaration contains a summary of the tyrrany [*sic*] exercised by the King of England—an indictment of twenty-eight counts—certainly justifying the determination to achieve the establishment of an independent government. It is well to keep alive the patriotic spirit by a commemoration of so great an event. Whether it is well to keep alive feelings of animosity, after the noble achievement, I have some doubt. It seems a little too much akin to our hanging up the conquered flags of other nations in St. Paul's. The people of Britain were to be held, according to the declaration, as "enemies in war," but "in peace, friends;" and it scarcely seems like the cultivation of peaceful relations, this annual enumeration of old wrongs. However, the wrongs *were* perpetuated; and we now have not much reason to find fault that a periodical complaint is made of a war-loving King, a profligate Ministry, and a corrupt Parliament, representing not the people, but the †boroughmongers.

The country around this place is what is called "rolling." To call it "hilly" would not describe it accurately, for the elevations do not deserve the name of hills. "Undulating" is not a much more appropriate designation, for it gives the idea of longer and gentler surface waves. "Knolly" or "hillocky" would be more accurately descriptive, if care were taken not to imagine the knolls or hillocks as very small. The soil, though in many places light and stony, bears good crops of clover, potatoes, Indian corn, and rye; the latter just about ready for the scythe. The cleared and cultivated land ranges in price from six pounds to twenty pounds an acre, according to proximity to the market, a few miles, so heavy are the roads, making a great difference in value. A man who possesses fifty acres close to the town, one who has one hundred at a distance of from one to two miles, and one who has one hundred and fifty at a distance of from three to four miles, are persons well to do in the world. The farm labourer has two shillings and a penny a day with board, and six shillings and three-pence a week extra if he finds his own lodgings and food.

Saratoga consists principally of a wide street, a mile in length, one side occupied by large and handsome hotels, with their gardens. On the other side are good shops and dwelling houses. The settled population is about 2,000, but in a full season there are as many as 3,000 strangers here, at one time, from all parts of the Union, but more especially from the south, to take the benefit of the waters, which are very efficacious in †bilious complaints. Our hotel, the "Union," is far from being the largest in the place, the "United States" being nearly twice the size, but it contains 220 bedrooms, can make up 300 beds, and its dining room can accommodate 350 persons. There is great attention and civility, and every possible comfort is provided at the charge of ten dollars, or two guineas, a week. At eight in the morning all meet at breakfast, at two for dinner, and at seven for tea, with additions, which is called supper. During the whole week I have seen no liquors taken except one pint bottle of †porter, which a gentleman shared with his wife, and on the celebration day there were only seen two persons drunk, of all the multitude that attended, one of whom was an Irishman, and the other a young American farmer. What with the medicinal water, the pure and mild but bracing air, the quiet, the rest, and the comfort of our hotel, Mr. Brooks is greatly renovated in health, and says he is quite ready to take his part, on his return to England, in the proposed new movement for the extension of popular rights.

There were faro tables, roulettes star games, and many other gambling gimcracks

ROBERT MCCOSKRY GRAHAM

Young Bob Graham (1830–1890) visited Saratoga in both 1848 and 1849, and kept a detailed diary with interesting observations, among them a relatively early discussion of gambling; only a small part of the useful material is quoted here. Son of a New York druggist, Graham was sent to Paris to study when he was 14. On his return to New York, and not very long before his first spa visit, he entered the counting house of Howland and Aspinwall. He was later in the insurance and gas businesses.

1848–1849
ROBERT MCCOSKRY GRAHAM

Robert McCoskry Graham, "Journal of Passing Events," volume 3 (1848–49). The New-York Historical Society. Transcribed by Field Horne. Biography is found in Helen Graham Carpenter, *The Reverend John Graham of Woodbury, Connecticut and his Descendants* (Chicago: The Monastery Hill Press, 1942), 485.

Wednesday, August 2d 1848. Saratoga

AFTER BREAKFAST I went with William to the bowling alleys[151]—after rolling a game a man came in the alley next to us, and commenced betting with a friend who appeared a stranger to him—that he would knock down 9 pins every roll (3 balls allowed) the bets were accepted and the roller had lost 10 dollars, he insisted I should bet with him, but I declined—at last William seeing him miss so often and rolling apparently as good as he could, bet him $1, that he could not do it—no sooner accepted than down fell 9 pins—in this way Wm lost $3 which however did not fall out of his own pocket as he had just gained $6¾—We went in a side room off the alley, there were †Faro tables, Roulettes Star games, and many other gambling gimcracks. After looking around a little he asked a man at the roulette to explain the game to him, which the fellow did with very good grace, and William said well Bob, we'll understand it better by taking a dollars worth of tickets, and taking a chance—in an instant the exchange was made. Wm put down his counter on 21 and in 3 turns of the roulette the ball dropped in 21—without saying a word the man handed him a $5 bill and $1¾ in counters which were all lost. We then left this chap—there are more of these †blacklegs around this place than any other I was ever in. While bowling a man will come to you "I'll bet you a dollar I'll tie your game, no matter what you make"—or I'll bet you 50 cents I make a spare or something of the kind—they are annoying as well as amusing—I noticed that whenever a gentleman came in the alley they all had their eyes on him—I was convinced that the man who knocked down the 9 pins for William could do just what he liked with the ball.

Tuesday July 31st 1849. Albany—Saratoga

Rose at 4½ as the Steamer arrived at Albany—took breakfast at the "Delevan House"—and took the cars for Schenectady arrived in Saratoga at ¼ of 10.—sent my baggage to Union Hall, and walked down there—entered my name in full upon the Register—Mr. Hathorn gave me a very good room "112"—Uncle Robert sent for me to come to his room—where I saw Aunt, Tim Read, Miss Read Mr. & Mrs. Stuart & joined a party going to the Bowling Alley—dined

"View of the Show Ground at Saratoga." Engraving, 1847, by R.H. Pease.

at 2—The old Union is now under the management of Messrs W. Putnam & H. H. Hathorn This house still retains the reputation of being the best kept in the Place—The United States Hotel is running over—all the fasion [*sic*] swarms there—as I am only to stay a few days I preferred the Union—Tim Read introduced me to a host of Gents—called on Mme de Dion—in the evening we retired to the smoking room and kept it up quite late telling stories and drinking †cobblers.

Wednesday August 1st 1849. Saratoga Springs.
I did not go down to breakfast, this morning until 9. Uncle Robert gave me lecture N°. 1—bowled with a large party of ladies & Gentlemen until near 12—wrote Father—& Loo before dinner. After dinner we had some delightful music from the "Saxonia Band" Herr Krauss the great Hungarian vocalist is here—Grass Widow sits next to me at table—Williamson Van Vechten, Clark, Stephens, Downing, Wheelwright Chambers &^c. were introduced to me—I joined Uncle Aunt Miss Read in a ride to the Lake—the roads a [*sic*] fine here—especially the plank road[152]—met Mr. Mrs. Stuart, Mr. Richards Mrs. Richards & Son—took †cobblers—I played some polkas on the Piano, & all danced around the room—Mr. Richards played the fiddles with his cane—walked down to the Lake and strolled around—finally I sat down by Uncle, Mr. R. Mr. Stuart, lis-

tening to their many stories & †*jeu de mots*—Old Mr. Richards was full of fun—came home in time for tea—Went over to a Ball at Congress Hall—Mrs. Little Mrs. Jackson were there I escorted them up to the U.S. Returned it was the stupidest affair of the kind that I ever witnessed none of the ladies could be persuaded to dance a Polka or †Redowa and very few †Cotillions—walked up to the U.S. at 9½ and rolled a game of ten pins with Joseph Howland—Mr. S. S. Howland is there also—I partook of a cold cut in Mr. Van Vechtens room when I returned—did not retire untill near 3. he told me some strange stories about engagements—Miss Melville & Miss Yates—

Thursday August 2d 1849. Saratoga Springs.

Late at breakfast again this morning—Uncle gave me lecture No 2—have concluded to get down by 8 in future—rolled tenpins until 11—went up to see Henriette MCarty—hop in ball room—met Jack Wilmerding & Riggs (the two †Dromios). rolled a string with them when I returned to the Union found Mr. Richards[153] "a corpse" he was taken ill at 10½—supposed disease of the heart he was treated for cholera—Mr. Leavitt went down to the City in the aft with Mrs. R. & the body—it has thrown a gloom over the house which every one seems to feel—Received 2 Boxes of Segars from Uncle [?Mintrim]—100 pressed Regaliers "Jeanne y Rosa" & 100 Washington La Norma—Smoked all the evening—did not go out—Mr. Whitewright arrived today—retired early—

Friday August 3d 1849. Fast day. Saratoga

This day has been set apart as a day of fasting and prayer by our worthy President. Uncle, Aunt & Miss R went to church, I remained in my room, & wrote until near dinner time—

Henry Clay is in town—at the United States though he lives at Marvins[154] private house—Went out to the Race course[155] with T. Read, Mr. Whitewright & Mr. Williamson in a fine carriage—Boyd the Canadian walked 6¾ say six & three quarter miles in one hour, & Jackson the American Deer ran Ten miles & three quarters in fifty eight minutes & fifty five seconds.

One of the handsomest villages in the state

J. C. Myers

About J. C. Myers we know only what is contained in the preface to his 1849 book. In May, June and July 1848 he toured the North and East, making notes on the spot, and revising them each evening. Myers protested that he did little to prepare these notes for publication, since he wrote them originally only for himself and his friends, "in a simple, plain, plantation manner." The author signed the preface at New Hope, Virginia, in the Shenandoah Valley, and the book was printed at Harrisonburg. His observations are detailed but impersonal.

J. C. Myers, *Sketches on a Tour through the Northern and Eastern States, the Canadas & Nova Scotia* (Harrisonburg, Va.: J. H. Wartmann and Brothers, 1849), 242–248.

I now made my way for Saratoga Springs, where I arrived on my route south from Canada. These springs are set on the west side of the noble Hudson, and within 4 miles of the beautiful Lake of Saratoga. They are celebrated as one of the greatest watering places in the world. There is here a town with a population of 3384; the buildings of the town are large and well finished, either of brick or frame; the latter being painted white, which make a very elegant appearance; being situated on a high commanding plain, and is in every sense one of the handsomest villages in the State of New York; the streets are broad crossing each other at right angles; the principle [*sic*] ones extending in a straight line far out into the country. The streets are all beautifully ornamented with shade trees; among which may be found Elm, Beach, Sugarmaple, White pine, Spruce pine, Cypress, Balsam, &c., which together with 4 large Pine Groves within half a mile of the town, perfume the air very agreeably. Two or three of these groves are furnished with seats for the accommodation of visitors.

The streets have side-walks about 12 feet wide, which are beautifully curbed and paved with patent bricks. There are hydrants[156] at almost every corner of the streets, to supply the town with fresh water, for the various uses of the inhabitants; these side-walks are adorned on one side with hydrants, white posts and beautiful shade trees; while the other is no less ornamented by the numerous marble and granite steps at the doors of the dwellings, surmounted by a splendid iron banister or railing, painted green or black; together with the numerous flowering boxes, bird cages, &c., renders these walks more delightful than those of other cities or towns.

The town contains 10 very large and elegant hotels, all of which are well conducted; the four largest of which are the United States Hotel, containing 480 rooms; Congress Hall, Union Hall, and Columbia Hotel[157]; which four hotels alone are capable of accommodating 4900 persons in a very comfortable manner.—The whole number of hotels combined are capable of accommodating a large number of visitors; in addition to which almost every house is a Boarding-house, of the first class; so that those vast crowds which collect together here from far and wide, find little difficulty in procuring good accommodations.

The principal mineral Springs at this place are ten in number, and known by the names of Congress, Washington, Columbia, Hamilton, Putnam, Pavilion, Flat Rock, High Rock, Iodine and Empire. Eight of these springs are fitted up in a very handsome style, with curbs or tubes inserted in the earth to the depth of from 30 to 40 feet, well secured against the admission of fresh water. These Springs are protected by a roof, supported by large pillars which are whitened as well as the ceiling over-head. The floors are two feet lower than the top of the curb. Near each of these springs are very large buidings [*sic*] used for bottleing water.

The most popular of these mineral waters is the Congress Spring, which is visited by thousands and thousands daily during the months of July and August.—This spring alone has been an independent fortune to the late Dr. Clark & Co., as vast quantities of the water is sold in bottles to citizens of our country who live at too remote a distance to attend the springs; in addition to which vast quantities are exported to foreign countries.

The town contains the Saratoga Academy[158], a frame structure, situated in a beautiful white pine grove on the main street about 200 yards from the town, which is a very flourishing institution. There are 5 large and elegant churches, each of which contains a very fine Organ; the Catholic church[159] however has the honor of having the finest. There are also many splendid dwellings in the town and its vicinity, among which is that of Judge Marvin[160], which is situated on commanding ground overlooking the whole town, and is one of the most splendid dwellings in the State of New York.—This gentleman

Saratoga Lake. Stereoscope view. Robert Joki Collection. Note the small steamboat tied up at the wharf.

is the owner of the great United States Hotel, and a vast deal of property in the town and its vicinity, together with a very large portion of the stock in the Saratoga Bank.[161] A large portion of the lands around the town are the property of this same wealthy man; many of the lands are laid out in lots from a fourth, to an acre each, and offered for sale at $1200 per acre[162]; at which enormous price some are sold. The soil is of an inferior quality, as the whole surrounding country is an elevated sandy plain, and was it not for the celebrated Mineral Waters, the whole plain, handsome as it is, would be comparatively a barren plain.

There are here a number of bathing establishments, where baths may be had at all times of mineral or soft waters, at any temperature. There are also for the amusement of persons, Swings, †Stooling Galleries, Bowling Alleys, Race Paths; and in one of the Groves there is a circular Railway of about 400 feet in diameter with two tracks, on each of which is a small car with a seat for two persons. This is propelled on the track by means of a crank which the passenger has himself to turn.

The Cemetery[163], about a mile from town, contains about 30 acres of ground: the whole of which is tastefully laid out, and contains many handsome Tombs and Monuments. At the distance of 4 miles is the beautiful little Lake of Saratoga, which is 20 miles long, on which are several handsome little steamers[164], on board of which a delightful pleasure ride may be had up and down the lake.

Everyone seems to be preparing for the busy summer

Lucy Louisa Cooke Lester

We met Lucy Louisa Cooke as a schoolgirl in 1839, newly-arrived from the country town of Milford in Otsego County. A second group of letters is from the months before and after her marriage on 20 September 1849 to Charles Smith Lester. They contain intimate glimpses of domestic life, including the strange Saratoga custom of taking "rooms" in a huge hotel for the winter.

May 1, 1849 to "Mother and Father"

I am seated at my little writing table in my own room with the windows both open and the sounds of hammers, railroad cars, and the voices of the busy world around me mark my ear and destroy the quiet which could be most agreeable & more suited to this pleasant day. The former occupants of the house next to us have gone out and the landlord is mending, papering and painting it for a new tenant. The house is full of workmen and you may imagine the din and confusion they make as the house joins on to ours. This is a great moving day—everybody is going to & from and the streets are crowded with loads of furniture going from one house to another. Everyone seems to be preparing for the busy summer and in a few weeks everything will be in order for the strangers.

June 3, 1849 to "Mother & father"

Our garden is a perfect little paradise just now. I wish you could see the beautiful variety of tulips we have—every color and variety that you can conceive of.

July 8, 1849 to "Father"

The reason why it is so much warmer here is that the heat is reflected so much from the hot sands. We are surrounded by those heavy sand plains and banks which make it very unpleasant. The roads are naturally so very sandy that the plank road which is now completed between here and Schenectady will be appreciated very much. The panic about the cholera has entirely gone and every one has become quite composed. We have had no new cases within two weeks and we

Lucy (Cooke) Lester with her family at High Rock Spring, *circa* 1865. Clockwise from upper left: her brother Joseph Cooke, her husband Charles S. Lester, their son James W. Lester, and Lucy Lester. Collection of Milford D. Lester.

hope that we shall escape having it here again. The village was in a great state of excitement on account of the cholera for about two weeks and the physicians spent about two thirds of their time in trying to convince people that they had not the symptoms of the cholera and needed no medicine. There are not a great many strangers in the village yet but the hotel-keepers are in hopes of seeing more before long. The reports of cholera were a great injury to Saratoga and I fear that there will be but few here. If we did not as a village depend so much upon the patronage of the strangers, we would desire [not] to see many this summer, but all are affected either directly or indirectly, the merchants as well as the hotel keepers.

July 22, 1849 to "Mother"
Our poor little garden was so dry that all the plants were nearly burned up and our cistern was so low that we could not spare the water to water it with. There are not many strangers here this summer which makes it much pleasanter though not so profitable. We are able to realize this summer how much we are (as a village) dependent upon the patronage of strangers. It seems quite strangely to see so few at the different hotels. We see the difference very plainly in church. Usually at this season the churches are crowded this summer they have not been even filled.

Sabbath afternoon [1849] to "Mother"
We have selected our rooms at the Columbian and they are being made ready for us. We shall have one good sized room for a sitting room and out of it a bedroom.

October 29, 1849 to "Mother"
I have just got settled in my new home for the winter and I thought that my first leisure moment should be spent in writing to you. We commenced moving this morning and got settled in time to dress for dinner. I must describe to you our rooms. They are in the front of the house and look out onto Broadway and across to the Warrens[165] who are directly opposite. Our sitting room is about as large as Libbie's bedroom and has in it two windows. Between them is a nice little table that Mrs. Lester lent us on which is a darling little †solar lamp that James gave us. Aunt Mary lent us her lounge the one that she had in the library and Elisabeth Lester lent us her large hurricane which we also have in the sitting room. We have a nice mirror that was in the room when we came and a rocking chair with four other chairs and a nice airtight stove. With all these our room seems quite filled up. Charles is having a bookcase made which we shall have here when it is done. In our bedroom we have beside the bed, a wash stand dressing table and a little bureau of Charles' which by the way is a dear little one. It is about as high as a table with four drawers in it.

April 28, 1850 to "Mother"
We shall be delighted with the maple sugar. I have been crazy all the Spring for some but have not been able to satisfy myself. It is the hardest thing to get here for there is little if any made in this vicinity.[166]

Indians in their tents, busily engaged making baskets

ELLEN BOND

On 9 July 1850, 23-year-old Ellen Bond of Cincinnati received a morocco-bound diary as a gift from her father. Her father inscribed it on the flyleaf, and on the first page Ellen wrote, "Journal of a trip made with my dear Mother Father & Sisters L. J. and Sue July 1850." The next morning they started out, taking an omnibus to the railroad "cars." At Sandusky, they boarded the Alabama, *and began their tour of the northeast: Niagara, Toronto, Montréal, Québec, Lake Champlain, Ticonderoga, Lake George and Saratoga, finishing with Newport and Boston by 27 August. Her father, William Key Bond, was a lawyer and a former congressman from Chillicothe, where the family had lived until 1841. The whole household made the trip: Ellen, the oldest, along with Lucy, 22, Josephine, 18, and Susan, 15. Ellen Bond's notes are vivid and personal, and almost certainly she intended them for no one but herself; only brief extracts from a long and interesting diary are quoted here.*

Ellen Bond, diary. New York State Library, Manuscripts and Special Collections. Transcribed by Field Horne. She was identified in the Federal Census, 1850, Cincinnati, Third Ward, page 469, through the courtesy of Roger Joslyn. Biographies of William Key Bond are found in standard references such as the *Biographical Directory of the American Congress 1774–1949* (1950).

Monday July 29th

I WAS ENJOYING a nice little nap, when another shower wakened me, & in a few minutes found ourselves in the depot at Saratoga, & now at the great U.S. hotel *the Hotel* of the place, crowded to overflowing, *only* 700 guests.

Music on the lawn after dinner promenading on the porches & through the grounds—this seems to be the only variety here. The grounds are kept in such beautiful order, that it is a pleasure to walk thro' them. they are so finely shaded too. I felt sad strolling through them, thinking of the sad fate of the old German Baron whose acquaintance I had made at Niagara. Here in the land of strangers & in the midst of vanity, [?reaction] & folly he died a few days before our arrival, walking in the yard fell down in a fit & died an hour afterwards—

Tuesday 30th July

Up bright & early: Luce & I were in Ma's room enquiring the road to the Spring—they were soon in readiness & joined us. The spring is two squares from the U.S. hotel. We met many going, & crowds there. here too the grounds are in beautiful order. We stepped forward with the crowd & helped ourselves from the boys who were busy dipping up the sparkling beverage. Drinking now two glasses each we walked through the grounds, bands playing finely—altogether it was an enlivening scene—Two glasses more returning & now home for breakfast good *déjeuner à la fanchette*[167] after breakfast out for a tramp through stores.

At the dinner table a paper going the rounds for subscribers for the Ball. Pa with the rest contributed a dollar for the hop & at half past nine all are at the †*qui vive.*

How it happened I am unable to say, but Miss Jones led off the first †cotillion with a young lady—The new & affectionate style of polka waltz chotish [†schottische] kept us all laughing. We consider we were more than compensated for the dollar.

172

Thursday 1st of August
After dinner a large party of us strolled through the town, dropping in some stores & then a visit to the spring & walk around the grounds. Luce tried the new rail road with Thomas S. working herself at a merry rate.

Friday
Dinner at 3 & †*toute de suite* Dr. Goodale & Luce called for us to join them in a ride to the Lake 4 miles in the Country. The Lake is really worth going to see—We found on reaching the house (the public *rendez vous* of the strangers) many carriages & a number of pleasure seekers like ourselves The Lake is just at the foot of the yard, so we walked down, saw several taking skiffs for a sail. We played a game of ten pins. Doc & I against L & Miss Briggs, & came off victors!

Saturday
Went with Luce to the jewellers' & had her ears pierced—I treated myself to garnet cuff pins—I find the dividend of my rail road stock very convenient!

Sunday Aug 4th 1850
Ma Luce Pa went to church. heard a sermon from the Arch Deacon of Jamaica.

Monday 5th Aug
Shall I ever forget the Gourmand with the crape on his arm. his grief is certainly intense, were I to judge from the quantities he disposed of at each meal—his generosity without bounds—after a thorough & indefatigible search through his pocket book he actually donated to his attentive waiter George ten cts, & left the table with his pockets full of nuts & raisins!

Sunday 6th Aug
After dinner a walk to Rock Spring with Mr & Mrs Hartshorne, Springer—this spring is really a curiosity. the waters coming out of an immense rock. We found here an old woman like the good Samaritan ready to supply us with a glass, & on Ma asking her how the rock happened there she replied "it was put here by the hand of

Providence." We returned to the hotel by way of the Pavillion & Iodine two other springs of note. I tasted the waters of all, found them very similar to the Congress water.

We walked out to the Indian encampment[168], found some few Indians in their tents, busily engaged making baskets—Lucy purchased a pretty fan from one of the squaws.

There were people here and there about the colour of a half worn saddle

JAMES P. THOMAS

In the summer of 1851, James P. Thomas (1827–1913) of Nashville came to Saratoga Springs as the hired servant of Andrew Jackson Polk. He was the son of a slave mother and a white father who was later a justice of the U.S. Supreme Court; his mother bought his freedom when he was six. He apprenticed as a barber, hired himself for wages, and established a successful business. Although his experience as a black man in Nashville was one of considerable latitude, he remained—under Tennessee law—nominally in bondage. In 1857, he settled in St. Louis, became a prosperous businessman and real estate investor and married a wealthy woman of color, only to lose his fortune in the 1890s. In 1903 he set about writing his autobiography and from it we gain some understanding of what Saratoga must have been like to an African American from the South.

James P. Thomas, autobiographical notes and recollections. Rapier Family Papers, Moorland-Spingarn Research Center, Howard University. Transcribed by Field Horne. It has been published as Loren Schweninger, ed., *From Tennessee Slave to St. Louis Entrepreneur: The Autobiography of James Thomas* (Columbia: University of Missouri Press, 1984), wherein Saratoga Springs is at 127–128

BUT FEW people traveled from the north, south, with servants, unless they were invalids, but during the summer months the people from the south would invade the northern cities and pleasure resorts with their servants. It made them quite conspicuous. When a Gentleman registered from some point south and gave notice that he wanted his servant property cared for, as the servant had nothing whatever to do it looked as his only use was to tell those who were curious to know something about his boss. How many slaves he owned, how many plantations he owned, etc. The question would always be in order, do you belong to him? Some would believe his report as to the servant being his property, others would not. Some would carry their own servants and say to them if any of those ask you if you belong to me, say no, or they will give me trouble by carrying you off. The people of New York did not often trouble peoples servants.

After four or five weeks in New York, We concluded, or I should say Col. Polk concluded to go to Saratoga. I was instructed to be prepared. I was ready and we went. The first impression of Saratoga would be that it was a charming place before fashion and folly got in. The season was at its height. The Bostonians seemed to go together. New Yorkers appeared to mingle more freely. Those from the City of brotherly love, or to be more explicit, Philadelphia, formed their clique. There were many southern people. They seemed easy and comfortable and dared to talk above a whisper. With all, well behaved.

There were many people who had just dropped in from the four points who nobody knew or cared to know. Nor did they care to be known and left as they came. Only stopped to see the show. Didn't need the water.

Many of the gay looking young men from the different cities I found were the fellows that took the lead in the fancy dances when the hops came off. But that close embrace and hopping business didnt quite meet the approbation of those conservative old fellows with young and pretty wives. They thought it abominable, but their wives and daughters seemed to like it. As usual, the old chaps held their peace.

There were people here and there about the colour of a half worn saddle, faultlessly dressed, with low quartered shoes, displaying rattlesnake looking sox. Their locks wavy such as I had often seen around Nashville on the heads of the servant Element.[169]

Upon the whole, the gathering looked stiff and formal compared with the guest at a southern watering place. But dinner was the time for the full enjoyment of some of the best that Saratoga offered, elegant dressing, elegant bill of fare, service unsurpassed.

A colored man, Mr Mason Morris, was the head waiter. He skillfully seated his hundreds guest. The United States was then the largest hotel in Saratoga. Morris had several years been the head waiter. When one of the guest told Morris that a friend of his had arrived and that he wanted him seated in his company, he would (Morris) look over his list, arrange it satisfactorily. In such cases he would be compensated.

Champagne corks would fly in every direction during the dinner hour. I noticed some persons would make an effort to force themselves on the attention of others by sending his wine with compliments, which would be returned unrecognized by the Gentleman it was sent to. It looked as there was some dissippation mixed with the health seeking course at Saratoga.

There was nothing alarming in it

MARIANNE FINCH

About Marianne Finch we know nothing except that she was in the United States as a delegate to the Woman's Rights Convention. During her visit to Saratoga in August 1851, she recorded her observations of the Indian Encampment. Though visitors, especially European ones, had always been curious about Indians (Solomon Mordecai encountered an Indian basket peddler in 1818, and Margaret Hall attended a musical performance by an Indian in 1828), the Indian camp became a fixture of the "season" only in the 1840s. The first mention of it is in Robert Playfair's book about his 1847 visit. It moved from place to place, and was finally given up shortly before World War I. Finch's description is particularly evocative and charming.

Marianne Finch, *An Englishwoman's Experience in America* (London: Richard Bently, 1853), 113–117. She is briefly identified in Max Berger, *The British Traveller in America, 1836–1860* (New York: Columbia, 1943), 200, but I have not identified his source, which does not appear to be internal to Finch's book.

THE NEXT morning I rose early, in order to visit some Indians, who were encamped in a wood about two miles from the village. I arrived about 7 A.M., and found several at their *toilette.*

One young lady was dressing her hair at the door of her tent. A young gentleman was performing the same operation under a tree; others were going through the process of ablution. There was nothing alarming in it; they were sufficiently civilized to do it on a very limited scale, using a bit of soap the size of a button, and a towel as

Indian Encampment. Stereoscope view by E. and H. T. Anthony and Company. Robert Joki Collection.

large as a knife-cloth, instead of swimming about in a river, as savages ought to do.

A very handsome girl, about eighteen, was brushing out her tent with a broom, made of green leaves. Her dress, like that of the rest of the women, consisted of a blue cloth skirt and pantalets of the same material, over which is worn a short loose dress of cotton. Her long black hair was parted down the centre, Indian-wise, and hung down her back in two plaits. She was tall and straight as the young pine-tree of her native forests. All her movements were beautiful, but I was especially struck with her walk—so free and graceful, yet so dignified. I have often thought of her since, when witnessing the mincing gestures of more civilized *belles.*

They were all employed and silent; even the little children were running about and playing as gravely and silently as their seniors worked.

The men were making bows and arrows, which was quite †*comme il faut;* but to see the old squaws sewing in spectacles, and the young ones handling needles and scissors, as daintily as boarding-school misses, seemed quite an innovation on the proprieties of Indian life, and has doubtless been duly †anathematized by the "friends of order" belonging to the race.

I made several attempts at a conversation with these gentle dames, but always found their knowledge of English was confined to the subject of currency. They told me exactly how many cents made a dollar; and on my taking up a †watchpocket that one of them finished while I was there, she showed me which of the pieces of silver in my purse would pay for it. On my telling her to help herself, she laughed, and took the piece of money she had pointed out, telling me to keep the pocket.

Returning to the hotel at a little past nine, I found nearly all the company had breakfasted, and many of the young ladies were dancing the polka in the drawing room.

Like harlequin in the pantomime, in they come again

CHARLES RICHARD WELD

A scientist by vocation and for 16 years the assistant secretary and librarian of the Royal Society in London, Charles Weld (1813–1869) was the son of Isaac Weld, who had himself visited Saratoga Springs in 1799, and brother-in-law of Alfred, Lord Tennyson. In 1850, Charles Weld began publishing a series of "Vacation Tours" books. The second of nine such volumes was his Vacation Tour in the United States and Canada, *for which he wrote a fine description of railway travel and the obligatory discussion of hotel meals.*

Charles Richard Weld, *A Vacation Tour in the United States and Canada* (London: Longman Brown Green and Longman, 1855), 64–77.

MY DESTINATION was Saratoga, to which I travelled by railway, passing through the picturesque district of the Green Mountains. The American railway car, as is generally known, is about forty feet long, eight and a half wide, and six and a half high, having seats, with reversible backs, for sixty passengers. The weight of a car of these dimensions is eleven tons, and the cost about 400£. It is supported at each end on four wheeled trucks, ingeniously mounted on swivel axles, enabling it to whisk round curves at the sight of which an English railway engineer would stand aghast. The locomotive is very unlike ours, being an uncouth-looking machine, with a prodigious bottle-nose chimney, and an iron-barred vizor-like affair in front, called a cow-catcher, though, as I can attest from observation, it is not at all particular as to the kind of animal it catches, or kills; for, as may be imagined, when an unfortunate beast is struck by the pointed guard, the chances are it is killed. As the railways, with few exceptions, are unprovided with fences, the herds and flocks turned into the forests are at liberty to roam on the track; sheep especially are fond of resorting to the line at night, which they find drier than the damp clearings. These animals, however, are not deemed formidable obstacles. An engine cleverly dashed through a flock of one hundred and eighty, the greater portion of which were summarily converted into mutton. Differing in outward form, the American engine differs also in its interior economy from our locomotive, feeding on wood, for which it has an insatiable appetite, instead of coal, which may account for the unearthly sound it emits, comparable only to the simultaneous braying of a dozen donkeys labouring under oppressive asthma. The English first-class railway traveller, accustomed to the courtesy of guards and the servility of porters, will seek in vain for their representatives in America. A conductor, unmarked by any badge of distinction beyond a small plate, which he only displays when the train is in motion (for up to that period he is an independent gentleman), shouts to the engine-driver, "All o' board;" a bell, attached to the engine, is rung violently, not to summon indolent or tardy passengers "on board," for they are supposed to be in the cars—but to warn people in the streets of the approach of the locomotive, and the train is off. Thus, the traveller has to look out for himself, and he is early made aware of the important fact, that if he trusts to others he will in all probability pay the penalty by being left behind. Through streets, across thronged roads, speeds the train, the only warning being a conspicuous notice—"Look out for the locomotive when the bell rings." The conductor's labours commence with the journey. Here again the value of time in America is made apparent; for as the functionary proceeds through the cars, calling out "Tickets," it will be noticed very few passengers are provided with checks. The conductor is, therefore, empowered to sell tickets, and this, with receiving them at the end of the journey, constitutes his principal occupation. When the train reaches its destination, the conductor removes his official badge, and retires into private life.

The process of watering the passengers, as it is called, is another feature peculiar to American railway travelling. A man or boy, often a negro, carrying a tin can, and tumblers in a frame, passes frequently through the cars, dispensing iced water to the numerous applicants for that indispensable refreshment during an American summer, which is provided at the expense of the railway company.

The rate of travelling is about twenty-four miles an hour. The stoppages are frequent, to take in wood, which burns more rapidly than coke. At these wooding stations, unfortunate horses may be seen toiling up an endless incline, which retrogrades beneath their feet, and sets machinery in motion to saw logs for the locomotives.[170]

The great event of the day at "the Springs" is dinner, which takes place at half-past three. This, at the United States Hotel, is a tremendous undertaking. Conceive sitting down in an enormous saloon, or, rather, four saloons at right angles to each other, with some 600 guests, waited upon by 150 negroes, commanded by a black †*maitre d'hôtel.* The operation of finding places for such a multitude—in itself no trifling task—being over, the waiters, dressed in spotless white jackets, extend their hands over the covers, and at a signal from their chief, stationed in the centre of the saloons, remove them simultaneously. Then arises a clatter of knives, plates, and forks perfectly bewildering, in the sharp rattling fire of which conversation is drowned and confusion seems established. But a glance at the commander-in-chief shows that, although his black troops are rushing hither and thither in hot haste at the bidding of impetuous Southerners or less irascible Northerners, he has not lost his authority. At a clap of his hands they fall into their places, and at another all the dishes are removed. Bearing these dexterously on their extended arms, they march in step to the side-doors, through which they disappear. Scarcely, however, are they out of sight when, like Harlequin in the pantomime, in they come again, each with three fresh dishes, with which they march to their appointed places. Then, with their eye on the commander, they hold a dish over the table, and pop it down at the first signal. With clap two the second dish descends; and at the third signal the tables are covered. So through the dinner; for even in the changing of knives, forks, and spoons the same regularity is observed. The whole thing is excessively entertaining; and, what between looking at the various manœuvres, and at the ladies' dresses, I fared badly in the way of eating. The fault, however, lay entirely with myself, for the abundance of dishes was almost overpowering. This admirable organization is, of course, a great economy of time; for, although no counting-houses are near, the guests, without any display of quick eating, were evidently desirous not to remain longer at table than necessary; and in less than an hour the rooms were deserted.

Such is a sketch of the life I saw at Saratoga,—highly amusing to contemplate for a short time, but presenting no temptation to the stranger to mix in for more than a couple of days.

No one expected a good season on account of the war

ELIZABETH PECK PUTNAM SHACKELFORD

Elizabeth Shackelford (1825–1885) left us a diary that provides a wonderful domestic look at Saratoga Springs during the Civil War. The daughter of merchant Rockwell Putnam and granddaughter of the spa's first hotelier, Gideon Putnam, she had studied at Albany Female Academy and, in 1851, married the Rev. John Wragg Shackelford, then rector of St. Mary's Episcopal Church, Brooklyn. At the time of the diary they had two children, Eleanor and "baby," whose name was Elizabeth. They were apparently staying with her parents for their home was in Newark, N.J., where Rev. Shackelford had become rector of the House of Prayer; that summer he was in Naples, according to the diary. The excerpts printed here describe Van Amburgh's Circus, a frequent attraction, and the Independence Day festivities.

Elizabeth Peck Putnam Shackelford, diary. New York State Historical Association, Cooperstown. Transcribed by Field Horne. An obituary, "Death of Mrs. Shackelford," is in *The Saratogian*, 11 March 1885; Rev. Shackelford's is in *The Saratogian*, 26 March 1902. Additional family details are from a biography of George R.P. Shackelford, Citizens Historical Association, 21 July 1945, in the Shackelford file, Saratoga Room, Saratoga Springs Public Library, and Eben Putnam, *A History of the Putnam Family in England and America* (Salem, Mass.: The Salem Press, 1891), 2: 58.

MON. JUNE [3]. Rainy morning rained all night. Ellie[171] could not recite early as her lessons were not sufficiently prepared. Studied them but baby too wakeful to hear them during her nap. Very warm heat kept waking baby—Menagerie passed through about 12 o'clock. Van Amburghs[172]—Pa and I went after dinner and took Ellie. I did not mind the walk as it was only just beyond Maxwells though it was so muddy Pa tried to get a cab; but we found it was previously engaged and we would have to wait too long. The tent was unusually large & covered with flags and there was a good collection of animals—Hannibal the largest elephant in the country and Lippoo Said the most educated one. We were in time to have a very good view of the animals before the exhibition and Ellie was much interested. She also enjoyed the monkey riding on the pony. The ponies were well trained standing on their hind feet almost erect and the second one stood on his hind feet with his front ones elevated on a box and fired a pistol which was fixed on the top of a pole by pulling a string attached to the trigger. The clown fell down pretending to be killed when the horse immediately fell down also and lay as if dead. He afterward wiped his nose on the clown †[?pocket] which lay on the grass & then picked it up & brought it to the trainer who managed him whom they called Mr. Nash who also appeared to be the teacher of Lippoo Said as he exhibited him—Hannibal was quite docile letting the keeper walk over him and put his head in his mouth and ride on his tusks but Lippoo Said danced and kept time with his trunk to music and let his keeper ride & climb over him, but they brought out a round box exactly the size of his feet all four. He put one foot fore foot on it then the other then his two hind feet and stood there. The[n] the keeper clim[b]ed up his tusks and swung on them & then they brought a long pole with a sharp end & stuck it in the ground & the elephant clasped his trunk around it while standing with all his feet on the little box and the keeper clim[b]ed the pole balancing himself on the very top holding on merely with his feet, a fine feat of gymnastics, and a good exhibition of the strength of the elephant as the pole was supported merely by his trunk his feet being all crowded on the little top of the box. After the exhibition we bought a book descriptive of the animals and took Ellie around again and she stood in front of the lions cage while they fed the animals.

Th. July [4] There were no bells rung here at sunrise but the bright morning sun & the boys with their little cannon in front of the house did and Ellie went to Julia's room at 5½ to throw some torpedos in to wake her; baby who woke early and we were able to go down to breakfast at 7—I gave Ellie the little pail with powder crackers and holder which I had saved for her since she used it two years ago in Newark and her grandpa had some more and enjoyed firing them very much. Baby was disposed to be afraid last evening at the noise & was going to cry when she heard them but I laughed and called them

Union Hotel dining room. *Frank Leslie's Illustrated Newspaper,* 9 July 1864.

"Pop" and took her to the window where the boys were throwing them at a dog who seemed to enjoy the fun and she soon became used to them & this morning enjoyed Ellie's and at last had courage to take the little wooden holder and fire one herself. When baby went to sleep we put them up and Ellie looked over her lessons and wrote and then painted Mother Goose till dinner time. We had dinner early and George[173] came in for his telescope to look at the comet this evening—He says they have 70 to dinner & last year had 250. We hurried on our things after dinner to go to see Union Hall table which was decorated with flowers, 5 tables the two end ones having arches of flowers in the centers with a gilt statue under of Washington. They do not put the meats on anymore but have them in the carving room and the entrees and vegetables in covered dishes and pineapple and some parts of the dessert on all the time; All these dishes were garnished with flowers and flowers in the napkins and the butter cut to look like pine apple. The next tables had pyramids instead of the arches and the center one had a figure of Liberty made of something eateable but looking like a bronze figure. Flags abounded on all the tables and in the chandeliers with †asparagus. It was all very pretty and it is too bad they have not more company but no one expected a good season on account of the war. We went through the grounds to Georges and chatted a few moments with the children who were on the steps with Lizzie then came round by the

Church to see whose funeral was taking place & found it was someone from the Clarendon[174] & Dr. Freeman had opened the Church & Lorin[175] was tolling the bell and the funeral was over. We did a little shopping at the stores and then to the Spring and around the largest circle and home past the Union & Lizzie walked a little way with Julia then the cannon frightened the baby who was tired and cried in the street & we came home & changed our dresses & Ellie fired some torpedos I bought her & I pressed some flowers—Then tea & Pa let off some †wheels he bought for Ellie & Fanny & her children came in time to see them. Tice has been here painting all day at the chairs & washboard & with another view at the comet we went to bed but the streets were thronged until 11—We were delighted with a long letter from Mr. S. from Naples which I glanced over to myself but did not get time to read to the family. Heard today of the death of Fanny Thompson's baby aged 6 months. She did not nurse it.

Alternate dashes of water and terrific screams

MARY C. CHARLES

Dr. Norman Bedortha[176] came to Saratoga Springs in 1852 to operate his Water Cure, the first of a new type of physician-operated boarding facilities. Mary C. Charles, a young woman from Sturbridge, Massachusetts, stayed there in 1863 after moving from the "Union." Her diary, only part of which is quoted here, is a delightful and whimsical look at life in a water cure. The splendid building it was occupying just south of the present Urban Cultural Park Visitors' Center burned to the ground in 1864 after a firecracker was thrown into a window.

A typescript of this diary has been in the collection of the Historical Society of Saratoga Springs for about 25 years; its donor is unknown, and the original has not been located.

Wednesday Aug 14

DID NOT SLEEP so very much. †Chloroform was consulted a good many times. I thought this morn we were firmly fastened at the Union. This eve finds us bag & baggage at the Water-Cure. We went out walking this morn & found Austin Hitchcock at the bowling alley—he said Mrs Stebbins & Julia were at his boarding place the Water Cure—So we called to see them on our way home & they set forth the advantages of their establishment in such eloquent terms we concluded to come here. Breakfast is at 7—dinner at 12½—tea at 5½—quite rural & [supposed] to be quite healthy—I could scarcely keep from laughing at the table—so plain & I may almost say [?s]tingy was everything food & ware—Cracked wheat & molasses stood sentry at regular intervals—Graham bread, wheat bread & gingerbread accompanied the aforesaid articles—Fortunately we dined at three at the Union & I had a good excuse for not being hungry.

Thursday Aug 15
This morn along with a parcel of diseased womankind I wended my way toward Dr. Bedortha's apartments for I had consented to undergo the ordeal of water. He felt of my pulse, scanned my tongue—looked exceeding wise, said he perfectly understood my case—all I needed was a thorough course of cold water treatment—At which he scribbled off some orders on a bit of paper. I ventured to suggest that very cold water did not agree with me [in] fact it went strongly against both my disposition & constitution & I more than hinted I should have my own way—so he rubbed out with his little finger some he had written & commenced again—This I was to carry to Ellen the bath girl. I having as little idea of who Ellen might be as who the man in the moon is. So stumbling my way through the dark alleys of the old part of the house by aid of the housekeeper—who I afterwards found to be Mrs. Dunn, I came to a room which from the musty smell I concluded must be neighbor to the bath room if not the room itself. It was the room—Upright in a row of tin tubs with white sheets round them & a wet cloth on their heads sat a row of the †dyspeptic forlorn-looking women I saw at table—Underneath another curtain—I caught from behind a curtain—this glimpse—somebody was undergoing some dreadful ordeal for there issued from thence alternate dashes of water & terrific screams. I ascertained this *was* Ellens bathroom & she informed me very graciously she would be ready for me in 15 minutes—I went to my room—divested myself of all extra apparel & my jewels—& again amid the labyrinth of passages caught a smell of the room—After assuming my seat in a tin tub with as much composure as circumstances would permit—I asked Ellen if I was to be dashed—having ascertained that was what they called the screams & throws of water—for I told her I

should submit to no such indignity—Much to my mental peace & I have since had reason to believe my bodily vigor I was told No,—I set 15 min.—in P.M. soaked 20—this is my first days experience—Meanwhile I get up quite an appetite for cracked wheat—have eaten a little oatmeal & a piece of gingerbread—Uncle took pudding this morn for desert & I told the girl to pass him the molasses—He looked grave as a judge. This eve we went to the different Hotels to see the dress & display—

Friday Aug 16
This day has passed pleasantly—Uncle informed me he thought this was sort of two-pence-half penny establishment—sort of second-class people—he would rather pay $3. per day at the Union in all of which I agreed with this difference I had the same opinion before I came.

Not a corner grocery to colonise in
GEORGE AUGUSTUS HENRY SALA

Perhaps the most amusing narrative of Victorian Saratoga is the one written by George Sala (1828–1896) about his arrival in the summer of 1864. Trained as a draughtsman, painter and etcher, he had come under the patronage of Charles Dickens in 1851. The great writer invited him to contribute weekly to the periodical Household Words. *It was under Dickens that Sala first went abroad as a special correspondent, to Russia in 1856. Later he wrote for such well-known journals as the* Illustrated London News, *the* Sunday Times, *and the* Daily Telegraph. *From November 1863 to December 1864, he was in the United States reporting on the Civil War. His biographer wrote, "His contributions exhibited unusual powers of observation, familiarity with many phases of low life, multifarious reading, capacity for genial satire, and at times a vein of sentiment imitated from Dickens."*

George Augustus Sala, *My Diary in America in the Midst of War* (London: Tinsley Brothers, 1865), 2: 257–293.

DETERMINED ON our arrival at the Saratoga terminus—which in Europe would be a palace in miniature, but is here, of course, a hovel—to cast no discredit on the head-quarters of American fashion, but to do the thing in style, we abandoned our luggage checks to a negro porter, telling him in a lordly way that we were going to the "States," and entered a sumptuous †barouche drawn by two noble grey horses with flowing manes and tails. It was just that kind of barouche you used to see in English country towns at election time, only, in lieu of two grey horses there were four.

I could not help fancying that the citizen in the straw hat and the "duster," or overcoat of yellow Spanish linen, who drove the barouche, made, as the door was slammed to, a gesture very nearly approaching the thrusting of his tongue into his cheek. It may have been, after all, that he was only shifting his "chaw" of "big lick"; but it looked uncommonly like derision. The truth is that we were perfectly unconscious of the fact that it is not five minutes' walk from the railway station to the "States," and that, the night being a remarkably balmy moonlight one, it was slightly an idiotic proceeding on our part—unencumbered with luggage as we were—to ride to our hostelry. There seemed to be also a touch of humorous contempt in the inquiry made by the driver as to whether we thought we could get in at the "States." We said that our rooms had been secured in advance. "Ah," quoth the driver, "you're lucky, you air. They were dreadful choked when the last train come in, I expect. They know how to pack, they do, there. They have colonised out, they have, and they have camped out, they have, till their aint ary a corner grocery left to colonise, nor a billiard-table to camp on. You air lucky, and here you air *at* the States."

He was by far the civillest and most communicative fellow, this driver, that I had met with during many thousand miles of American travel; yet his remarks and his manner made me gloomily distrustful of what was to come. My diplomatic friend could only murmur: "They promised to reserve the rooms." It was midnight. The ladies' entrance to the "States" was closed. The general entrance only remained open. I feared for the worst. You don't know what it is, arriving in an American town, and being unable to obtain accommodation. To have the key of the street to the Great Desert of Sahara is Paradise compared with such a position. I had not nerve enough to descend from the barouche to ask the awful question. My diplomatic friend was good enough to do the needful.

The worst *had* come. Not a bed. Not a billiard-table. Not a corner grocery to colonise in; although what "colonising" was I did not learn

The Railroad Terminus as it was from 1864 to 1869. Franklin Square and the Marvin residence are to the left.

until afterwards. We might "camp," it is true; but it must be camping out †*à la belle étoile*, with the turf for a couch and the stars for our canopy. In other words, the United States Hotel was full. They had kept their compact with us. Oh, they had kept it, with a vengeance! They had waited until the last train—the regular train; but this, it appeared, was an exceptional, abnormal, non-Appleton-authorised, out-of-the-way train—so they said, at least. A senator, or a corn-cutter, or a †shoddy-contractor, I am sure I don't know which, was now comfortably ensconced in our apartments—liquoring-up probably in our parlour, flinging his boots, confound him! outside our bedroom door. They were really very sorry. It was a pity they had not known about the train, or that it had not come in a little sooner. Why didn't we telegraph from Troy? Telegraph from Jericho! Malediction upon that Harlem River Railroad!

"Expect you'd better try Congress Hall," quoth the barouche-driver, "or Union Hall. They're both full, they du say; but they might find a corner."

Despair! To add to our anguish, our names, in expectation of our coming, had been duly entered by the clerks in the portentous Guests' Ledger at the "States." We were branded and ticketed—we, bedless and supperless wanderers—as sojourners at the "States."

Clarendon Hotel. *Saratoga, and How to See It* (1873)

Cards would be left upon us to-morrow morning. We had not even the wretched consolation of saying that we hadn't chosen to stop at the "States." And the luggage? It was coming joltering in a van to the place where we couldn't find a bed. We had to fee another negro porter to keep watch and ward over it till we roamed forth in quest of other shelter. In England, when a traveller suffers such a disappointment as this, he generally makes up his mind, in dudgeon, to sleep at the Railway Hotel, go back to town by the first train in the morning, and write a furious letter to the *Times*. But alas! There is no Railway Hotel at Saratoga[177]; and this was Saturday night, and no trains whatever run anywhere on Sunday. In this frightful conjuncture an idea suddenly struck my diplomatic friend, and a ray of hope beamed on his countenance. "We'll try the Clarendon," he exclaimed. The barouche-driver didn't think much of the proposition. "The Clarendon," he echoed. "I thought you wanted a fashionable house. Why, the Clarendon's out of the world." We might have explained to the driver that, to an English mind, the very meaning of the word Clarendon conveyed an idea of fashion in its most exalted sense; but, time pressing, we deemed it better merely to reiterate our desire to be conveyed thither. The Clarendon was, perhaps, ten minutes' drive from the "States." I glanced gloomily forth from either side of the barouche, to see if Saratoga looked anything like a watering-place. To my mind it didn't: it had more the appearance of Jersey City gone a short way out of town—say to Peckham-rye—and much overtaken by dust. Beautifully in bars of pale silver as the moon shone on the scene, I could see that the main street was inch-deep in dust, and that the trees and the herbage were powdered thick with pulverous particles. "Sarytogy's a big thing on dust, and that's a fact," remarked the communicative driver, divining perchance my thoughts. I have remarked that the night was delightfully warm and balmy, yet I could not help noticing a pervading and sometimes oppressive odour of something burning. I asked the driver if there had been a fire at Saratoga lately. "The Water Cure[178] was burnt up on the Fourth"—the glorious Fourth he meant—he replied †sententiously: "Fireworks did it. Our citizens are death on rockets. It was a first-class blaze. Nobody was sorry, for to see those miserable cusses that were going through the water cure, sitting outside the establishment with death in the very soles of their boots, was enough to make a man drown himself. Why couldn't they drink the waters and be cured in a legitimate manner? Wasn't the Empire Spring[179] good enough for them? This is The Clarendon. I expect you'll get in, for the door's open, and if they couldn't room any more guests they'd pretty soon close up, I guess. *And now hold on till I get your pay.*"

The concluding portion of his remarks, respecting "holding on" was not uttered in any disrespectful manner. It was a mildly but firmly authoritative reminder that he had conveyed us quite far enough on credit, and that, to prevent misunderstandings, he would like to see the colour of our greenbacks before he took us any farther. The driver was quite right in his generation. Once established as regular guests at any reputable hotel, we could have engaged him at any time, and he would have trusted us for any amount of drives for the next fortnight to come; but in our present transitory and vagabond state—†*sans feu ni lieu,* as it were—we might have been a select party of "confidence men," or swindlers, with one lady as a †blind, and delusive luggage, containing nothing but brickbats and corn-cobs. So we "held on," and he got his pay.

Our hearts danced within us at the intimation that there was plenty of room at the Clarendon. The landlord turned out to be an old acquaintance of my diplomatic friend—at least he he [*sic*] had been a clerk at the hotel in New York most frequented by the diplomatist. He was a superb landlord, with a silky-white moustache, the which, with his shining bald head, closely-fitting blue surtout, and general half-military, half-aristocratic mien, gave him the appearance of a colonel of the Old Guard †*en retraite*. I was introduced to him, and he shook me warmly by the hand. We should have the best rooms in the house, he said. An enchanting landlord! We made bold, albeit with fear and trembling, to observe that we had had neither dinner nor tea, and that one of our party was very nearly fainting for want of sustenance. Promptly did this pearl of landlords undertake to supply us "right away" with supper. Clearly a unique landlord.

I am afraid however that the subscriber's incorrigible habit of seeking to inquire at inopportune moments into the nature of things resulted, ere I had been five minutes in the house, in my falling at least fifty per cent. in the landlord's good graces. He had †inducted us into a very neatly furnished parlour on the ground floor—or first floor, as our cousins term it—and was listening with conscious pride to our †encomia thereupon, when the state of the walls unluckily attracted my attention. They were covered with a coat of seeming enamel, of a delicate white, and as smooth and polished as glass. "What a beautiful effect!" I exclaimed. A frown passed over the handsome countenance of the unique landlord. "They're just plastered." he remarked curtly, "waiting to be †frescoed, and till we get more guests at the Clarendon we can't afford to have 'em frescoed. That's what's the matter." Whereupon he retired, slamming the door behind him. "Now you've done it," said my diplomatic friend, ominously; "not a bite shall we get to-night." My heart misgave me, and I wished the walls had been as those of Balclutha[180], and desolate before I criticised them.

It was close upon one o'clock in the morning, but the unique landlord bore no malice, and ere long we were summoned by one of the courtliest black waiters I ever came in contact with to the dining-hall, where a supper of ham, sardines, crackers, bread, butter, tongue, and cranberry sauce was laid out for us. The courtly negro was the head waiter, and gave us delicately to understand that he had got out of bed expressly to wait upon us, and that it was an honour and pleasure to do so. To our delight, he waived the stereotyped inquiry as to whether we would take tea or coffee, and "'spected vat ver gemblemens ud like to partook of somffin strong an' comfable right away." We acquiesced so far as regarded the future of the verb to partake, and he produced the strong and the comfortable in the shape of bottled stout. He informed us, with a waive of the napkin which the elder Vestris[181] might have envied, that we needn't be "'ticlar" as to the sounding of the gong for meals in the morning, and that "lowances" would be made for "gemblemens from foreign parts," an intimation inexpressibly grateful to tired travellers. "An, Lor lub yer," he finally whispered as he reconducted us to the door, "Saratoga's dreffel for gentility, *and gemblemens can get drinks all day Sunday.*" Another worthy servitor, groom of the chambers, as black as a patent-leather boot, and nearly as shiny, ushered us to our sleeping apartment. The unique landlord, however, visited us no more that night. I caught a glimpse of him through a little glazed aperture looking into his private office. He was scanning the pages of the guest-ledger, with a grave and, as it seemed to me, a sorrowful mien. My guilty conscience hinted to me that his glance might have been arrested at my name, and he musing, "Always, always the same. He can't even come to a quiet hotel at a watering-place without making unpleasant remarks upon the walls." Although it is just probable that the unique landlord was only lamenting the paucity of arrivals by that night's train. Let me hasten, however, to record that neither by word nor by gesture did this excellent person betray any outward consciousness of my having, however inadvertently, wounded his feelings. His behaviour to us, during the week we remained at Saratoga, was marked by the extremest courtesy and consideration, and when we left he disdained to charge me so much as one cent for the use of the enamelled parlour, for which I had expected to be charged at least five dollars a day.

The main thing is dressing up, dressing up, once and again and forever

ERNEST DUVERGIER DE HAURANNE

A young Frenchman of unusual powers of observation wrote letters, which he never intended to be published, to his father during an eight-month tour of the northern states and eastern Canada in 1864 and 1865. Despite a notably realistic attitude, there was nothing ill-humored about this liberal opponent of Napoleon III's regime. Ernest Duvergier de Hauranne (1843–1876) was well-educated, fluent in English, and thoroughly familiar with the great work of de Tocqueville. He came to study American political life first-hand, and be-

came a Republican sympathizer during his visit. While there is nothing unique about his observations on Saratoga Springs, they are rendered with a sharp focus yet absent the haughtiness of many of his British counterparts as social critics.

Ralph H. Bowen, ed., *A Frenchman in Lincoln's America. Huit Mois en Amérique: Lettres et Notes de Voyage, 1864–1865* (Chicago: The Lakeside Press, 1974), 1: 140–141. Biography is found in the introduction.

Saratoga
July 25. 1864

IMAGINE A flat, sandy, uninteresting region, a big village of wooden buildings separated by long avenues: this is Saratoga, a watering-place and pleasure spot which is, so to speak, the Vichy of America. Standing opposite the railroad station is an enormous barracks, built partly of wood and partly of brick: this is the United States Hotel, the center of polite society in Saratoga. You enter through a sort of portal made of thick planks and come into a courtyard planted with trees and flanked by two immense wings; on one side you look out onto the railroad and on the other the view is enclosed by a vast white building. A covered porch, to which innumerable staircases lead, has been built all around the enclosure. The windows of a colossal dining room, and a room crowded with ladies dressed in the height of fashion, open onto the back. The interior corridors resemble those of a prison. The suites are wretched—scarcely furnished at all: each room has white-washed walls, two wooden chairs and a crude wardrobe made of rough lumber. In these bare surroundings, bejewelled idlers disport themselves in white waistcoats and silken dresses. The day is passed in the drawing room where the guests assemble by the hundreds, treading on one another's toes or sitting about in groups. A confused din of shuffling feet and mingled voices arises from the promenade; it is like a ground bass above which a frightful clatter of plates, knives and glasses breaks forth at mealtime. Finally, to complete the uproar, a small orchestra takes up its station daily under the trees and pumps out dance tunes to the accompaniment of train whistles and the roaring of the locomotives. In the evening, formal gowns and expensive black suits make their appearance. Then the band withdraws to a large, empty room, furnished only with wooden chairs, where it plays without intermission or let-up until the early morning hours. The men gather in the barroom and discuss business; the hotel is like a stock exchange for the use of bro-

U.S. Hotel Dining Room. Stereoscope view by T. J. Arnold. Robert Joki Collection.

kers who come up from New York to spend the weekend here with their families. All in all, it is the most terrible pandemonium that civilization has ever invented to be passed off under the name of pleasure. The Americans call this "the country;" living in such barracks open to the entire world, milling about like sheep between the ballroom and the locomotive—this represents for them the charm of the out-of-doors. I detest those so-called pleasure resorts where our society people go during the summer, taking with them as many trappings of Parisian life as they can cram into their luggage; and ours are truly rustic retreats in comparison with this †phalanstery where a thousand human beings eat, drink and dance in a crowd at fixed hours. It took the most advanced people on earth to perfect this modern way of tasting the delights of fashionable upper-class life!

As for the women, the main thing is dressing up, dressing up, once and again and forever. One young lady who is most "in the swim" changes her *coiffure* three times in a single day. All watering places are for "flirtation" first and foremost. More than one of these elegant young ladies will catch a husband in the scuffle. More than one of these stylish young loafers, once he has acquired a sufficient fortune, will be peering into these muddy waters in search of the pearl for which he has prepared a costly setting. It is a marriage market where the deals are concluded in the full glare of publicity. So much the worse for those who might wish to escape the eyes of the crowd. In this democratic world everyone eats out of a common bowl; people are moved about by the shovelful like so many inanimate objects and the whole society is simmering in the same pot.

Here and there in the midst of the bedlam I have run across a few amiable and distinguished people from New York who are becoming my regular companions. As for the run of the public, nothing is simpler than to put oneself on its level: it is enough to throw overboard a little art and literature or to keep it under lock and key. Business and politics take up the entire conversation—but it isn't the brilliant, almost philosophical conversation to which we are accustomed. Here the ideas of a man of the world are scarcely any more elevated than those of a man of the people; it is the same solid common sense, but rather dull and unappetizing. It is the same with their minds as with their clothes and houses: prevailing fashions are not to be violated, colors are uniform, and when you come upon an occasional exception to the rule—an attempt at color or originality—you can count on its being a masterpiece of bad taste. I am inclined to compare the Americans with their machines, which are powerful, but somewhat crudely put together—excellent for turning out articles of workaday quality for common use, but not suitable for producing the imaginative creations and articles of luxury that we have in Europe.

Today it is all hushed in morning
SALLY ANN KNICKERBOCKER

Seth Hill (1842–1930) was farm boy from Porter Corners when he enlisted in Company H of the 153rd New York Volunteers just after his 20th birthday. He served three years and was promoted to sergeant. His brothers Erastus, Christopher, John and George also served. After the war he returned to Porter Corners, married and adopted a son. He carefully saved the letters he received; one of them, from his sister Sally describing the reaction to Lee's surrender and to the assassination of Lincoln, is quoted in full.

Sally Ann Knickerbocker, letter to Seth Hill, 23 April 1865. Punctuation added. Collection of Robert Joki. An obituary of Seth Hill is in the *Saratogian*, 31 May 1930.

Sunday Morning ten o'clock Apr the 23 1865
My Dear Brother

I now take my pen to answer your kind and ever welcome letter which I recievd some weeks ago. we ar all well here at present and hope this will find you all right. we have been very uneasy about you but ar assured at last that you ar safe once more. Dalkams folks ar all well. Mariette came from Mothers yesterday. She sais Ma is miserable. don't think she will live long. I wish she would come and stay with me or sister until some of you get home for she is not fit to be left a lone at all. She mite let out the garden and shut up the house. it would be better for her a good deal. when you write to her tell her you think she had better do so as it is not safe for her to be alone. I think some times she will die there all alone.

I got a letter from Fred the other day. he sais he thinks you feel above him since you have been promoted for he rote to you in Feb and has heard nothing from you since. he sais he is a going to enlist in the Regulars for three years longer. I am going to write to him to day and tell him if he wants to kill Mother to do so. I don't know what to think of him some times. a little over a week ago our Vilage was all jou [*sic*] and tumult Bells wer rung cannon fired Bonfiers burnt in the streets horns blowd hands clapd voices shouted joy to the surrender of Lees Armey. to day it is all hushed in morning. our President has fallen by the hand of an assassin and the land is drapt in Morning to day. last wensday all busness places were closed and survice in all of the churches and nearly every house in the Vilage trimd in morning. every body had on the Badg of Morning. that his Murderer may be speadily cought and brought to justus is the prair of every loyal heart. his remains ar to be in Albany Wensday and there is to be a special train from here at half price. I should so much like to go down. don't know but I shall. prehaps shall never be eny the poorer for it.

Seth I did not think you was drunk. I only said so for fun. I told Ma you had made a mistake. those virses I thought first rate Well dear Brother I hope there will be no more fighting and soon you will all be home. I shall have to bring my letter to a close as I have got severl to write to day. Write as soon as you get this. good by for this time my dear Brother and believe me as ever your affectionate sister

Sally Ann Knickerbocker

PS Johny sends love to you he sets here trying to make a ring

He who carried an empty sleeve or a scar on his face was a lion in Saratoga
JOHN EDWIN HILARY SKINNER

A special correspondent to the Daily News *of London, Hilary Skinner (1839–1894) began reporting on foreign places in 1864, traveling with the Danish army. In the following year he visited the United States, Canada and Mexico; the volumes he published about that journey provide us with a vivid perspective on Saratoga at peace in the aftermath of the Civil War.*

J. E. Hilary Skinner, *After the Storm; Or, Jonathan and his Neighbours in 1865–6* (London: Richard Bentley, 1866), 1: 61–65.

THOSE WHO declare that the scenery of the United States is monotonous should make some of the excursions from Albany mentioned in a previous chapter. Half a dozen watering places would be within easy reach, and at any of them the traveller might not only enjoy pleasant society, but might see how Americans do not live when they are at home. He might if only his purse were long enough, go to Saratoga and take part in a score of fashionable pastimes.

Never was the place so madly merry as in 1865. One large hotel had been reduced to ashes[182], which made the street near the railway station somewhat dreary. But other hotels were flourishing, and the trains brought new swarms of excursionists to fill every hole and corner in the ugly village. Prices were fabulously high. A man might hope to get shaved, have half an hour's drive in a carriage and buy a cigar, for a pound sterling—but nothing more! Saratoga did not want poor people, and took a very effectual means to keep them away. Great was the flirting, and the dancing, prodigious the consumption of champagne! Officers returned from the army, with wealthy merchants from east and west, met †"shoddy" and "petroleum" in eager rivalry. If the officers could afford to stay long enough, they were sure to win, as they deserved, the greater share of ladies' favour; while he who carried an empty sleeve or a scar upon his face was a †lion in Saratoga.

The races[183] of this season were unusually good, and I regretted that I had not time to wait for them. Talking of horse races, there is no doubt that what concerns sport is making rapid progress in America. The grave Puritan spirit of New England, which objected to

Saratoga Race Course. Woodcut by Winslow Homer. *Harper's Weekly*, 26 August 1865.

trivial amusements, has been overborne by the modern demand for relaxation, even in New England itself. New York State has exhibited cosmopolitan eagerness in such matters, and Saratoga was always gay.

One great difference did I observe between the Springs in 1860, and in 1865. Southerners had formerly been the leaders of fashion at this and other summer resorts in the North. Their elegant †equipages and profuse expenditure made them conspicuous in the eyes of the most careless lounger; whilst on looking beneath the surface and learning who governed society, it became clear that Southern influence and opinion had deep root amongst well-dressed Northerners. So it was at the Saratoga of 1860. But when five years had passed, secession and war had rooted up the old associations, fresh names were held in honour, and fresh families displayed their wealth. The planters of other days were killed or ruined, society had abhorred a vacuum, and their place was supplied by oil and shoddy. What did it matter to Saratoga, viewed as a village hungering for spoil, to whom its mineral waters were given? There was no falling off of custom at the hotels; no abatement in the demand for carriages to drive to the Lake.

I spent a pleasant week at that hotel, now lying in ashes, during the by-gone period of Saratogan life. We had prominent men from both sections of the country staying in the house, and one evening in particular, when some strolling musicians performed before a group of laughing guests, there were citizens standing side by side convulsed with merriment, who have since been deadly enemies. They were then persuaded that, although differences of opinion existed between North and South, no bloodshed need be feared. Poor human foresight! I have often thought of that evening when telegrams announced some desperate battle in Tennessee or Virginia.

To the Union flock the men and women of the vulgar fashionable world

SIDNEY GEORGE FISHER

Frank and plain in style, the diary of Philadelphian Sidney George Fisher (1809–1877) reveals the changes brought about by the Civil War. A graduate of Dickinson College, Fisher practiced law for many years but, in his forties, became interested in farming on his Maryland plantations. He also grew sympathetic to slavery; in the year before the Civil War he published "an erudite plea for white supremacy." Fisher thought that the increase in wealth and the ease of travel had drawn the vulgar multitudes to Saratoga Springs and, as Newport and Long Branch grew fashionable and attracted the "best" society, the spa was becoming notable for the worst. Nevertheless, Fisher was a traditional health seeker and concluded, "I am sure the water & the air together did me much good."

Nicholas B. Wainwright, ed., *A Philadelphia Perspective: The Diary of Sidney George Fisher* (Philadelphia: Historical Society of Pennsylvania, 1967), 529–531.

DR. KEATING advised me strongly to spend a week before going home at Saratoga. He thought the waters there would have a very good effect after the sulphur water at Richfield, of which I drank five or six tumblers a day, & in which I took a daily bath. I determined to follow his advice, and on the 21st of August with him left Richfield at 1 o'clock & reached Saratoga the same evening at 7 o'clock.

I had a pleasant visit to Saratoga. I was with an agreeable party & enjoyed the novelty of the scene & the various attractions of the place. Before breakfast I went to the Congress spring & drank two tumblers, took a walk in the beautiful park, & then drank two more.

At 12 took a bath at the Putnam mineral spring[184], very delightful & stimulating, and drank a glass of the water or that of the Washington spring, both strongly †chalybeate, and also saline &, like the water of the Congress spring, cold, clear, sparkling, effervesing & very refreshing & exciting, very different from the same waters as we get them here in bottles. Dinner at 2. In the afternoon at 5 or 6 a stroll in the park or in the Pine Grove. In the evening, Keating & I generally went to the Clarendon to talk nonsense with Mrs. Randall & Miss Allen.

Saratoga is very much enlarged since I was there last, about 18 years ago. There are streets & hotels on the ground then open fields. Before railroads made travelling universal, it was the chief watering place of the country & the resort of the best society from North & South. The prestige thus acquired & its natural advantages afterwards, as wealth increased & travelling became fast & cheap, attracted the newly made rich & would be fashionable pleasure seekers, & lovers of show & vulgar aspirants to good society, and Saratoga continued to be for many years the central point of attraction during the summer months for the crowds that travel for health or pleasure. Of late, however, Newport & Long Branch & other watering places have become fashionable & diverted from Saratoga much of the best society, and now it is notorious for assembling the worst. It is easy of access, the hotel accommodations are large, & the habit of going there had become established. A crowd attracts, for it tempts many tastes & interests by the offer of gain or pleasure. Some years ago politicians went to Saratoga to discuss party measures & attract adherents. It has ceased, however, to be a theatre for such display & intrigue and now the society of the place may be divided into two classes, quiet, respectable people who go to drink the waters & breathe the wholesome air, & a crowd of sporting men, fast men, gamblers & adventurers, the †*demi-monde* in short, male & female, who attend the races & gather together for their various objects of pleasure & profit.

Two or three years ago the two largest hotels, the United States & old Congress Hall, were burnt.[185] On the site of the latter a new & much larger is building & will be ready for company next year. A hotel is also to be erected on the lot occupied by the United States, so there will soon be room enough for all comers & they will no doubt be in numbers sufficient to fill all the houses, for the advantages of Saratoga are so great that it must always be a place of resort. These advantages are, in my judgment, the various springs of delicious

The United States Hotel under construction. *Frank Leslie's Illustrated Newspaper,* 5 July 1873.

water, fountains of health, the pure, dry air, the park & the surrounding country, which, tho not remarkable for striking scenery, is rural, wooded, & pleasant for rides & drives & contains a very pretty lake. At present, the chief hotels are the Union, the Clarendon, the Everett, & three or four others of less note, & any number of boarding houses. To the Union flock the men & women of the vulgar fashionable world, gamblers & †demireps, some of the latter unmistakably women of the town. I went there two or three times & walked in the evening thro the immense drawing rooms, I was never more disgusted. There was no elegance or beauty, but coarse, low, vice & vulgarity. The men looked like the thieves & the women like the whores that many of them were. I here saw John Morrissey[186], the noted pugilist, gambler, *burglar,* rowdy, & member of Congress, & with him Heenan[187], the celebrated prize fighter. The latter, a fine specimen of athletic strength, a magnificent animal; the former of powerful make & with a gross brutal countenance & most depraved & guilty look. He was worth noticing as one of the representatives of the great & gorgeous city of New York, the "metropolis" of the country, and as a very remarkable phenomenon of our politics, a scientific factor revealing the nature of democracy.

The Clarendon is the best house in the place. It is a handsome building, spacious, with extensive & broad piazzas, & comfortable reading & smoking rooms for gentlemen, has large, well-kept shady grounds, and is very well managed. The best company go there now & to the Everett house.[188] Altogether, Saratoga has special attractions and will no doubt increase in size & improve in the style of its accommodations every year. The springs alone will always bring there a large company. I am sure the water & air together did me much good. Probably, this will not be my last visit.

The use of rouge and white paint is very prevalent among the women
GEORGE ROSE

There's a great deal of criticism in the writing of George Rose (1817–1882), but it's delivered with the geniality of a comic rather than the imperiousness of a social critic. Indeed, after Oxford and careers as a minister, tutor and playwright, he launched himself as a monologuist in 1866, writing under the pseudonym of Arthur Sketchley. Most of the monologues purported to be the views of an illiterate old woman of the lower middle class, not unlike the later "Josiah Allen's Wife" of Marietta Holley. He visited America the year after he began the series: his book of travels was unrelated to the monologues but partook of the same acute satire.

Arthur Sketchley [George Rose], *The Great Country, or Impressions of America* (London: Tinsley Brothers, 1868), 256–265.

SARATOGA has no beauty of position to recommend it, though it is not an unpleasant place; the streets are lined with trees, which afford a grateful shade to the dusty walks. The glory of Saratoga has much departed "since the war."

In former days the wealthy inhabitants of the South used to seek here a retreat from the heat, and yellow fever, by which summer is distinguished in their own latitudes; and in those days the toilettes of the ladies, and the equipages were gorgeous in the extreme. The hotel at which I stopped was called the Union, and very like a barrack and a bathing establishment combined.

It is built and arranged for summer residence, the rooms are large and full of windows and doors. I'll not say anything about the living at this hotel, or I shall gain the reputation of being devoted to the pleasures of the table; which I do not deserve, for though I hold that man to be a fool, or worse, who says that he does not know the difference between good and bad food, yet I do not think dinner the one great and all important event of a man's daily life. I feel bound to state that those who ought to be judges in the matter of good living, assure me that "before the war" the food at the hotels was excellent. I can only conjecture that the contending armies ate all the provisions and slew the cooks; hence the existing state of things which unhesitatingly I pronounce to be detestable.

The company at Saratoga was what is termed "style," by which is meant very over-dressed, jewel-bedizened, loud-talking women, and men displaying every eccentricity that the male wardrobe is capable of being brought to. There was not a crowded attendance at the dinner-table; and one very magnificently attired "gent" made a confidant of my neighbour, and indulged him with many particulars concerning the character and career of a lady sitting close by, which if not edifying, were interesting to a foreigner, as enabling him to judge as to the desirableness of bringing his female relatives to a fashionable place. There was some reason for the "gent's" disclosures, as he was a discarded lover of the lady who, at the moment, was the idol of an individual in a black velvet coat, a shirt that defies description, and jewellery so massive as to make me think it must be a fatigue to carry it about.

The lady was a work of art, powerfully, if not beautifully, painted; even her eyes were picked out with black. Her dress was of the palest blue, very much †vandyked at the bottom, and her feet were encased in very small high-heeled bronze boots of the brightest hue. Her hair was a little overdone, for she had such a lump at the back, that it gave her the effect of going about with a small †porter's knot on her head. I believe that subsequently she had the "gent" who persevered in circulating idle tales about her nearly flogged to death; some say she cow-hided him with her own hands; but I do not vouch for the truth of this statement. I saw her at the Lake with her companion playing at bowls, and am inclined to think, by her excessive vivacity, that she had been indulging in fried potatoes[189], for which the restaurant adjoining the Lake is famous; they are cut marvellously thin, being fried quite dry, and they serve to give a relish to the champagne, which is largely consumed at this place.

I was much struck by the very great number of men whom I saw both here and elsewhere, with hair, whiskers, and moustache dyed; it gave them a fierce appearance, and added to the conviction I entertain most strongly, that in a few more generations numbers of the Americans will have returned to the Indian type.

The use of rouge and white paint, another characteristic of the savage, is very prevalent among the women, as also an inordinate love of beads and feathers.

Some of these fair creatures are artless and primitive, as though born in a wigwam.

I observed one (as she sat waiting for her breakfast) cleaning her nails with a penknife she had borrowed of a friend; whilst a rival beauty, in order to shame her, produced a little box, with a file and pumice stone, and commenced the same operation.

There were some strong-minded females at table. I saw one who had not cleaned her nails, pinch every peach on a plate, and having selected the only two that were eatable, hand the dish to a neighbour. Let me here observe that I consider the American peaches as much over-rated as every thing else in the country, whether fish, flesh, or fowl. I had heard so much of the peaches, and one informant on the subject said, "I reckon 'twill about astonish you Britishers to see our pigs fed with peaches." When I became acquainted with the peaches I felt sorry for the pigs.

Within a short distance of Saratoga is an Indian camp, but as the tribe is almost entirely composed of white men, and some declare they speak with a brogue, a very deep insight into Indian manners and customs cannot be expected to be derived from a visit to their wigwams. During the season there are races at Saratoga, a circumstance that by no means increases the select nature of the visitors, nor the high character of the place.

Was discharged from the Union today on account of their getting white help

EMMA WAITE

A pocket diary for 1870 gives us a window into the world of an African American hotel worker. Emma Waite was an itinerant, discharged when a hotel found a white worker to replace her, always looking for the next situation in New York or Brooklyn for the winter. Yet she had strong ties of friendship and, perhaps, blood to other black and mixed-race Saratogians, such as the Hunters and the Ostranders, and she bought a plot for herself in Greenridge Cemetery (we do not know if she was ever interred there). The diary descended in the Hoke family of Canajoharie. It gives us a unique perspective on hotel help through the eyes of a sensitive and intelligent woman of color.

Emma Waite, diary. New York State Library, Manuscripts and Special Collections. Transcribed by Field Horne with punctuation added. The small "gem" photograph acquired with it, which has been hitherto identified in publications as that of Emma Waite, is probably a friend of the diarist rather than Waite herself; the marking "Emma Waite" on the reverse was done by a librarian at the time of acquisition to associate it with the diary.

[MAY] MONDAY 30. Very warm and sultry. I attended the decoration[190] of the Soldiers Graves to day.

Tuesday 31. Still very warm. through work at Mrs Jacksons tonight

[June] Wednesday 1. Very plesant for the first of June. I went to the cemetery this afternoon and cleared up my lot.

Thursday 2. Plesant but very warm. went to work at the Union Hotel this morning.

Friday 3. It still continues warm and plesant, it is very dry and dusty. was discharged from the Union today on account of their getting white help.

Sunday 5. Very warm. went to Sabath school this afternoon and up to Mrs Ostranders and to Church[191] in the evening.

Monday 6. Not quite so warm as it was. cloudy off and on and this afternoon a little rain. was up to see Charlie Lattimore[192] this morning and also had my hair cut.

Wednesday 8. Sunshine and rain. attended a Wedding this afternoon.

Thursday 9. Quite plesant. the Methodist Sabath School went on an Excurcion to Luzern today[193]

Sunday 12. Just cool enough to be plesant. I attended Sabath School and Church.

Tuesday 14. Plesant so far. I commenced work at the Congress Hall today. I dont know yet how I shall like it. I feel quite unwell today.

Wednesday 15. Showery. I do not feel much better than I did yesterday.

Friday 17. quite plesant. I do not like my situation much. I am almost burnt up already

Tuesday 28. Very very warm. I dont know what I shall do if it keeps as warm as this long. their was a thunder shower a while ago.

Wednesday 29. Not quite so warm as it was yesterday. Maggie Williams died yesterday afternoon.

Thursday 30. Quite warm and dusty. I attended the funeral of Maggie Williams this afternoon.

[July] Monday 4. Very plesant. it does not seem much like the 4th of July as there is no celebration here.

Sunday 10. quite plesant. the people are beginning to come in to the races

Monday 11. Rather cloudy all day but very warm and sultry. I am almost dead with the heat. I left the Congress tonight

Tuesday 12. Cloudy but sultry. it rained quite hard in the night. I commenced work at the Continental Hotel[194] this morning.

Continental Hotel. *Saratoga, and How to See It* (1873)

Tuesday 14. This is the first day of the races. it has been plesant with the exception of a little shower

Friday 15. Very plesant. one of the horses[195] and his rider was killed at the race today.

Sunday 17. Very plesant indeed, I am getting along quite nicely, so far

Monday 18. Plesant, rather warmer than yesterday. the new washwoman tried to get up a [?room] with me tonight.

Thursday 21. Very plesant. I attended the prayer meeting this evening

Monday 25. Still very warm. it is blue Monday again. my friend Emma was discharged today. I was very sorry to have her go.

Tuesday 26. Still warm. I am feeling very miserable.

Wednesday 27. quite plesant. I don't feel any better.

Thursday 28. Very warm all day and raining this evening. I have been feeling worse today. there was a [?hop] here last night, Mr De Mars made me a present of a splendid bottle of port wine today

Friday 29. It rained hard this morning but it cleared off splendid. I feel a little better than I did.

Sunday 31. quite cool and pleasant, we had to get up a very heavy dinner today.

[August] Monday 1. Came in very plesant. I am quite tired tonight. Maggie had to leave to day on account of her Mothers being sick & I had to turn into the pastry work until she comes back.

Tuesday 2. Rather cool but splendid working weather.

Friday 5. A splendid day. I drove down to the lake this evening and had a splendid drive. it was beautiful moonlight and the roads were in splendid condition. I stopped and saw—Anna.

Saturday 6. A very nice day. I have had a bad headache all day and have felt miserable. Sophia Hunter came home today from Oberlin.[196]

Thursday 11. Another very warm day. the house has filled up today.

Friday 12. It rained quite hard this forenoon but cleared off nicely afterwards. the races commenced today.

Sunday 14. Plesant and cool, a very busy day. Daisy my poor little kitten got killed today by the †dummy. it made me feel very bad indeed. I attended a party last evening at Mr Hunters.

Sunday 21. Cool and plesant. I have had to work very hard to day on account of my assistant going on a bender.

Wednesday 24. Threatening rain. the girls are to have a ball here to night.

Thursday 25. Raining hard this afternoon. the ball took place last evening and was a perfect success. they all looked very nicely.

Friday 26. Rather cool after the shower. I attended the lecture of Rev. H.H. Garrett[197] this evening and was highly delighted. there was a large and highly enteligent audience present. the Circus[198] came today

Sunday 28. quite plesant. I attended Church this evening to hear Mr Gilberts last Sermon in this place

Tuesday 30. Cooler after the rain. I saw Mr Smith today and he wants me to go to Lansingburg to live with them this winter.

Wednesday 31. Very pleasant. I attended a party at Mrs Hunters this evening.

[September] Friday 2. Still plesant. a number of the help are gone away. John Leary was here tonight drunk and brandishing a knife and useing threatening language. Mr de Mars sent for an Officer to arrest him but he ran away

Saturday 3. Quite warm and close, a boy that lived opposite to us was killed by the cars today. I was invited to a party this evening but could not attend on account of sickness.

Tuesday 6. Rather cooler. the fair commenced today.

Wednesday 7. quite cold all day but plesant. the Republican State Convention meets here today to nominate a Candidate for Governor. Speeches are being made and cannons fired and a great time generally.

Thursday 8. Still cool but plesant. Mr Hunter received a dispatch to come to New York. he intends to start in the morning.

Friday 9. Plesant. Mr Hunter went to New York this morning and I have been Chief Cook

Saturday 10. Raining this morning, but cleared off cold. Mr Hunter returned this morning. I lost my place at Lansingburg today

Monday 12. Still plesant. Emma Knight left for home tonight

Wednesday 14. Very plesant, I finished my seasons work at the Continental this afternoon

The company is dreadfully mixed

HENRY JAMES

One of the greatest of American authors, Henry James (1843–1916) needs no introduction. His essay on Saratoga Springs, published in The Nation, *is unlike most of the other excerpts in this anthology in that it is a work of formal literature. But it was, it appears, written on the scene and from personal observation, and it seconds the sentiments of many of his contemporaries, especially the critical English.*

[Henry James], "Saratoga," *The Nation* 11 (August 11, 1870): 87–89. It was slightly rewritten and republished in *Portraits of Places* (Boston: Houghton Mifflin, 1883), 324–327.

SARATOGA, August 3, 1870

ONE HAS vague irresponsible local previsions of which it is generally hard to discern the origin. You find yourself thinking of an unknown, unseen place as thus rather than so. It assumes in your mind a certain shape, a certain color which frequently turns out to be singularly at variance with reality. For some reason or other, I had idly dreamed of Saratoga as buried in a sort of elegant wilderness of †verdurous gloom. I fancied a region of shady forest drives, with a bright, broad-piazzaed hotel gleaming here and there against a background of mysterious groves and glades. I had made a cruelly small allowance for the stern vulgarities of life—for the shops and sidewalks and loafers, the complex machinery of a city of pleasure. The fault was so wholly my own that it is quite without bitterness that I proceed to affirm that the Saratoga of experience is sadly different from this. I confess, however, that it has always seemed to me that one's visions, on the whole, gain more than they lose by realization. There is an essential indignity in indefiniteness: you cannot imagine the especial poignant interest of details and accidents. They give more to the imagination than they receive from it. I frankly admit, therefore, that I find here a decidedly more satisfactory sort of place than the all-too-primitive Elysium of my wanton fancy. It is indeed, as I say, immensely different. There is a vast number of brick—nay, of asphalte—sidewalks, a great many shops, and a magnificent array of loafers. But what indeed are you to do at Saratoga—the morning draught having been achieved—unless you loaf? *"Que faire en un gîte à moins que l'on ne songe?"*[199] Loafers being assumed, of course shops and sidewalks follow. The main avenue of Saratoga is in fact bravely entitled Broadway. The untravelled reader may form a very accurate idea of it by recalling as distinctly as possible, not indeed the splendors of that famous thoroughfare, but the secondary charms of the Sixth Avenue. The place has what the French would call the "accent" of the Sixth Avenue. Its two main features are the two monster hotels which stand facing each other along a goodly portion of its course. One, I believe, is considered much better than the other—less prodigious and promiscuous and tumultuous, but in appearance there is little choice between them. Both are immense brick structures, directly on the crowded, noisy street, with vast covered piazzas running along the façade, supported by great iron posts. The piazza of the Union Hotel, I have been repeatedly informed, is the largest "in the world." There are a number of objects in Saratoga, by the way, which in their respective kinds are the finest in the world. One of these is Mr. John Morrissey's casino.[200] I bowed my head submissively to this statement, but privately I thought of the blue Mediterranean, and the little white promontory of Monaco, and the silver-gray verdure of olives, and the view across the outer sea toward the bosky cliffs of Italy. Congress Spring, too, it is well known, is the most delicious mineral spring in the known universe; this I am perfectly willing to maintain.

The piazzas of these great hotels may very well be the greatest of all piazzas. They are not picturesque, but they doubtless serve their purpose—that of affording sitting-space in the open air to an immense number of persons. They are, of course, quite the best places to observe the Saratoga world. In the evening, when the "boarders" have all come forth and seated themselves in groups, or have begun to stroll in (not always, I regret to say, to the sad detriment of dramatic

Interior of the Casino. *Every Saturday*, 9 September 1871.

interest, bisexual) couples, the vast heterogeneous scene affords a great deal of entertainment. Seeing it for the first time, the observer is likely to assure himself that he has neglected an important feature in the sum of American manners. The rough brick wall of the house, illumined by a line of flaring gas-lights, forms a harmonious background to the crude, impermanent, discordant tone of the assembly. In the larger of the two hotels, a series of long windows open into an immense parlor—the largest, I suppose, in the world—and the most scantily furnished, I imagine, in proportion to its size. A few dozen rocking-chairs, an equal number of small tables, tripods to the eternal ice-pitchers, serve chiefly to emphasize the vacuous grandeur of the spot. On the piazza, in the outer multitude, ladies largely prevail, both by numbers and (you are not slow to perceive) by distinction of appearance. The good old times of Saratoga, I believe, as of the world in general, are rapidly passing away. The time was when it was the chosen resort of none but "nice people." At the present day, I hear it constantly affirmed, "the company is dreadfully mixed." What society may have been at Saratoga when its elements were thus simple and severe, I can only vaguely, regretfully conjecture. I confine myself to the dense, democratic, vulgar Saratoga of the current year.

You are struck, to begin with, at the hotels by the numerical superiority of the women; then, I think, by their personal superiority. It is incontestably the case that in appearance, in manner, in grace and completeness of aspect, American women vastly surpass their husbands and brothers. The case is reversed with most of the nations of Europe—with the English notably, and in some degree with the French and Germans. Attached to the main entrance of the Union Hotel, and adjoining the ascent from the street to the piazza, is a †"stoop" of mighty area, which, at most hours of the day and morning, is a favored lounging-place of men. I am one of those who think that on the whole we are a decidedly good-looking people. "On the whole," perhaps, every people is good-looking. There is, however, a type of physiognomy among ourselves which seems so potently to imperil the modest validity of this dictum, that one finally utters it with a certain sense of triumph. The lean, sallow, angular Yankee of tradition is dignified mainly by a look of decision, a hint of unimpassioned volition, an air of "smartness." This in some degree redeems him, but it fails to make him handsome. But in the average American of the present time, the typical leanness and sallowness are less, and the individual keenness and smartness at once equally intense and more evenly balanced with this greater comeliness of form. Casting your eye over a group of your fellow-citizens in the portico of the Union Hotel, you will be inclined to admit that, taking the good with the bad, they are worthy sons of the great Republic. I find in them, I confess, an ample fund of grave entertainment. They suggest to my fancy the swarming vastness—the multifarious possibilities and activities—of our young civilization. They come from the uttermost ends of the continent—from San Francisco, from New Orleans, from Duluth. As they sit with their white hats tilted forward, and their chairs tilted back, and their feet tilted up, and their cigars and toothpicks forming various angles with these various lines, I imagine them surrounded with a sort of clear achromatic halo of mystery. They are obviously persons of experience—of a somewhat narrow and monotonous experience certainly; an experience of which the diamonds and laces which their wives are exhibiting hard by are, perhaps, the most substantial and beautiful result; but, at any rate, they are men who have positively actually lived. For the time, they are lounging with the negro waiters, and the boot-blacks, and the news-venders; but it was not in lounging that they gained their hard wrinkles and the level impartial regard which they direct from beneath their hat-rims. They are not the mellow fruit of a society impelled by tradition and attended by culture; they are hard nuts, which have grown and ripened as they could. When they talk among themselves, I seem to hear the mutual cracking of opposed shells.

If these men are remarkable, the ladies are wonderful. Saratoga is famous, I believe, as the place of all places in America where women most adorn themselves, or as the place, at least, where the greatest amount of dressing may be seen by the greatest number of people. Your first impression is therefore of the—what shall I call it?—of the *muchness* of the feminine drapery. Every woman you meet, young or old, is attired with a certain amount of splendor and a large amount of good taste. You behold an interesting, indeed a quite momentous spectacle: the democratization of elegance. If I am to believe what I hear—in fact, I may say what I overhear—a large portion of these sumptuous persons are victims of imperfect education and members of a somewhat narrow social circle. She walks more or less of a queen, however, each unsanctified nobody. She has, in dress, an admirable instinct of elegance and even of what the French call *"chic."* This instinct occasionally amounts to a sort of passion; the result then is superb. You look at the coarse brick walls, the rusty iron posts of the piazza, at the shuffling negro waiters, the great tawdry steamboat cabin of a drawing room—you see the tilted ill-dressed loungers on the steps—and you finally regret that a figure so exquisite should have so vulgar a setting. Your resentment, however, is speedily tempered by reflection. You feel the impertinence of your old reminiscences of Old-World novels, and of the dreary social order in which privacy was the presiding genius and women arrayed themselves for the appreciation of the few—the few still, even when numerous. The crowd, the tavern loungers, the surrounding ugliness and tumult and license, constitute the social medium of the young lady whom you so cunningly admire: she is dressed for publicity. The thought fills you with a kind of awe. The Old-World social order is far away indeed, and as for Old-World novels, you begin to doubt whether she is so amiably curious as to read even the silliest of them. To be so excessively dressed is obviously to give pledges to idleness. I have been forcibly struck with the apparent absence of any warmth and richness of detail in the lives of these wonderful ladies of the piazzas. We are freely accused of being an eminently wasteful people: I know of few things which so largely warrant the accusation as the fact that these consummate *élégantes* adorn themselves, socially speaking, to so little purpose. To dress for every one is, practically, to dress for no one. There are few prettier sights than a charmingly dressed woman, gracefully established in some shady spot, with a piece of needlework or embroidery, or a book. Nothing very serious is accomplished, probably, but an æsthetic principle is considered. The embroidery and the book are a tribute to culture, and I suppose they really figure somewhere out of the opening scenes of French comedies. But here at Saratoga, at any hour of morning or evening, you may see a hundred brave creatures steeped in a quite unutterable emptyhandedness. I have had constant observation of a lady who seems to me really to possess a genius for being nothing more than dressed. Her dresses are admirably rich and beautiful—my letter would greatly gain in value if I possessed the learning needful for describing them. I can only say that every evening for a fortnight, I believe, she has revealed herself as a fresh creation. But she especially, as I say, has struck me as a person dressed beyond her life. I resent on her behalf—or on behalf at least of her finery—the extreme severity of her circumstances. What is she, after all, but a regular boarder? She ought to sit on the terrace of a stately castle, with a great baronial park shutting out the undressed world, mildly coquetting with an ambassador or a duke. My imagination is shocked when I behold her seated in gorgeous relief against the dusty clapboards of the hotel, with her beautiful hands folded in her silken lap, her head drooping slightly beneath the weight of her †*chignon*, her lips parted in a vague contemplative gaze at Mr. Helmbold's well-known advertisement on the opposite fence, her husband beside her reading the New York *Sun*.

I have indeed observed cases of a sort of splendid social isolation here, which are not without a certain amount of pathos—people who know no one—who have money and finery and possessions, only no friends. Such at least is my inference, from the lonely grandeur with which I see them invested. Women, of course, are the most helpless victims of this cruel situation, although it must be said that they befriend each other with a generosity for which we hardly give them credit. I have seen women, for instance, at various "hops," approach their lonely sisters and invite them to waltz, and I have seen the fair invited most graciously heedless of the potential irony of this particular form of charity. Gentlemen at Saratoga are at a premium far more, evidently, than at European watering-places. It is an old story that in this country we have no leisured class—the class from which the Saratogas of Europe recruit a large number of their male frequenters. A few months ago, I paid a visit to a famous English watering-place, where, among many substantial points of difference from our own, I chiefly remember the goodly number of well-dressed, well-looking, well-talking young men. While their sweethearts and sisters are waltzing together, our own young men are rolling up greenbacks in counting-houses and stores. I was recently reminded in another way, one evening, of the unlikeness of Saratoga to Cheltenham. Behind the biggest of the big hotels is a large planted yard, which has come to be talked of as a "park." This I regret, inasmuch as, as a yard, it is possibly the biggest in the world; while as a park I am afraid it is decidedly less than the smallest. At one end, however, stands a great ball-room, approached by a range of wooden steps. It was late in the evening: the room, in spite of the intense heat, was blazing with light, and the orchestra thundering a mighty waltz. A group of loungers, including myself, were hanging about to watch the ingress of the festally minded. In the basement of the edifice, sunk beneath the ground, a noisy auctioneer, in his shirt and trousers, black in the face with heat and †vociferation, was selling "pools" of the races to a dense group of frowsy betting-men. At the foot of the steps was stationed a man in a linen coat and straw hat, without waistcoat or cravat, to take the tickets of the ballgoers. As the latter failed to arrive in sufficient numbers, a musician came forth to the top of the steps and blew a loud summons on a horn. After this they began to straggle along. On this occasion, certainly, the company promised to be decidedly "mixed." The woman, as usual, were a great deal dressed, though without any constant adhesion to the technicalities of full-dress. The men adhered to it neither in the letter nor the spirit. The possessor of a pair of satin shod feet, twinkling beneath an uplifted volume of gauze and lace and flowers, tripped up the steps with her gloved hand on the sleeve of a railway "duster." Now and then two ladies arrived alone: generally a group of them approached under convoy of a single man. Children were freely scattered among their elders, and frequently a small boy would deliver his ticket and enter the glittering portal beautifully unembarrassed. Of the children of Saratoga there would be wondrous things to relate. I believe that, in spite of their valuable aid, the festival of which I speak was rated rather a "fizzle." I see it advertised that they are soon to have, for their own peculiar benefit, a "Masquerade and Promenade Concert, beginning at 9 P.M." I observe that they usually open the "hops," and that it is only after their elders have borrowed confidence from the sight of their unfaltering paces that they venture to perform. You meet them far into the evening roaming over the piazzas and corridors of the hotels—the little girls especially—lean, pale, and formidable. Occasionally childhood confesses itself, even when motherhood stands out, and you see at eleven o'clock at night some poor little †bedizened precocity collapsed in slumbers in a lonely wayside chair. The part played by children in society here is only an additional instance of the wholesale equalization of the various social atoms which is the distinctive feature of collective Saratoga. A man in a "duster" at a ball is as good as a man in irreproachable †sable; a young woman dancing with another young woman is as good as a young woman dancing with a young man; a child of ten is as good as a woman of thirty; a double negative in conversation is rather better than a single.

An important feature in many watering-places is the facility for leaving it a little behind you and tasting of the unmitigated country. You may wander to some shady hillside and sentimentalize upon the vanity of high civilization. But at Saratoga civilization holds you fast. The most important feature of the place, perhaps, is the impossibility of realizing any such pastoral dream. The surrounding country is a charming wilderness, but the roads are so abominably bad that walking and driving are alike unprofitable. Of course, however, if you are bent upon a walk, you will take it. There is a striking contrast between the concentrated prodigality of life in the immediate precinct of the hotels and the generous wooded wildness and roughness into which half an hour's stroll may lead you. Only a mile behind you are thousands of loungers and idlers, fashioned from head to foot by the experience of cities and keenly knowing in their secrets; while here, about you and before you, blooms untamed the hardy innocence of field and forest. The heavy roads are little more than sandy wheel tracks; by the tangled wayside the blackberries wither unpicked. The country undulates with a beautiful unsoftened freedom. There are no white villages gleaming in the distance, no spires of churches, no salient details. It is all green, lonely, and vacant. If you wish to seize an "effect," you must stop beneath a cluster of pines and listen to the murmur of the softly-troubled air, or follow upward the gradual bending of their trunks to where the afternoon light touches and enchants them. Here and there on a slope by the roadside stands a rough unpainted farmhouse, looking as it its dreary blackness were the result of its standing dark and lonely amid so many months, and such a wide expanse, of winter snow. The principal feature of the grassy unfurnished yard is the great wood-pile, telling grimly of the long reversion of the summer. For the time, however, it looks down contentedly enough over a goodly appanage of grain-fields and orchards, and I can fancy that it may be good to be a boy there. But to be a man, it must be quite what the lean, brown, serious farmers physiognomically hint it to be. You have, however, at the present season, for your additional beguilement, on the eastern horizon, the vision of the long bold chain of the Green Mountains, clad in that single coat of simple candid blue which is the favorite garment of our American hills. As a visitor, too, you have for an afternoon's excursion your choice between a couple of lakes. Saratoga Lake, the larger and more distant of the two, is the goal of the regular afternoon drive. Above the shore is a well-appointed tavern—"Moon's" it is called[201] by the voice of fame—where you may sit upon a broad piazza and partake of fried potatoes and "drinks;" the latter, if you happen to have come from poor dislicensed Boston, a peculiarly gratifying privilege. You enjoy the felicity sighed for by that wanton Italian princess of the anecdote, when, one summer evening, to the sound of music, she wished that to eat an ice were a sin. The other lake is small, and its shores are unadorned by any edifice but a boat-house, where you may hire a skiff and pull yourself out into the minnow tickled, wood-circled oval. Here, floating in its darkened half, while you watch on the opposite shore the tree-stems, white and sharp in the declining sunlight, and their foliage whitening and whispering in the breeze, and you feel that this little solitude is part of a greater and more portentuous solitude, you may resolve certain passages of Ruskin, in which he dwells upon the needfulness of some human association, however remote, to make natural scenery fully impressive. You may recall that magnificent passage in which he relates having tried with such fatal effect, in a battle-haunted valley of the Jura, to fancy himself in a nameless solitude of our own continent. You feel around you, with irresistible force, the serene inexperience of undedicated nature—the absence of serious associations, the nearness, indeed, of the vulgar and trivial associations of the least picturesque of great watering-places—you feel this, and you wonder what it is you so deeply and calmly enjoy. You conclude, possibly, that it is a great advantage to be able at once to enjoy Ruskin and to enjoy what Ruskin †dispraises. And hereupon you return to your hotel and read the New York papers on the plan of the French campaign and the Twenty-third Street murder.

The entire room together with its ten or twelve inhabitants rose gently upwards

FRIEDRICH RATZEL

Ironically, the breeziest and yet most detailed account of a visit to Saratoga was written by one of the most competent intellectuals to record his impressions of the spa. Friedrich Ratzel (1844–1904) was sent to America in 1873–74 by the Kölnische Zeitung *to report on the industrialization of America and the changes since the Civil War's upheaval. With complete freedom to choose itinerary and subjects, he covered the nation, sending articles to Germany. Two years after his return, he published some of the essays in book form. The work, while little appreciated at the time, is one of the earliest books by a geographer to stress American urban history. Ratzel later left journalism and taught geography, first at the Polytechnicum in Munich and then, until his death, at the University of Leipzig.*

Stewart A. Stehlin, ed., *Sketches of Urban and Cultural Life in North America by Friedrich Ratzel* (New Brunswick: Rutgers University Press, 1988), 66–73. Reprinted by permission of Rutgers University Press.

THE EARLY September evening on which we arrived in Saratoga was clear and as warm as summer, the streets were bright with the light from illuminated windows, a profusion of bright light poured out of the open hallways of the hotels, along with the sounds of well-known dance music intermingling in the distance with all sorts of dissonances, which then faded away. In this village, tree tops towered over houses, fluttering shadows of trees and bushes covered all the places the light could not reach, and a cool, crisp breeze, like the one that usually emerges from forests and fields at sunset, pervaded the whole place. Gigantic elms lowered their branches before windows in which the most varied types of golden jewelry, precious stones, and pearls were displayed, and a grove of trees, which seemed to lead into a dark valley, stood on one side while the other side was filled with rows of shops stacked with the requirements and needs of a large city. It was a remarkable combination of unspoiled nature with traces of overrefined culture combined according to the recipe we know from Baden-Baden and Interlaken, yet altered by new ingredients, which this restless people's keen sense of taste requires.

The coach stopped in front of a long veranda, or piazza, whose roof rested on tall, thin pillars, while decorated rounded arches connected the pillars and numerous torches illuminated the surroundings.[202] Many people were sitting in rocking chairs, smoking; others were walking around engaged in lively discussion; and still others were gazing out into the night. We went up the broad steps, crossed the piazza, and entered a room that was illuminated from above and again supported by pillars that went up to the height of several floors. Several men were standing here behind a long table. One of them pushed a large book towards us in which we signed our names and where we came from, whereupon another man gave each of us a numbered key. Then several colored men picked up our baggage to take it up to the floor where our assigned rooms were to be found. We entered a little room, paneled in dark wood, whose walls were lined with padded seating and sat down in the midst of a very quiet group of people who were obviously waiting for something. After a few minutes, the entire room together with its ten or twelve occupants rose gently upwards, gliding from floor to floor, letting some people out and taking others in, finally letting us off on the floor with numbers 703 and 705—the highest room numbers I have ever had. The rooms were small and simply furnished; for us unpampered hikers, they were fine enough. My companion, an American familiar with the customs of his countrymen, told me to put on my very best clothes, whereupon we again went down to the ground floor and entered the dining room where once again a colored man respectfully opened the doors for us.

Here were numerous serving and dining tables set up for several hundred guests. Since it was already late, only a few were occupied, and several dozen waiters, colored, as in all the best places, were standing around in the large room in a bored fashion. They say here that the Negro is a born waiter, but those at this hotel had nothing of the grace, nothing of the disposition, nothing of the hidden virtues and capabilities that make the European waiter such an interesting phenomenon for the observer of human nature. Here they work like machines. They scarcely finish what was required of them before falling back into a leaden inertia in which they remain until a new command galvanizes them into new efforts. As they stood there, staring ahead with all their limbs hanging loose, they looked so limp and tired that one almost hesitated to disturb them. At our entrance, one of these men, who rose from his meditative position with a jolt, offered us the menu which had everything on it that hungry stomachs or a spoiled palate could demand, from oysters to roast beef. Across the way from us sat a man who had tea, oysters, roast salmon, a beefsteak, and six varieties of bread in front of him, and whoever wanted ten times that amount could have had it. Most people are less demanding and allow the proprietor to make a good profit in return for the pleasure of knowing that they have the possibility of enjoying a splendid meal every day.

From the dining room we went towards the large common room, where at any time of the day one finds people playing music and dancing and where in the evening fashionable society meets to see and be seen. The dressed-up ladies and gentlemen, amongst whom there were quite a few children moving about, the vacuity and dreariness one notices in so much of the conversation and movement, and the incessant poor piano playing all make this room a very unpleasant spot, although for the majority of the guests it is really the center of activity in such a place. In a luxury-class establishment such a scene in the common room does not seem out of place, but rooms providing such activities are found in every hotel of any importance, even in the lonely areas around Lake George and Lake Champlain where they do not fit in with the surroundings at all. It is very difficult to live alone here for very long, since the rule of sociability completely dominates. This rule, upon which the very popular boarding-house style of life is based, permits many families to give up for years the comfort of private family dwellings to live in inns and hotels. The individual seeks his relaxation and enjoyment by doing something with or at least being in the company of a group. The bedrooms in such an establishment are seldom such that one enjoys spending time in them. On the other hand, it is rare that the common rooms are not equipped with all the comforts in keeping with the circumstances.

This room was the only place in the entire hotel where I saw no spitoons standing about, where, in other words, no smoking was permitted. In all other areas, one could find these symbols of a more relaxed sociability in ample abundance, and I often had the opportunity to admire the dexterity with which the men, without taking much time to aim, hit the mark, or how as they were sitting they stretched out a leg in order to bring these "inseparable companions" over towards them. This household article is a glazed earthen vessel with a crater-like opening inclining towards the center, similar to what one finds on ocean liners.

The reading room, smoking room, and barroom are the meeting

Congress Hall as it was after 1868. Stereoscope view by W. H. Cipperly. Robert Joki Collection.

places of the male guests of such hotels, and all three are heavily frequented. In the last of these they stand or sit before the bar, behind which the barkeeper mixes up all kinds of little drinks that are imbibed in this country—some to cool off with, some to warm up with. They are sometimes very strange concoctions but generally not bad tasting. On this evening my friend tasted and then presented me with a milk punch that was made out of milk, brandy, ice, and herbs. Later I got to know still other nice mixtures of this type like iced claret (red wine, ice, slices of lemon and pineapple), sherry †cobbler (sherry, ice, lemon slices), various types of grog, and similar drinks. The iced drinks are sipped through straws.

The next morning we took care of the few things worth seeing in Saratoga. Congress Park, a grove full of beautiful trees in which the most famous of the Saratoga springs, the Congress Spring, originates, provided us with shade, and we walked along its winding paths northwards to a so-called Indian settlement where Indians and half-breeds who come down from Canada in the summer offer braided and hand-carved trinkets for sale and demonstrate their skill at archery. The settlement looked exactly like a section of one of the gypsy camps of Hungary. Though apparently often racially mixed, the inhabitants showed by their deep golden or bronze facial color, their little black eyes, their pitch black bristly hair, and their broad cheekbones (the last trait also appeared to be very pronounced in

"The Appearance of the Office of the Union Hotel, on the Arrival of the Steamboat Train from Albany." *Frank Leslie's Illustrated Newspaper,* 12 August 1865.

the half-breeds, who had the most European blood) that they belonged to the original inhabitants of this land. On Lake George we later found an opportunity to visit a similar settlement and to speak with several Indians, one of whom, as serious and monosyllabic as one would picture him à la Cooper[203], was carving away on his wooden arrows, while another, who had an exceptionally good-natured, broad-smiling and yet still not quite ingenuous facial expression, enjoyed showing and telling us, but in short and phlegmatic words, how the little baskets are woven out of ash wood and the arrows carved out of oak and hickory. In one hut some young girls were singing and laughing while busy with some sewing, and in spite of their broad faces, they did not look at all unattractive. These people were dressed like we are, but they do as they wish with articles of clothing. The preference for loud colors and, in part, the awkwardness in adapting to our clothing, which we notice among the gypsies, can also be seen here among these people. The Canadian Indians speak mostly a French †*patois*; the men in addition can speak English. They looked well nourished and happy, and even today they do not appear in any way to envy the race that overcame and displaced them in this land, a few pale, melancholic specimens of which, their drinking glasses in their hands and a few pints of water from the Congress or Columbian Spring in their stomachs, are already wandering about—a feeling I completely sympathize with in the red men.

We went from spring to spring but found them everywhere pretty much all the same, the water having the same salty, prickly taste (kitchen salt, bicarbonate of lime, magnesia, †natrium, iron, and lithium and not insignificant quantities of carbon dioxide in various proportions to other components are found in most of these springs). The people went to and fro, letting the boys who were dispensing the water fill their glasses, looking generally drowsy and intent on taking the cure. However, the cure routine was apparently not taken very seriously, for in comparison to the large number who are always there, only a few were taking their morning drink.

Except for the springs, nature did not endow this place with anything outstanding: Saratoga is an unattractive, low hilly area, and many larger cities in this country are quieter and have fresher air and more attractive, greener, shadier streets than this well-frequented spot. But there is something intriguing about the temporary transplantation of big-city life to the confines and tranquility of the village. Saratoga in summer is little New York; the high society from the big cities of the Atlantic seaboard, particularly from New York, which at home feels itself scattered and spread out among the general populace, for a few weeks comes together here, along with everything else that goes with its life style. Every individual is pleased to see his own personality flatteringly reflected in the mirror of the resplendent high society. The many people who do not come here with an ailment are looking for this part of Saratoga life. One can probably assume that a visit to such a place is seen more as a necessity, much in the same way that close, lasting social contacts among the better circles are viewed as usually more difficult in this country due to the many fewer sharp class distinctions existing here than in Europe.

To conclude, it is not to be forgotten that Saratoga also has its impressive aspects. To live at a hotel that has 1,364 feet of frontage, one mile of piazzas, 2 miles of halls, 13 acres of carpets and marble floors, 824 rooms, 1,474 doors, and 1,891 windows is certainly a great pleasure; $2.50 a day[204] is not too much to pay for the feeling of living in the biggest of hotels, especially if it is in America and one is an American.

1874
HIRAM
FULLER

It is most elaborately furnished in blue, gold, and water-coloured silks

HIRAM FULLER

Hiram Fuller (1814–1880) had a purpose in writing his Grand Transformation Scenes in the United States. *Massachusetts-born, he had been the publisher of the New York* Evening Mirror *in the 1840s and 1850s, and a popular special correspondent under the pseudonym of Belle Brittan. But on the eve of the Civil War he took so strongly pro-Southern a stance that he found it necessary to leave the United States. He went to London and continued to espouse the Confederate cause, in consequence losing his friends and nearly ruining himself. Though his attempt to regain his popularity with his final book was not a success, he did write a valuable and detailed account of Saratoga and of its newly rebuilt United States Hotel.*

H[iram] Fuller, *Grand Transformation Scenes in the United States; or Glimpses of Home After Thirteen Years Abroad* (New York: G.W. Carleton and Co., 1875), 116–127.

AFTER PASSING a few restless hours in one of the *St John's* numberless "Bridal State-rooms," with its spacious and sumptuous bed, "not made for slumber," we reached Albany, the State capital, 150 miles from New York, at five o'clock A.M., and at seven o'clock took the cars for Saratoga, arriving at half-past nine o'clock. And here was a transformation scene indeed! Four new hotels[205], capable of accommodating an aggregate of 6000 guests, with their beautiful gardens, seem to have crowded everything out of town, occupying the whole space of the old village. With rooms engaged in advance at the "United States," the newest and the grandest of all these grand hotels, the long *queue* at "the office" of ardent room-seekers did not alarm us. Breakfast was ready, and so were we. The dining-room covers half an acre, seats 1000 persons at table, who are received by an army of 200 "coloured gentlemen," but not, as formerly, dressed in the cool, clean white linen uniform. Considering that the hotel had just been opened, that its forces had not sufficient time for organisation and drill, and that there were no less than 1500 persons to room and feed, the administration was wonderfully efficient and generally satisfactory. The "United States" occupies the site of the old hotel of the same name, which was destroyed by fire[206] nine years ago, and the phœnix that has recently risen from the ashes, at a cost of a million of

The Regatta at Saratoga Lake. *Frank Leslie's Illustrated Newspaper*, 31 July 1875.

dollars, is hailed by the public as a favourite work revised, and improved in type, and greatly enlarged in margin. There is no watering-place hotel that I have seen, or heard of, either in Europe or America, that equals it in size, accommodation, and comfort. Saratoga has one principal street, Broadway, on which the hotel has a frontage of 230 feet. It is built in the form of a hollow parallelogram, the sides extending 715 feet, embracing a garden, handsomely laid out in walks, and lined with trees and plants. When enlivened with playing fountains, and illuminated with gas jets, the garden of the "United States" will look as gay as a little *Mabille*.[207] There are 768 sleeping-rooms, besides 65 suites, each of which has from one to seven connecting rooms, with baths, &c. The dining-hall measures 212 by 52 feet, with a ceiling of 26 feet; has eight chandeliers, which, with the 38 side-brackets, give a total of 276 burners. The drawing-room is 87 by 50; ceiling, 26 feet; has 14 windows, and 75 gas-burners. It is most elaborately furnished in blue, gold, and water-coloured silks, with heavy †lambrequins of light-blue silk. The furniture of this room cost 20,000 dollars. The ball-room is 112 by 52 feet; has three chandeliers, 83 burners, and 30 windows. The †Enunciator is 20 feet in height, and cost 10,000 dollars. It registers 916 rooms. The carpets were furnished by A. T. Stewart & Co.[208] The parlour carpet is an

Axminister of 500 yards, and cost four dollars per yard. There are two passenger elevators in the hotel. The piazzas measure 2700 feet in length, and the lawn cover three acres, on the south margin of which are located 63 hotel cottages. The firm which manages this magnificent establishment is Ainsworth, Perry, Tompkins, & Co. Mr Marvin[209], who has been connected with the hotel business in Saratoga since 1830, and who for some years represented the district in Congress, is the principal stockholder in the new concern, and still keeps his eye on the management from the force of habit; while Major Field[210], who has been the popular "room clerk" of the hotel ever since he was three feet high, is still at his post, with pen behind his ear, and the same cordial "glad to see you" on his lips. The sewage and "w. c." improvements of the "United States," a matter of fundamental importance, hitherto shamefully overlooked in Saratoga hotels, are worthy of all praise. But we are a long time in getting to the Regatta[211], which, by the way, I shall leave to the sporting papers to describe. It was announced to take place at 4 P.M. on the 16th, and not less than 20,000 people, perhaps twice this number, gathered on the borders of the Lake as eager spectators of the contest. Owing to a little roughness of the surface of the water, the race was postponed until the following day at five o'clock, and again postponed, for the same reason, until the third day at ten A.M., when the "event" actually took place, but in presence of a greatly diminished crowd of "assistants." The result was a general disappointment; at the same time, it created a whirlwind of rejoicing, Columbia—the New York City College crew—having only taken to the water within the last two years. There was a great deal of betting on the match; even the New York Stock Exchange suspended the regular business for pool transactions on the Regatta. The "fouling," and consequent unpleasantness between Harvard and Yale, were the only clouds in the brilliant *fête*. The moral effect of all this excitement I do not propose to discuss; but leave that to parents, guardians, and college professors. No doubt †"muscular Christianity" is a good thing; but the habit of betting is not a good thing. There is also a possibility of over-training and over-straining. One of the rowers in the victorious boat fainted on passing the winning-point, and had to be carried ashore.

There are so many that go there for the summer looking for work

KATE DRUMGOOLD

The spiritual memoir was a common type of document in early America but, in Saratoga Springs, so many people came to play that it is relatively rare. An exception is the remarkable autobiography of Kate Drumgoold, a young African American woman who worked three summers in the 1870s. Born a slave in Virginia, her mother was sold away from her but, in a marvelous example of resourcefulness, she made her way back to Kate after the war's end, determined to reclaim her and give her an education. They went to Brooklyn where Kate worked as a domestic in order to put herself through boarding schools, at Wayland Seminary in Washington and at Harper's Ferry, and she taught for 11 years. In achieving her desires, she cultivated an attitude of gratefulness that comes through in her vignettes about the white Saratoga women who treated her well.

Kate Drumgoold, "A Slave Girl's Story," *Six Women's Slave Narratives* (New York: Oxford University Press, 1988), 41–44.

WHEN I FOUND that I could get through school in a given time as I had studied hard, if I had the money, I told Miss L. A. Pousland, that I would not be there to work any more, as I had a place in Saratoga Springs for the Summer. She felt bad to lose me, but as she knew that I could make more money for three months at the Springs she wanted me to have my heart's desire, so I came on from school and went to see her and then made ready for the Springs, getting one of my sisters to go with me and taking such things as we could. We were there too soon and we had to wait for work, and I went around and made myself known to the white people. They soon called on me to come and do work for them, and the first was a Mrs. Carpenter, a good lady. She then got her married daughter to have me to work for her family and they were a fine family. Her daughter's husband was a grand †studio man on Broadway, doing a good business. Then she sent me to another friend of hers, and my sister and I could live for a while. When the rush came I did not forget the one who had helped me, but went to her two days out of a week, for she had her house filled with boarders, and the Summer was all a blessing to her and her family.

There was Mrs. Purdy, who was another one of my friends, for I did work for her laundry for three years, and she said whenever I came to the Springs and wanted work to come to her; if the house was filled there was room for me. So you see how God did open the way for me in that strange and lonely place, where there are so many that go there for the Summer looking for work. I went out of the house where we were stopping and got the washing and brought it home to my sister, for she would not go out of the house as she had not been from the place where she lived before. I got her to go with me to help me with the work, and it was coming in so fast I had to get a white lady to help us get through, for the colored people said that we would not get work as the laws were passed to keep the New York workers out[212], and I told them that they would have to pass laws to keep the rich people of New York from coming there to board if they should keep the workers out; so I did not hear to that, and found the way for I had the will, and where there is a will there is always a way. So much for the first Summer.

Well, the second time I went up alone. I say alone, I mean that my sister did not go, but the Lord did go with me that Summer, for I did not go to the house where my sister and I was for they tried to discourage us the first time. I always mark one that is an enemy to me and shake the dust off of my feet and let the Lord do for that one what He thinks is best.

Well, for the third year I was there with the Lord and He was surely there with me. I did not do any work on the Lord's Day, but tried to teach them. When they made me an offer of larger pay for the work done on the Lord's Day, I told them that in six days the Lord made the heavens and the earth and He rested on the seventh day, and I felt that if He needed rest on that day I was sure that I must have rest. So the Sunday work was not carried on any more in that laundry. He said that the Lord had sent me to that laundry for the bettering of all in it. The gentleman was from Philadelphia and his name was Mr. Cheek.

So you see how the Lord preached His word through me, a feeble one of the dust, and what can not the Lord help us to do if we only trust in Him and if we strive to live for His honor and glory while on this side of Jordan?

Mrs. Purdy had one daughter, and a lovely girl in music, and her name was Kittie Purdy. She was sought to play everywhere as she was a fine player, and everyone thinks her a very pretty girl. Her mother is a perfect lady, for she used to be so kind to her help. She never was late in any of her meals for the help and she always sat down with us and eat with us. She was as jolly as any one at the table and she always called me her bird, for I was on the wing of song from the time I began my work until my work was finished, and then I would start home as happy as any one could be. Then I would be the first to greet her in the mornings always and she used to say that I brought to her a great deal of comfort each hour and drove all of her business cares away. I used to feel glad that I, although a working girl, could be of some love and comfort to some one, and it makes me feel glad to-day that God in His love to me and for me can own such a feeble one.

In Hungary there are some ten spas with more effective waters

Aurél Kecskeméthy

Aurél Kecskeméthy (1827–1877) was a lawyer in Buda, now part of Budapest, and active in political and government affairs. In 1857, he became editor-in-chief of the official government newspaper, Sürgöny [Truth]. *His account of a visit to America in 1876 was a kind of anti-travel treatise, in which he took pains to point out to Hungarians that, although America was full of curiosities, Europe was much more cultured and really nicer. He returned home ill and was able to finish his book shortly before his death.*

Aurél Kecskeméthy, *Utazás Éjszak-Amerikában* (Budapest: Tettey Nándor és Társa, 1884), 241–244. The quoted passage was translated for this book by Walter von Schrenck-Szull through the courtesy of Margot Archer of Williamstown, Mass. Ivan P. Vamos provided the initial summary through the courtesy of Holly Schwarz, and Dr. S. Vardy supplied a biographical note on the author.

After 24 hours we had exhausted all the pleasures Newport, Rhode Island, had to offer and left for Boston, and consequently a few days later for Saratoga. Jumping over [my story of Boston] I will take the reader right to Saratoga.

There is nothing to say about the surrounding area of Saratoga. It is a flat land, mountains are visible only in a distance of half-a-day's travel. There are avenues with young trees planted, leading into every direction. At a distance of one hour leading to the South, there is Lake Saratoga. There is a nice little island.[213] The shore is a few †fathoms high, the heavy trees look – one could think – like planted park trees. The lake is not small: 9 miles long and 3 miles wide.

The bathhouse is a simple wooden house set up in the water of the lake. The entertainment building with a large terrace is built on the shore. In a distance of half an hour there is the Congress Spring (a spring or fountain) and there is the Sulphur Spring—the first one contains iron, the second one contains of course sulphur—there is finally the Geyser Spring. The latter is shown on wood- and steel-engravings and on photographs pushing a one-foot-wide stream of water into the sky, and gives the impression of a miracle of nature, whereas in reality it is a thin streak of water shooting up just a few feet high by the artificial pumping artesian well. This one is at least ordinarily walled around, the other springs are just left in their primitive state. The waters of these springs then meet in a swampy pool. In Hungary there are some ten spas with more effective waters, in much more beautiful environments, but they are neglected and only known to the people of their area, and nobody speaks about them.

There is a quite visible difference between the fashions of Saratoga and Newport. In Saratoga there are few private gardens and villas, but you find there more large hotels. Here everything is planned for a large number of visitors. The Hotel Grand Union, where we are staying, covers not less ground than the Károly Barracks in Pest [Budapest], four-five stories high, and there are several more of the same size. In the courtyards there are wing buildings, and what is left is being used for gardens, trees offering shade, fountains, and fragrant flowers. You may imagine how pleasant all this is, when the temperatures in the shade outdoors reach 28–30 Celsius on the thermometer! The large parlor and the concert hall are the ideal of the public halls of hotels or steamboats, called by the Americans "most splendid saloon." The furniture consists of some 40 sofas, 200 armchairs, and an equal number of smaller chairs. This furniture is upholstered with covers of parrot colors. You find yellow, dark green, orange, pink, coffee, light green, sky-blue, indigo-blue, dark-red, flame-red—really, any possible color covers, but all of it expensive wool, silk, damask, and velvet fabrics. The furniture pieces are pell-mell set up mixed, all over the room near the walls, and also in the center. On the floor carpets of all colors laid over the entire floor of the room; at the walls sparkling mirrors; gilt chandeliers.

In addition, there are smaller parlors for ladies in even more extravagant colors.

The daily program in Saratoga is the following: early in the morning drinking the water of the various springs. The ladies are already dressed up in their fashionable clothing. Between 8 and 10 general breakfast in the beforementioned dining room of the hotel; after this the ladies retire to change into better dresses; the gentlemen are sitting in rocking chairs, smoking their cigars, falling asleep. Between 12 and 2 lunch is being served; the ladies arrive again in different dresses. After lunch the ladies sit, or rest on sofas at the corridors facing the windows opening to the garden. They are in conversation with each other, or with gentlemen; they watch the passers-by and make a great effort—especially the older ones—to act "ladylike," that is, what they consider to be "ladylike." Some have a book; some of the men are flirting; others smoking their cigars, or chew tobacco, sleep, or are playing cards. Games of chance are played on a large scale, though they are forbidden by the law, but the card-playing rooms are set up in a way that strangers may not enter unless they are introduced by a member of the club. At the entrance you change your money, buying chips, coins made of copper or ivory. The games are for chips only, not for currency, which has the advantage that in case of a police raid it may be used as a sufficient excuse. At this spa, as well as in clubs of larger cities, card games are played in very high sums. Some people would lose thousands, easily made previously in business, mostly in the fashionable game called †"faro."

Between 5 and 7 there is a fight among 1400 people for their dinner. This is followed by a change of clothing; a carriage drive to the lake, rowing, flirting; there is a ball every night lasting almost to the next morning, where the young ladies show up without their father, mother, or aunt, which is not "shocking," it is customary. Every day there are flirting and small scandals. If someone would like to go into a more thorough and entertaining study of the American spa life, he would be advised to read the typical novel, *Ellen Story*, by Edgar Fawcett (publ. E.J. Hall & Son, New York[214]).

The type of the Saratoga society is what in America they call †"shoddy," or in Vienna they would call it *"schnuss,"* in Hungarian we would say it is a phony gentry, a wild aristocracy. They are rich people without culture, or established base in society, whose money is mostly dated yesterday, and seldom secure for tomorrow. This type of people you would find just the same in the whole world everywhere, but their number in America is quite high; their influence is consequently so general, that it begins to stick even to the better class people.

Indeed, you need American nerves to stand for weeks the noise of being pushed around this spa, what some even consider fun.

The Sunday is above all "genuine American." In the morning pious sermons to be followed by the celebration of the Sunday. In order to make it possible for the servants to celebrate a Holy Day, the lunch is fixed for 1 o'clock and is shorter than usual. The front doors of wine- and liquor-stores are closed, you can only enter through the back-door. Music is forbidden.

However, since this big silence is in the long run boring: they have concerts in the nice and shady garden (ticket 25¢). So that nobody be scandalized, they call it "Sacred Concert," at which allegedly only church-music is being played, but of course from all sort of operas, for example, when I was there, among others, they had parts of Verdi's opera *Nabucco*, and they did not miss to indicate on the program: "Nabucco, subject, the Book of Daniel." These Americans are a strange kind of saint!

The dresses of the ladies are most extravagant

M. DAVENPORT

The identity of this English visitor has not been established but, in his book, Under the Gridiron, *he provided acute and breezy observations about society at the spa in the centennial year. He was especially taken with the children of the social aspirants, and his description makes a fine companion to a familiar magazine engraving of the same scene.*

M. Davenport, *Under the Gridiron: A Summer in the United States and the Far West, including a Run through Canada* (London: Tinsley Brothers, 1876), 117–124.

WHILST HERE, the Grand Union inaugurate [*sic*] a new species of entertainment, by issuing invites to a grand garden party, to which as guests we receive an invitation.[215] The balconies around are draped with divers colours, and an immense American banner, with

Children's party at the Grand Union Hotel. Stereoscope view. Robert Joki Collection.

many smaller ones, decorate the trees. Swings have been erected for the children, and a platform for their dancing. At four P.M. the band strikes up, the company now fast assembling. They are quite a study, and we have the pleasure of seeing all the pick of American society.

The children are dressed superbly, the smallest dots of all being little clouds of lace. Young ladies, of the more advanced age of seven and upwards, are costumed like little women, with high boots, silk stockings, and jewellery, all wearing necklaces, earrings, bracelets, and rings.

Two little eight-year old blondes waltz together in such beautiful style, that they are the admired of all admirers, and appear like fairies in flesh and blood.

When the platform is filled, with some eighty children dancing, the effect is really charming, and they all have a self-possession that nothing seems to ruffle. The absence of anything like shyness is noticeable with all.

Two children of about eleven, a girl and boy, particularly attract our attention; the former in deep blue–hat, silk dress, silk stockings, boots, fan, &c., all †*en suite;* the latter, a handsome fair boy, is in appearance, a little courtier, come out of one of Sir Peter Lely's pictures—jacket to the waist, with belt and breeches to the knee of deep blue velvet, blue silk stockings, shoes with buckles, and deep lace collar, back and front, with cuffs of same materials.[216]

The girls are all exquisitely got up, regardless of cost, and dressed like princesses, with gold †vinaigrettes and fans by their side, and kid gloves with six or eight buttons even at the age of five. Their nurses are in attendance, and all uniformly dressed, with mob caps.

The dresses of the ladies are most extravagant, but as a rule in excellent taste. In an assemblage of some two or three thousand, there are of course some exceptions, and a few have overdone it altogether. The display of diamonds is something extraordinary; they are the rage with New York society, and some of the millionaires' wives are carrying thousands and thousands upon their persons. For the first time in our travels, we note here many excessively stout ladies, some ludicrously so. The girls are elegant, but I can see many who promise in a few years to pull down the scales with their mammas. Their great anxiety seems to be how to sit down gracefully, rather a difficult matter under existing fashions, and incurring a kind of side movement, followed on rising by a general spasmodic pulling out of puffs belonging to the †panier or whatever the †excrescence in the rear is now styled.

The papers here comment upon the great lack of "marrying young men" coming forward with offers, but excuses them for the natural fear they experience as to the necessary funds being forthcoming.

Certainly, to see some of the girls, with hundreds of dollars trailing in the dust, it would shake the nerves of any man unless he have expectations from Uncle †Crœsus.

Taken altogether, the variety of costumes have a charming effect of colour, and many twine a white gauze cloud round their heads, with the ends streaming, after the manner of brides.

The appearance of our own sex needs no description; they are simply the †antipodes of all that is bright and gay, being dressed in decent mourning, and serve as a foil to the gay colours before mentioned.

What a menu! I count eighty-five dishes, not one less

GUSTAVE DE MOLINARI

Belgian born Gustave de Molinari (1819–1912) was the most adamant spokesman of the liberal viewpoint in French politics, trusting completely in free competition to solve every problem. He came to the United States in 1876 to visit the Centennial Exposition in Philadelphia, but he also visited Boston, New York, Charleston, Savannah, New Orleans and Chicago, as well as Saratoga Springs. He was generally favorable toward America and Americans, and was awed by the Grand Union Hotel, although his book identified a variety of shortcomings.

Gustave de Molinari, *Lettres sur les États-Unis et le Canada Addressées au Journal des Débats à l'Occasion de l'Exposition Universelle de Philadelphie* (Paris: Hachette et Cie, 1876), 137–155. Translated for this volume. Biography is found in John Eatwell *et al.*, eds., *The New Palgrave: A Dictionary of Economics* (London: Macmillan Press, 1998) 3: 492, located through the courtesy of Martin Bruegel of the Institut National de la Recherche Agronomique, Paris.

WE TAKE THE Saratoga train, and arrive before midnight at this favored rendez-vous of American society. We descend at the *Grand Union*, a leviathan hotel next to which the largest hotels of Europe are like the cascade of the Bois de Boulogne next to the cataract of Niagara. It is worth the trouble to describe, this *Grand Union hotel.* The omnibus from the railroad brought us to the foot of a building as large as a barracks, with two wings surrounding a park; cast iron columns 20 meters high support, along the whole length of the exterior and interior facades, the roof of a large *piazza*, which has a total length, if I can believe my *Panoramic Guide*[217], of not less than one mile (1.25 km). You climb by a vast staircase to an immense parlor where the essential services of the hotel are concentrated: the reception and information offices, the post office on one side, the four windows of the cashier's office, the office of carriage rental and the telegraph on the other. You write your name on a voluminous register, they give you a key that you place in your pocket, and which the "advice" posted conspicuously requests that you not take with you when you leave the hotel. Despite the crisis, *Grand Union hotel* is sufficiently peopled. They gave me no. 1315, on the second floor. I have the choice between four elevators and stairs for getting upstairs. The elevators are elegant rooms where 20 people can be without rubbing shoulders. A bell, and the machine is at your command. You pace the long corridors, entirely covered with carpet, like the drawing rooms and the bedrooms; there isn't less than 10 acres, again according to my *Panoramic Guide.* For example, my bedroom, in which the white walls are lit by a nib of gas, lacks a bit of elegance, even though—a particularity rare enough in American hotels—the gas light is tempered by a frosted glass globe; the bed is hard, and the furniture is reduced to a toilet table and a walnut armoire. It is true that you don't spend much time in your bedroom. You descend to the ground floor, where there are "2 square miles" of drawing rooms, sumptuously decorated, with wall hangings and furniture garnished with satin; lecture rooms, billiard rooms, a *bar-room;* and, finally, a dining room, in which 600 people can sit with ease, and in which a Parisian restaurateur would not be embarrassed to shove 2,000. The dining room is the center, and one could say the spirit, of the hotel; they only serve three meals a day: breakfast, dinner, and supper; but what meals! the festival of the wedding of Gamache is, in comparison, a meal of Petit-Manteau-Bleu.[218] We enter, after having dropped off at the door (without cost) our hat and our cane to the care of a negro. A battalion of negros and mulattos, in black vests or jackets and white ties, provide the service. One sees them advancing in procession, their fore-arms filled, and carrying on their flat palms a platter filled with dishes. A subordinate waiter detaches himself and politely designates for you an empty straw chair, where you see a colleague. You sit, and they place in front of you a menu and a glass of ice water. What a menu, good God! I count 85 dishes, not one less, from the *mock turtle with †quenelles* and the *†consomme printanier à la royal,* through the series of fish, meats boiled, roasted and seasoned, entrees, the *vegetables,* to *vanilla ice cream* and *watermelon* at the end. And I have the right to make them serve me everything! I only use that right with moderation, and here in front of me is a large platter of meat, surrounded by a dozen small covered platters of the most varied *vegetables,* potatoes, large peas, green corn, boiled rice, fresh tomatoes, but only one plate. It is the American habit to eat at the same time, on the same plate, meat, fish and vegetables combined. Frightful habit! They entrusted me with a *napkin,* which has already arrived more than once in my pocket, my having mistaken it for a handkerchief. I am watching myself so as not to give the attentive and

Grand Union Hotel as it was after 1872. Stereoscope view by Baker and Record. Robert Joki Collection.

polite negro who serves me a bad opinion of the †probity of the white race; they give me back at the exit my hat and my *umbrella*, without question, and I find myself again under the *piazza*, where the hotel band has started to play.

I am going to take a tour on the "Broadway" of Saratoga,—all the American cities have their Broadway. This one is garnished with stores selling fashions, confections, hairstyles, alternating with *tobacconists*, (almost all Jewish[219]), and office of railway ticket sales. On the sidewalk, a screen ornamented with a giant red foot teaches me that Dr. Pray extracts painlessly corns, callouses, and molars.[220] Here is a Parisian hairdresser who comes from New York to Saratoga for the season. The season only lasts seven weeks, and he pays 400 dollars to rent his narrow store. That's expensive, but he sells enough hair to realize a good honest profit. The hair is imported from Europe, chestnut hair comes from Normandy, Brittany and Auvergne; black hair from Italy; blond hair from Germany and Sweden. Some elegants have on their heads, for $300, imported hair, and an old lady paid $200 for two tresses of white hair, the most expensive. I can well judge, this same night, the effect of imported hair on the heads of the charming misses who join all points of the Union in their grand matrimonial march. There is a ball at the *Grand Union hotel* and at the United States, its rival. I have taken care not to miss, but it's a double deception: one certainly meets there very beautiful misses and ladies sumptuously dressed who reasonably well encouraged the commerce of imported hair; but I do not see a single †"kangaroo" and that's despite the effort of several couples who decide to make a tour of waltzing. Men and women dance without gloves! At midnight the band disappears: we are on Saturday, and you can't dance on Sunday. I come back to no. 1315. My bedroom is not made, and the next morning my boots are not polished. Is this an accidental negligence, or a general measure of revenge of our negro servants against the white race? The bell is electric, and I ring and ring in vain without discovering this mystery. I leave to entrust my boots to one of the poor barefoot youths of the white race who crowd the sidewalk with their polishing box, *blacking*. I pass Sunday drinking the iron-filled and sulphurous water from the fountains, and in walking under the shade of *Congress Park*, where gushes the most celebrated of the springs of Saratoga, *Congress Spring*. In the evening, I demand my bill from one of the four cashiers of *Grand Union hotel*. I leave 10 dollars, 5 dollars per day[221]—and that's really nothing. Just think: two miles of parlors, ten acres of carpet, four elevators, three meals a day, eighty-five dishes at dinner, plus a concert during the day and a ball at night, all for 5 dollars! it is true that they didn't change my plates, that my napkin resembled a handkerchief, that they didn't make my bed, and they neglected to polish my boots. But these are details, and *Grand Union hotel* is no less a colossal manufactory of comfort and one of the most characteristic creations of the American genius.

Turning away quite a good many now and everything is lively

FREDERICK CARLOS FERRY

Fred Ferry (1868–1956) was the second son of a Braintree, Vermont, farmer. The family moved to Randolph during his childhood; but from 1885 to 1887 he spent his summers in Saratoga Springs working for his aunt, Clarissa J. Dyer, proprietor of the Vermont House and of the farm which supplied its table, located at Splinterville in Greenfield. He kept a daily diary which tells us a great deal about life and work in a smaller, family-run hotel. In later life,

Ferry was graduated from Williams College in 1891, went on to study at four great European universities, and ultimately served as the president (1917–38) of Hamilton College.

Frederick C. Ferry, diaries. Archives and Special Collections, Williams College. The passages are quoted from Chamberlain Ferry, ed., *Diaries of Frederick C. Ferry 1873 to 1888* (1991). See also Edward M. Ferry, *The Charles Ferry Family in America* (Northampton, Mass.: The Author, 1978).

MAY 22, SATURDAY—In A.M. I helped Levi whip carpets, cleaned the croquet ground, went to the Bank and got $150 for Aunt M. then to the PO and sent 20 to Mrs. Rodgers, etc. In the P.M. Levi and I washed in the dining room and Julia and small Anna helped some. Then L. and I drove to the farm. Allie and Perley went to town in the eve.

May 27, Thursday—Another cloudy and rainy day. Aunt M. and the girls are fast preparing for the coming convention. I help them quite a good deal. School is going rather unpleasantly because of reviews. Mr. and Mrs. Carey of Boston came to spend some time at the house.

Jun 1, Tuesday—Went to the village with Perley. The painters took Mouse and went to the Granger place and so Perley had to remain down until night. I helped Aunt Marenda take boarders up to their rooms. In the eve I went to the first annual meeting of the Am. Home Missionary Society. Sermon by J. Brand of Iowa. Bed at 11.30 P.M.

Jun 2, Wednesday—House well filled. Perley down all day. A few more boarders came and Aunt M. sent some away because the tables were full. I attended another meeting which was excellent and said to be the best ever heard. I helped Uncle Foster shut up at 11 P.M. Heard Sankey[222] sing this eve.

Jun 3, Thursday—Last meeting this eve. Many paid their bills tonight so as to leave early in the morning. Perley down all day. Studied Geometry at Elmwood Hall[223] with Mabel, Mamie and Theo this eve. Helped shut up at 10.30 P.M. Got my new pants at Hall's today and paid $6.50.

Jun 7, Monday—Went back to village with Perley this morn. Only about forty boarders and many of those leaving today. Mrs. Matthews, daughter, and friend went home but Mr. E.J.M. is to stay a little longer. Found I had passed my Geometry examinations at 51 out of 56.

Vermont House. *Saratoga, and How to See It* (1873)

Jun 19, Saturday—Took a shirt, pair of cuffs, and collar to Yet Sing's laundry[224] and then we all rehearsed before Mr. Massee at the Town Hall. Then I walked to the farm only riding a little way with Mr. Morehouse. Studied worked in garden and went over to Granger place. Papa and I took a long ride with Major and Sarah.

Jul 9, Friday—Perley staid here until after dinner. I busied about the house settling bills and so on. Very excellent young people are here at these conventions. Saw Misses Tompkins and Potter a few moments at Elmwood Hall.

Jul 10, Saturday—The conventionists left today. House about half full. Perley did not remain down long. Smith the hired man went home because of poor health.

Jul 11, Sunday—Attended church both morning and evening. Perley helped about the dinner and then he and I went to the farm. Mamma is having one of her regular headache spells. Allie and Arthur brought me back to the evening preaching.

Jul 12, Monday—Some boarders coming and I had my usual routine of chores. Perley does not stop any after breakfast but goes right back.

Jul 13, Tuesday—Boarders coming and going. I helped about the three meals as usual. Aunt M. is feeling quite well.

Jul 22, Thursday—A very fine day. Perley went back early and I done the carving, freezing †cream, etc.

Jul 23, Friday—Nothing new. Did my usual work. Boarders coming and going. About one hundred and ten at dinner.

Jul 27, Tuesday—Rainy early all day. In the eve Miss Tompkins and I attended a concert at the park. Had quite a pleasant time.

Jul 30, Friday—The Rankin party from St. Johnsbury registered here tonight.

Jul 31, Saturday—Sat up until after 11 P.M. waiting for Frank Evans and party of Boston. They came.

Aug 4, Wednesday—Twelve came today. Late nights and early mornings are my bill of fare.

Aug 6, Friday—Turning away quite a good many now and everything is lively.

Aug 13, Friday—An excursion in town from Bethel[225] today and Aunts Hannah and Mary came and I carried them to the farm.

Aug 20, Friday—Perley brought Aunts H. and M. down this evening to the entertainment in the parlors by Mrs. Whitney, Mr. and Mrs. Spear, Miss Evans and Dr. MacAuley. After this I accompanied them through the parlors of the U.S. and Union.

Aug 24, Tuesday—Braintree and Randolph excursion today. Among those who came I saw Wales and papa, D.V. Page, Miss C., Bover, Ned T., Harry Beedle, Harris Bass, R. McDougell & w, Nelson Scott & w, Uncle Hiram, and son. I spoke to Uncle H. for the first time in several years. Dav. Adams, Mertin, and Alvan W. and Ness at farm tonight.

Aug 26, Thursday—Mrs. Whitney sang in the parlor this eve. She said if she had thought of it some she would have invited me as escort. Papa, Mamma, Lou, and Ethel came down to it. I dug up to fix a water pipe on Front St. all alone today.

Aug 28, Saturday—Through Mrs. Whitney's kindness I obtained an invitation to the Grand Union Garden Party and went with Mrs. Comstock and Mrs. Hobarth. 'Twas a grand affair and I enjoyed it much. About 7,000 were present.

My negro waiter quickly won my sympathy

Carlo Gardini, 1880s

Dr. Carlo Gardini made no fewer than four trips to the United States between 1878 and 1886, remaining at least eight months each time, to observe closely the American people and their way of life. His interest had been awakened by the writings of James Fenimore Cooper and of Carlo Botta, whose 1809 work, Storia della guerra d'indipendenza degli Stati Uniti d'America, *was the first history of the Revolution by a European. Gardini wrote his delightful book expressly for the edification of his countrymen; thus, it is less intimate and more prone to analysis than most European travel accounts.*

Carlo Gardini, *Gli Stati Uniti* (Bologna: Zanichelli, 1887), translated in Oscar Handlin, *This Was America* (Cambridge: Harvard University Press, 1949), 346–348. See also Andrew J. Torrielli, *Italian Opinion on America as Revealed by Italian Travelers* (Cambridge: Harvard University Press, 1941).

If Newport occupies first place for ocean bathing in the United States, Saratoga must take the palm for its mineral waters. Two powerful attractions draw the Americans, particularly those in high life, to the latter town. On the one hand there is the therapeutic value of its springs, which were secretly used even by the Indians, who venerated them as gifts of the Great Spirit; on the other there is the splendor and richness of its hotels and the irresistible fascination of the enchantress we call fashion.

There may be mineral baths in Europe pitched by nature in sites more pleasant and more beautiful than those in Saratoga, but there is no place on earth that can equal the New York resort in the splendor of its establishments and in the overwhelming luxury that surrounds the families of the millionaires who frequent it, especially at the height of the season. There are about 11,000 permanent inhabitants in the town; but the number triples from the first of June to the middle of September, a period in which lodgings are most difficult to secure.

Saratoga boasts the finest hotels in the United States, and that means in the world. The best known are the United States Hotel, the Grand Union Hotel, and the Congress Hotel, which like most of the others are located on Broadway, the main street. There they profit by

United States Hotel as it was after 1874. Stereoscope view by McDonnald and Sterry. Robert Joki Collection.

day from the shade of fine maple trees, and by night are illuminated by electricity.

The Congress and the Columbia are the most popular springs. These may be found in Congress Park where they flow in the shade of two magnificent wooden pavilions, connected with each other by a kind of colonnaded gallery.[226] There is also a kiosk for the orchestra, which is made up entirely of more or less skillful Germans who, paradoxically, seem to play only Italian tunes. I tried the waters of the Congress Spring and found them slightly sour but not unpleasant.

The Saratoga hotels are open only during the summer. To avoid the inconveniences of the season they are almost all situated in the midst of large splendid gardens, and built with thick walls to keep the excessive heat out of the living quarters. As in the houses of the southern cities, they have files of spacious and elegant columns built into both the exterior walls and the walls surrounding the inside courts and gardens. These colonnades are topped with parapets in the form of a gallery. These piazzas, as the Americans call them, supply a place where the travelers may enjoy the open air while they remain protected from the rain and from the heat of the sun.

Every night the United States Hotel, like the other two mentioned above, presents an impressive spectacle. The spacious interior garden, adorned with trees and fountains and lighted by electricity, is crammed with the flower of aristocratic society—three-fourths,

Birdseye View of Congress Park and Springs as they were after 1876. Stereoscope view by W. H. Sipperly. Robert Joki Collection. Taken after the park was redesigned by Frederick Law Olmsted, this view shows the elaborate Stick Style pavilion housing the springs.

women elegantly dressed—who listen to the music played in the center. Part of the crowd stroll in the aisles among the blossoms; part is seated on chairs around the numerous tables scattered here and there, and engages in lively and jolly conversation. In the piazzas is the same luxury, the same happiness, the same movement. From the open doors of the parlors, and from the other regally furnished rooms, pour streams of light. There is dancing in the ballroom. There I tried the †"Boston," which seemed to be a kind of waltz embellished with a graceful circular motion. Apparently, however, the American aristocracy do not consider it altogether dignified to indulge in this diversion; I was told that even at the evening garden parties, in which they dance on a platform built over the garden, only a very few men participate.

Walking through the halls, the garden, the piazzas, I had the opportunity to study high society, more so than in New York, in Boston, or even in Newport. And I could particularly note the difference in character between the two sexes, a difference so great that one might suppose them members of two different races.

The men have a rigid temperament; they speak little; and all, whatever their title—senator, governor, general, colonel—dress always in morning clothes, except for a white cravat which they wear everywhere. In the salon the American male is a fish out of water; not one of them will deny that his true place is the office, the countinghouse, or the political meeting.

The women, on the other hand, are full of spirit, chatter freely and coquettishly, yet do not go too far. They seem in their natural element. The alpha and omega of their daily routine is to rise, to eat, to talk, to change their costumes three or four times, and to sleep. When they come back in the morning from the mineral waters they have a substantial breakfast at about ten; then sit on the rocking chairs on the piazzas until it begins to be warm; then go to their rooms to change for lunch, which is at two. At the end of that meal they again retire to their chambers, and steal a nap on the sofa. At about six they reappear in traveling clothes, and ride in a carriage to Lake Saratoga, some seven kilometers away by a beautiful road lined with trees. There they may have an ice before they come back in time for supper. At nine they dress for the evening, almost always in gowns, half-décolleté and not seldom edged with lace, the value of which might easily come to 100,000 lire. After an hour they descend to the piazza by the steps, a journey which reveals to best advantage their elegant shoes, on which there are often buttons or buckles made of diamonds.

It is then that the life of the hotels really begins. The elegant people who live in the United States Hotel go to the gardens, the parlors, and the piazzas of the Grand Union and the Congress hotels, while in return those who live in the latter two come to the United States Hotel. Thus the women give each other an opportunity to observe and criticize the clothes and the jewels of their rivals and to make full show of their own.

In the United States Hotel, as in most of the best American establishments, the waiters are Negroes. A European entering the dining hall is to some degree always surprised to see the long line of Africans in gala dress, their shining white linen strangely in contrast with the color of their skin, a color which varies in all the gradations from ebony black to the lightest shade of coffee.

The menu boasts a long list of foods in all languages, including the Indian. It is not only startling by comparison with the strict diets which are generally imposed in health resorts in Europe, but indeed demands that you be endowed with the stomach of an ostrich to eat, without indigestion, even half of what is put before you.

My Negro waiter quickly won my sympathy. I asked his name and was told it was Tom, a name very common among his race. He spoke with such assurance, moved with such swiftness, that he seemed to act as if propelled mechanically. He was almost always smiling so that his very white teeth showed, and on his breast shone a gigantic diamond that could not possibly have been genuine.

The conversation at our table was concerned first of all with the fair sex in Saratoga, and then with the names of all the people who had become the season's rage through charm, eccentricity, or luxury. Then it turned to the great doings of the aristocracy of the hour and to politics, and finally it moved on to our hotel. One of my table mates, a pure American and therefore endowed with a special sense for figures, knew exactly the area of the plot on which the building stood, the number of halls, rooms, corridors, piazzas, doors, and windows, how many kilometers the carpets, telephone, telegraph, and electric wires would measure if laid end to end, how many tons of food were consumed in a day, the horsepower of the elevators, of the laundry, pumping, and other machines, the candlepower of the gas and electric lights, and the size of the great, complex army of administrative and service personnel. And to make all this interesting to me, he added that the many millions invested in the construction and equipment of the United States Hotel brought its stockholders a return of more than 5 per cent a year, despite the fact that it was open only during the summer months.

That which, however, made me open my eyes wide with surprise was the assertion of my companion about the Jews. These people, he said, would not be admitted to the best Saratoga hotels, not even were they the Rothschilds[227] in person. In the land of democracy, where freedom of laws and of religion reach their †apogee, I would have thought such restrictions fantastic. However, these were the facts, and one must come to believe that anti-Semitism has roots so deep and so strong in America that it will be impossible to extirpate them.

Saratoga is a very nice place but oh how the money does go

ARTHUR FREDERICK ALDRIDGE

Arthur Frederick Aldridge (1861–1923) left England "under a cloud" and came to New York City where he secured employment on the Mail and Express *at 23 Park Row under the assumed name of Alfred E. Moore. There he met a typewriter, a strong-willed and principled young woman named Georgina Warhurst (1865–1932). They fell in love and became engaged; when he confessed to her his deception she broke off the engagement, but he won her back and they were married in 1889. He wrote for the* Herald *and the* Sun *as yachting editor. They made their home in New York City and in Brooklyn, had three children, and lived happily until his death. When he was sent to Saratoga Springs in 1887—indeed, whenever they were separated by geography and sometimes when they were not—he wrote loving letters to her. They are unusually intimate documents, even for personal letters.*

Alfred E Moore (pseud.), letters to Georgina Warhurst, 28 April 1887 to 20 August 1889. Collection of their granddaughter, Barbara Weakley of Arlington, Vt. Excerpts were published in Barbara C. Weakley, "Letters Evoke Old Saratoga," *Times Union* (Albany, N.Y.), 9 August 1987, page G-1.

Congress Hall
Saratoga Springs
July 21, 1887

My darling Georgina,

I ARRIVED HERE all safely at 9 o'clock this morning, just about the time you were going to the office. Salmon and I (S. is on *The World*) shared a nice stateroom on the boat. Last night it was very pleasant, but this morning it rained very hard and they had to postpone the races.

I begin to think I am a big man already. I am receiving so much attention that it surprises me. Are you not afraid that your Alfred will come home spoiled?

For the present I am at Congress Hall, a very nice hotel. If I can make favorable terms I shall stay here. The regular charge is $4.00 a day.[228] The place is very full and there are lots of people I know. If you were here my darling I should enjoy myself immensely. I would not lose you to have all the wealth there is in Saratoga.

[July 22] I will give you the programme of my day so far. Rose at 8 o'clock. Went to the spring and drank Congress Water. Breakfast at 9. Visited hotels and collected some news. Races at 11, over at 3, then dinner at 4:30. Wrote articles for *The Mail* and at 6 the pleasantest duty of the day, wrote to you.

This evening there is a hop here and fireworks in the Park. I shall have to attend both I suppose. Last night I went to the Clubhouse[229] to watch the gamblers. If I had gone a year ago I should certainly have taken a hand myself at something or other, but last night I did not. The temptation was great, but my promise to you was too sacred to be broken.

[July 24] It is rather hard work gathering the items I have to write, there is so much running about for them. In yesterday's *Mail* I had lots of stories. They were short ones about cutlery, neckties, trunks, chain bracelets, medallions, floral jewelry and the Saratoga gossip.

Last night I had to go to a ball at the United States Hotel and another at the Clarenden. It was too hot to dance, and there was no one I would care to dance with present. I just studied all the society beauties and belles and was disgusted with them.

[July 26] Although I have to go about in all this excitement, it is not pleasure to me, and I am already heartily sick of it. I am disgusted at the heartless flirting that is being carried on here by both men and women. Love is too sacred to be trifled with in the way they do here. Girls sit and talk to men whom they know are in love with them and then toss them to one side, as a child would a ball. The men do the same thing.

In the evening the men play †faro, roulette and other gambling games. If I had the amount of money that is lost here in one evening you and I would do nothing but enjoy ourselves for the remainder of our lives and try to do good for others. It rained so hard last night that the races have been postponed again and everything is very dull! I have been asked to make up a poker party this afternoon. The fellows will be very mad if I don't go, but I am not going.

[July 29] Saratoga is a very nice place but oh how the money does go. My expenses for the first week were $35. All the hotels are close together here. The United States is the best and then comes Congress Hall. Here they can accommodate 1,100 guests. There is a handsome ball room in the hotel and a very good band plays morning and evening.

The roads are very good for driving, and the horses are all very

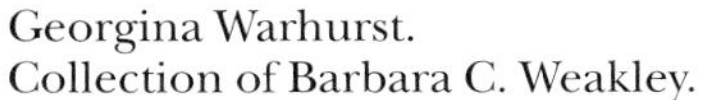

Georgina Warhurst.
Collection of Barbara C. Weakley.

Arthur F. Aldridge.
Collection of Barbara C. Weakley.

good and fast. I think the stay here is doing me good. I have already gained seven pounds.

How are things going at *The M&E?* Coates has been giving me a very good show, and as a result I am quite a big man at this hotel. All the girls in the place want me to give them nice notices. Did you notice the one I wrote about Miss Wolff? She bought 20 copies of the paper and sent them to her friends. Since then I have hardly dared show myself on the piazza; everyone wants a nice notice. Some of them go to the proprietor of the hotel, Mr. Clement, and ask him to introduce them.

Are you jealous? You need not be, my darling one, life is too short to bother with them much. The whole lot of them are not worth as much as your little finger. I wish I had a chance to write a paragraph about you, then I would write something worth reading.

[August 2] This morning I had to attend to the Republican State Committee, then I attended to the Republican Editors who met today, next I drove out to the race course and did my racing. At 1 o'clock I drove back to the hotel, found out what the Committee had done, and got back to the races without missing anything.

[August 3] I have now to go to the hop at the Congress this evening, and I shall be plagued to death by requests to give some nice notice in the papers. I can hardly walk down the piazza in the evening or in fact at any time of the day without being asked by some to write a personal. I think I shall write a number already except for the name, some for blondes and some for brunettes. I think if I remain a journalist I shall try and come here each year, there is lots of money to be made.

I have written letters for three other papers this year, and if I had made arrangements sooner than I did this year I could make $100 a week. Now I am making $60. That is doing very well, is it not? And if it would only last I would soon have a home for my Queen.

[August 11] The great horse Hanover[230] raced here today and as usual won just the same way that he did when he won on Suburban Day. Some of the ladies in the house have been losing very heavily on the races here, so today I told them I would give them some points if they wanted to bet. They were very pleased, took my advice and won $300, and now they think I am a perfect mascot.

[August 19] Some visitors here have heard of my entertainments in London, and last night a number of ladies asked me to get up and manage an entertainment in the hotel for the benefit of some charity. The performers all to be amateurs. I said I would and have secured the Ball room for the entertainment. It seats 700 people. To manage this alone means a lot of work but another lady suggested that a one act farce be given and Mrs. Hewitt and I are going to write one for the occasion. This in addition to all my work. Tonight I have a hop to attend to—the Children's Carnival.[231]

[August 21] You can't imagine how busy I am. The farce is written and is called "Left at the Post." We are having a little trouble in suiting everyone. It is very likely that I shall throw over the amateur company and obtain a company of professionals for the play and then I shall put Lillian Russell and Helen D'Arwray in the first part of the programme. I am now making arrangements for the Town Hall.[232] It seats 1,200 and I think it can be filled. I mean to make it a success if possible.

[August 22] Next Saturday night the Grand Union Garden Party—the event of the season—takes place. Today I had two papers to send the races to in addition to *The Mail*, and then the work for this play and concert is something awful. A company of amateurs are ten times worse than professionals. Today two ladies withdrew because the part did not make them out nice enough, and I had to find two more. I think the company is now complete. The concert com-

"The garden party on the lawn of the Grand Union Hotel, August 5th." *Frank Leslie's Illustrated Newspaper*, 30 August 1879.

pany is a good one. There is a xylophone solo and an orchestra of 14 pieces. The tickets are going like hotcakes. Judge Hilton has 50, Capt. Jake Vanderbilt 25, Berry Wall 25.

[August 28] The great show is over and you can't think how glad I am. This was one of the most trying I ever ran, but I think it made a big hit.

My troubles began on Wednesday when two of the company suddenly threw up their parts. Mrs. Hewitt forgot her lines and I had to prompt her. She got to the end, somehow staggered off the stage and fell down unconscious. I was dressing as a jockey at the time.

I rushed down from the dressing room and found the curtain down and a crowd of strangers on the stage. I dreaded to look at the morning papers expecting to be called over the coals, but they gave me a lovely notice.

[August 29] Tomorrow is the last day of the races and I am very glad of it. My love for horse racing is all gone now that I don't bet on them, but I have gained a great deal by giving up that bad habit. I have won your love. Goodbye now my dearest one.

From your loving Alfred

Swimming holes had their differences
Robert Sloane Wickham

In A Saratoga Boyhood, *his self-published memoir, Robert S. Wickham (1877–1956) paints an idyllic picture of being a boy in the late Victorian era. The son of a lawyer who died when Robert was in his early teens, he grew up at 24 Walton Street. His mother moved to Binghamton about the time he entered Cornell and, after practicing in Brooklyn, he returned to Binghamton where he remained the rest of his life. He also authored* Friendly Adirondack Peaks.

Robert S. Wickham, *A Saratoga Boyhood* (Binghamton: The Author, 1948), 100–121. An obituary notice is in the *Binghamton Press*, 4 January 1956, 43; the Cornell University Alumni Office has records on his career and avocational activities.

In winter no parental objection was made to our outdoor activities, but in summer, when thoughts of swimming had displaced sliding and skating and ice boating, we were forbidden to go near the water. After the cruel words were spoken we would go out in the back yard, so Mother would not hear us, and chant:

Mother, may I go out to swim?
Yes, my darling daughter;
Hang your clothes on a hickory limb,
But don't go near the water.

There was no sense in it!

We went just the same, and were then stumped by a problem. When we got home Mother would sometimes ask us where we had been. It bothered us to think up, quickly, a good answer that would end the discussion. We finally thought out a plan so we wouldn't have to tell a complete lie about it.

We would casually stop at several places, maybe at Olin's house, on our way to the swimming hole, not staying anywhere very long, and then when the question came on our return, we would answer almost truthfully by mentioning the places where we *had* been—at Olin's for instance. It wasn't necessary to tell *all* we knew. Later we didn't even stop at Olin's, but just walked through his yard on the way.

Our first swimming hole was in a little creek up near the Ten Spring Woods, in a cow pasture, where we built a brush and sod dam, backing the water up so that we had a hole all of four feet deep, with a nice sandy bottom and high banks from which we could dive.

Fragments of torn undershirts could be seen, here and there, among the alder bushes along the bank. The bigger boys, whom we could not whip, would tie our shirts in a hard knot when we weren't looking, wet it, and pull the knot tighter. Then when we came out to dress and tried to untie the knots with our fingers and teeth, the chorus would begin—

Chaw raw beef!
  Beef is tough!
Chaw all night
  And you'll never get enough!

If one of us tore up his shirt trying to untie the knot and threw it away, he had a problem on his hands. When he reached home he could get into the house and up to his room all right, without the absence of a shirt being noticed. But there would be one missing when the laundry was checked over sometime, and he had to be mighty fast and good with his tongue to turn the question when asked what had become of it. Often it was very difficult to explain to Mother about the missing shirt being old and all worn out anyway, so that it didn't fit, and wouldn't stay on, and how it just *had* to be thrown away.

Ere long we had learned to swim and dive and had become regular little water rats. Later I told Mother that I could swim, explaining very carefully that some older boys, friends of mine who were big and strong and knew all about swimming, had taught me where the water was shallow and it was perfectly safe, watching and helping me all the time until I learned. This heart to heart talk made it easier to go afterward—the question where I had been did not come so often.

Swimming holes had their differences. There was the "Three Sisters," three small ponds in upper Woodlawn Park, the water running down over rocky ledges between them. There the water was shallow and warm. We would walk out to these ponds occasionally on Saturday and spend the afternoon in the altogether, building a raft of old fence rails and posts with some nails we brought along, poling it around, diving, swimming, and then loafing on the rocks in the sun.

Woodlawn, or Hilton's, Park, an estate of about sixteen hundred acres[233], was situated on the outskirts of the village to the north. It was occupied during the season, but its gates were open all the year round. At least half of it was woodland, with curving well-kept gravel carriage roads, laid out through it, and open to the public. Upon the shore of Denton's Vly[234], one of the ponds of the property, there was a boathouse, and on looking in through its windows we saw several three or four feet long neatly rigged model sail boats. A flock of sheep, tended by a Scottish shepherd in plaid and kilts with his collie dogs, nibbled in one of the fields of the park during the summer. Pure bred cows grazed in its pastures. Spirited horses and smart equipages, including a tallyho coach, stood in its stables and barns. Fancy pigeons were kept in a cote—tumblers, pouters, Jacobins, fantails. The "Three Sisters," where we went swimming lay in the upper, more secluded and less frequented part of the estate.

"Eaton's" swimming hole, in a creek about a mile and a half away from our homes, we avoided. A gang of toughs frequented it—the "Rock Gang"—and if we went there we were likely to get ducked, clothes and all, or have a fight on our hands.

"William's" was quite a way out, in a little valley stream behind a brickyard. Nobody bothered us there. One Saturday afternoon, we walked out to it, and after a plunge to get our hair wet so we wouldn't get headaches in the sunshine, we roamed around in the fields and came upon some cows grazing in a pasture. We approached them carefully, and finally succeeded in milking one, squirting the spurts of warm milk into the open mouths of each of us in turn. Then we began laughing and squirted the stream all over each other's bodies.

So intent were we on our fun that we did not notice the approaching farmer until he was almost upon us. He yelled and ran for us, but we dashed around and through some bushes to our piles of clothes, hastily grabbed them up and got away, scattering as fast as we could run across the fields and through the woods in different directions. We joined up again when the danger was over.

Our favorite hole was "Putnam's"—"Put's" for short. It was the nearest one to our homes and was more secluded, being hidden in a thicket of tall alders in a creek out beyond Judge Putnam's house[235] on the northwestern outskirts of the village. After a big rain, when the creek was swollen, it was fun to go there and swim and float down on the yellow flood. We had to watch to avoid submerged barbed wire fences across the creek. The flood carried us under a stone bridge and on down for a long way through fields and woods. We returned along the bank, being careful not to let anybody see us in our naked pelts.

Another hole we liked was at the Geysers, near the old stone gristmill, about a mile and a half south of the village. The stream there, the outlet of the Geysers' pond, ran under a large arched stone tunnel through a tall earth embankment which carried the tracks of the railroad over it. A dam had been built a short distance down stream from the tunnel. It was built of big timbers bolted together, anchored into the banks on each side, and the spaces between the criss-crossed timbers were filled with stones. A double row of thick planks, spiked horizontally on the up-stream face of the timber framework, held back the water.

A timber and plank raceway led over to a big undershot water wheel on the side of the old stone mill. When it was running, we could hear the big millstones grinding the wheat and corn that was fed in between them by wooden chutes coming down from the large grain bins.

The water in the hole above the dam was deep. We would climb up on the steep bank by the side of the stone arch, go out on the limb of a tree, and take off for some wonderful dives, down, down, into the dark cool depths below. Then we would swim up under the arched tunnel a long way and float down on the slow current nearly to the dam, to climb out and dry off in the sunshine, flat on our back on the plank spillway.

The people want the earth and the stars for their goods

Benjamin Franklin Perry Leaphart

After the Civil War ended, Southerners returned to Saratoga, but never again did they dominate its society. An intimate letter from a 27-year-old banker to his mother in Columbia, South Carolina, is among the last of the letters available to us. Like many Southerners, "Perry" Leaphart (b 1867) found much to dislike in the North, particularly the more open interaction between the races, however inequal they may yet have been. In later life, Leaphart married and had a family, was elected president of a Columbia bank, and established the Columbia Clearing House Association to facilitate the clearing of checks between banks.

Benjamin F. Perry Leaphart, letter to Martha Leaphart, 19 August 1895. Janney-Leaphart Papers, South Caroliniana Library, USC, Columbia. It is written on printed stationery of the Grand Union Hotel, Saratoga Springs. Transcribed by Field Horne with punctuation added.

1895
BENJAMIN
FRANKLIN
PERRY
LEAPHART
254

Aug. 19, 1895

Dear Mother:

YOUR LETTER OF 15th was forwarded me from The [?Denis], and I was glad to hear from you. I wired you from here this morning and presume you received it. Saratoga is certainly a place only for people who don't want to do any thing but make a show. I went to the races, and saw five which were considered very good, there is a law against gambling & betting, but it was going on lively and a sporting man who chanced to sit next to me kept me posted. The attendance was about as large as we have at our state fairs and among the crowd many men women & negros, both male & female; Just here I will say that I have seen enough of society here, when I saw a couple, middle aged lady & gentleman meet two darkies and the whites lifted their hats and bowed as reverently as Mr. Sadler could have done. I have seen vehicles of every description & style, and horses with cut tails, some about as long as my hand. I have been drinking Congress water all day & feel pretty full, not drunk. It rained here early this morning and was so cold that I had to get out my over coat, and find others doing likewise. The hotels here are grand as large as our squares and piazzas with large columns from the ground up to the roof and four & five stories high. Rates $5 & $4 50.[236] So after spending a day here having seen the races & society and women change their dresses three times a day the last now, which is almost no dress at all, nude, I think I have seen enough. The style is the less you have on at 8 PM till 12 50 AM the more fashionable you are.

I have seen lots of pretty novelties but dare not purchase as the people want the earth & stars for their goods.

I will leave here tonight for Montreal and after spending two days there, will start back to New York and then home. Love to all, hope all keep quite well, and am glad the meals are what you like.

Your affectionate son

Perry

The racetrack was a playground made to order for youngsters

FRANK SULLIVAN

Saratoga's greatest humorist, Frank Sullivan (1892–1976), was born and raised on High Street [now Frank Sullivan Place], near the Clubhouse Gate of Saratoga Race Course. His reminiscences of a racetrack boyhood were published many years ago in The New Yorker, *for which Sullivan had been hired by Harold Ross, its founder, in 1926. Sullivan had begun his writing career as editor of the* Saratoga Springs High School Recorder, *went on to work for* The Saratogian *and, after Cornell, moved to New York where he became part of the famous Algonquin Round Table. But he loved his hometown and he returned in 1935, living on Lincoln Avenue for more than 40 years until his death.*

Frank Sullivan, "A Saratoga Childhood," *The New Yorker,* 18 September 1954, 98–107.

BACK IN THE NINETIES, High Street, in Saratoga, was a thoroughfare one block long, accommodating six dwellings, a greenhouse, a large barn in which hay was stored, and a number of small boys, including me. It was on the outskirts of the village—a lane unadorned by macadam, curbing, or other urban frills. In winter, it was as remote and snowbound as one of Willa Cather's prairie hamlets. In summer, it was verdant but dusty, except when washed by rain or when the village sprinkling cart, an equipage second in fascination only to a circus †calliope, deigned to squirt its way along it, with an admiring escort of youth in its wake. High Street ran its brief course north and south. At the south end, a providence alert to the interests of small boys and girls had placed Mrs. Crary's store[237], where a complete line of licorice sticks, jawbreakers, and other penny candies fashionable in that day was on sale. At the north end was an expanse known as the Rye Lot, where circuses set up when they came to town, and to its east, beyond the back yards of the five houses, among them my family's, that stood on that side, was the Saratoga Race Track, stretching far out into the distance. The race track was a playground made to order for youngsters. It lent itself wonderfully to all sorts of games, especially those needing plenty of room. The horse barns provided unlimited hiding places, the steeplechase jumps served admirably as forts, and the harrows stored in the paddock in the off season made fine Roman chariots.

High Street came into its own late in July, when the race track began to fill with horses and the neighborhood with racing folk. From then until September, we youngsters lived in a carnival atmosphere of glamour and excitement. There were few points of similarity between our education and the education of Henry Adams. I imagine we were better-posted on turf matters than Henry was in his youth. We could always tell you what jockeys like Arthur Redfern and Grover Cleveland Fuller and Freddy Taral were up to, or who had won the Saratoga Cup the year before, or what the racing colors of James R. Keene were. We mingled daily with real jockeys, some of them not much bigger than we were, though already well known or on the way to becoming so. These jockeys were heroes to us, and familiarity did not make them less heroic. If one of them gave one of us an old jockey cap as a souvenir, the fortunate youth was as transported as a boy of today would be if Yogi Berra gave him one of his catcher's mitts. One August a few years ago, after I had returned to Saratoga to live, a small and usually hatless neighbor sported a gay silk jockey cap, which his mother said she could hardly get him to take off at bedtime. I understood how he felt.

A man named Gottfried Walbaum[238] owned the Saratoga Race Track in those days, and ran it on the most informal lines. The races began at eleven-thirty in the morning, and if any resident of High Street wished to view them, he simply strolled through the gate beyond Mrs. Crary's store; there was very little fuss about tickets of admission. The larger stables had their own kitchens, and around those kitchens hung a rich and tantalizing aroma of watermelon and fried chicken, with hints of homemade ice cream in various flavors. The bosses of the kitchens were colored chefs who were invariably aware of a small boy's fondness for watermelon and generally ready to indulge it. In September, it was quite a comedown to return to the simple fare our mothers provided. As for the horses, I do not recall that we formed any intimate friendships with Hermis, or Africander, or any of the other Native Dancers of that era. We were not allowed to take any liberties with those high-strung thoroughbreds, but we knew quite a few of the dogs, cats, goats, banty roosters, and other stable pets that served as their mascots and companions.

East of the race track lay Yaddo[239], the estate of Spencer Trask, which was then, and still is, a beautifully wooded park, dotted with lakes. Around 1900, Yaddo was a great place for chestnuts in October, for skating in January, for wild strawberries in late June, and for swimming in July and August. At the swimming hole, we were usually joined by stableboys from the race track. We country boys regarded these lads as men of the world, who had been around and seen life, and we listened bug-eyed to their tales of adventure in places far away. Sex figured occasionally in these powwows, and there was one swashbuckler of perhaps thirteen whose tales of his conquests among the sirens of a hellhole called the Barbary Coast would have unnerved Dr. Kinsey himself. It never occurred to us naïve appleknockers from High Street to doubt one word this puberal Don Juan spoke, or to suspect that his boasted prowess was the figment of a gifted imagination, stimulated by eavesdropping on the conversations of rowdy elders.

In August, all the householders on High Street with spare rooms rented them to racing folk, who liked to live in the neighborhood because it was so handy to the race track. The extra income helped lay in many a barrel of potatoes and many a ton of coal against the winter. Our house was a mansion of ten rooms, for which my father paid a rent of eight dollars a month[240] when the mood seized him, and in August it was always crowded with delightful characters, who commanded my enthusiastic admiration. That house had a happy knack of constantly being able to stretch itself to take in a few more, including friends of ours who decided the nicest time to visit the Sullivans was in August. The family slept anywhere, or nowhere. It didn't matter. There would be plenty of time for sleep next winter. My pallet in August was a mattress on the floor. This modified form of roughing it I looked upon as a welcome novelty and part of the seasonal fun.

When August ended, the races ended, too. Overnight, the horses, the jockeys, and all the pleasant racing folk vanished. The carnival was finished, the fanfare and †tantivy of the bugles were stilled, and a quiet that was deafening dropped on High Street. It was too sudden and sharp a letdown for us youngsters—worse than the one after Christmas. Even now, the first two weeks of September are a vaguely lonely time for me, and I know the feeling stems from those September days on High Street when all the excitement and fun seemed to have gone suddenly out of the world.

Frank Sullivan the boy. Frank Sullivan Papers, Historical Society of Saratoga Springs.

When the horses left town, a few Saratoga youngsters usually left with them, fired with dreams of becoming rivals to Tod Sloan. Most of them didn't get very far, but a handful made careers for themselves, like Jimmy Donohue, from White Street, who became a well-known rider and, after that, a successful trainer. The August invaders sometimes bore off Saratoga girls, too, as when young Sam Hildreth, the trainer, fell in love with one of the pretty Cook girls from our neighborhood and persuaded her to become Mrs. Hildreth. Then Hildreth's colleague Frank Taylor married Mrs. Hildreth's sister, and then another horseman, Tom Welch, married Pearl Kelly, a cousin of the Cook girls.

Venturesome boys were not the only Saratogans who skipped town in the wake of the four-footed Pied Pipers. Early one September, my father and two friends of his grew so homesick for the horses that they took off for a weekend at the old Sheepshead Bay track, saying they would be back Monday. The weekend proved so charming that it extended itself to a week, and after that the three sportsmen found themselves in Maryland, enjoying the fall racing there. By the time they got back to Saratoga, a month had passed and the frost was on the pumpkin. Feeling that the situation called for some fast diplomacy, my father started talking before my mother could, telling her of a beautiful shawl he had brought her from New York. But when he looked for the shawl it was not to be found, and it turned out that he had left it on the train.

Eventually, we youngsters would adjust ourselves to the quieter tempo of High Street in the fall. School began, as a counter-irritant to the letdown, and there were other compensations, like the rudimentary form of football we played on the Rye Lot, and the pear tree we raided in Mr. Ryall's yard. The pears were small and hard, but to our robust palates they were golden fruit; Mr. Ryall[241] liked them, too—possibly because they were his. He was a whiskered patriarch, spry for his age, which we boys deemed to be a hundred or so, and when we stole his pears, he was obliging enough to take after us with rake or hoe and cries of vengeance. That gave an agreeable fillip to life on High Street in the pear season.

One fall day, a throng of workmen invaded High Street, camped in shacks on the race track, and started to pull it apart. Some wealthy sportsmen had bought the track from Gottfried Walbaum and were bent on enlarging and improving it on a grand scale, in time to open the following August.[242] The enlargement involved the purchase of all of our side of High Street, and the five houses there were either razed or moved away. In the spring, our house was placed on rollers and, in a confusion of shouting workmen and straining horses, swung majestically up the street and over a block to a new site, on Nelson Avenue. By that time, though, we ourselves had moved—two blocks in the other direction, to Lincoln Avenue, where I live today. Before writing this fond tribute, I walked over to High Street to see how it is faring. Shrubbery grows where Mrs. Crary's store was, and a copse of beeches under which horses are saddled before the races stands about where our house did. The approximate site of Mr. Ryall's pear tree is now the base of operations in August for the functionaries who summon motorcars for the clubhouse patrons. The Rye Lot was taken over by the race-track people years ago and serves as a parking space. High Street now accommodates a greenhouse, two stables, and one lonely, shabby, unoccupied dwelling. I came away feeling like Oliver Goldsmith after he had revisited sweet Auburn, loveliest village of the plain.

Endnotes

Sources Cited by Author's Name

Durkee, Cornelius E. *Reminiscences of Saratoga* (Saratoga Springs: The Author, 1928)

Joki, Robert. *Saratoga Lost: Images of Victorian America* (Hensonville, N.Y.: Black Dome Press, 1998

Kay, John L. and Chester M. Smith, Jr. *New York Postal History* (State College, Pa.: American Philatelic Society, 1982)

Kettlewell, James K. *Saratoga Springs: An Architectural History 1790–1990* (Saratoga Springs: Lyrical Ballad Book Store, 1991)

Swanner, Grace Maguire. *Saratoga, Queen of Spas* (Utica: North Country Books, 1998)

Sylvester, Nathaniel B. *History of Saratoga County* (Philadelphia: Everts and Ensign, 1878)

1. On his return journey, Kalm again recorded this tale, identifying his French source as M. St. Luc de la Corne (1712–1784), an officer in the Canadian army. (Benson, ed., 603)
2. Old Saratoga, now Schuylerville, was settled by Bartel Vroman no later than 1689, and mills were built by the Schuyler family in 1709 or 1710 on the south side of Fish Creek. By 1745 there was a village of 30 families, probably near the mills. The village was attacked by French and Indians on 17 November and destroyed. (Sylvester, 260)
3. The Reformed Church at the present Schuylerville was used as a hospital for British troops in 1777 and was taken down many years later. (Sylvester, 272)
4. Sylvester identified Gordon's house as being where Eugene Wiswall then lived (1878), presumably the house marked "H. Wiswold" on the 1866 atlas plate of Ballston, where the Middle Line Road crossed the Mourning Kill. (Sylvester, 247)
5. That is, the Hudson River.
6. By the time this letter was written Washington had indeed visited the springs, as shown by dal Verme's journal.
7. Should be "King Bladud" or "Bleiddudd" who, according to legend, was healed of leprosy at the Roman city of Bath. (John Clark, "Bladud of Bath, The Archaeology of a Legend," *Folklore* 105 [1994]: 39–50)
8. Rev. Eliphalet Ball came from Bedford, Westchester County, N.Y. in 1770 and settled at Ballston Center. (Sylvester, 246–247)
9. Probably a reference to Milton Center, where the Middle Line Road crossed Kayaderosseras Creek, or Milton Hill, about a mile south.
10. Salmon Tryon's tavern on the hill south of the Old Iron Spring was "a log house, to which he added a small frame with one room only and a bedroom. To these buildings Tryon added a store for the sale of dry goods and groceries." (Sylvester, 229)
11. Benjamin Risley, who came to Saratoga Springs from Hartford in 1790; his daughter Doanda married Gideon Putnam. (Sylvester, 152)
12. Henry Walton (1768–1844) was then living in Ballston. For his later career, see *infra.*

13. What is described is called a chair table; made as early as the 1630s. These objects functioned by raising or lowering the back, and were popular in houses with limited space. (Helen Comstock, *American Furniture* [New York: Viking, 1962], 32).
14. That is, High Rock Spring.
15. Now Schuylerville.
16. Probably the Second Lutheran ("Trinity") Church, on the southwest corner of Broadway and Rector Street. It served a Dutch congregation, and was burned on 21 September 1776 along with Trinity Church (Anglican). (*New York Gazette and Weekly Mercury*, 30 September 1776; *Iconography of Manhattan Island*, 5:1020–26)
17. MacMaster's Inn, southwest corner of Front and Court streets, built 1792.
18. This is the earliest description of Union Hall, which Gideon Putnam erected in 1800–02; its sign is in the collection of the Historical Society of Saratoga Springs. Enlarged and remodeled, it became the Grand Union Hotel. (Sylvester, 165–166)
19. About 150 feet south of the High Rock, the Barrel Spring was discovered in 1792 and got its name when Jacob Walton embedded a barrel around it for bathing. It was later called the Seltzer Spring. (Sylvester, 164; Swanner, 84)
20. Discovered soon after the High Rock, the Flat Rock Spring was at the northeast corner of Lake and Maple avenues, and disappeared after the Pavilion Spring was tubed in 1839. (Swanner, 64)
21. Congress Hall was erected in 1811–12 by Gideon Putnam; the Pavilion was built in 1819 on the site of the present City Hall. Milbert may have made several visits, or he may have updated his information for the benefit of his readers. (Sylvester, 167)
22. This reference is puzzling. Owl Pond is the old name for Lake Lonely, as shown on a manuscript map of the town of Saratoga Springs, prepared by John H. Steel, 12 January 1829, but there is no mountain nearby. A tiny pond northwest of Lake Lonely later assumed the name Owl Pond. (Map of Saratoga Springs by John H. Steel, 1829, New York State Archives, Series A4016, Reorganized Files of the Surveyor General's Office)
23. This amount was equivalent in buying power to $6 in 2000.
24. Steamboat service between New York and Albany was initiated by the successful demonstration in 1807 of the *Clermont* by Robert Fulton.
25. The reference is to Congress Hall, the largest of Saratoga Springs hotels at the time.
26. Moses Myers (1752/53–1835) was the son of a Dutch immigrant to New York City; he lived and died in Norfolk. (Malcolm H. Stern, *First American Jewish Families* [Cincinnati: American Jewish Archives, 1978], 218)
27. Judge Henry Walton (1768–1844) was the son and nephew of proprietors of land in Saratoga Springs. After an education in England from 1780 to 1788, he settled in Ballston in 1790. About 1815 he came to Saratoga Springs and built Pine Grove, his house on Broadway. While living in New York City in 1823 he rented Pine Grove to Reuben Hyde Walworth, then sold it to him in 1826. In the following year Walton built a stone mansion called Woodlawn on the approximate site of Jonsson Tower. He practiced law and developed much of the village north of the division line between his lots and those surveyed in 1810 for Gideon Putnam, visible in the slight bend in Broadway north of the Adelphi Hotel. (Sylvester 137, 191; Saratoga County Deeds J:448, N:474; "Map of Woodlawn," Walton Papers, New York State Library)
28. On 27 May 1795 Jacobus Barhyte of Saratoga County, yeoman, bought 200 acres in Lot 13 of the XVI Allotment of the Kayaderosseras Patent from Peter R. Kissam, merchant. He developed his fishing resort on the present Yaddo property. He died 22 December 1841, aged 79. (Saratoga Springs Deeds B2:36; *Saratoga Whig*, 28 December 1841, 3)

29. The Sans Souci Hotel, built 1803–05 on the northwest corner of Front Street and Milton Avenue in Ballston Spa, was that village's most important hostelry.
30. Probably either William Meade, *An Experimental Enquiry into the Chemical Properties and Medicinal Qualities of the Principal Mineral Waters of Ballston and Saratoga in the State of New York* (Philadelphia: H. Hall, 1817) or John H. Steel, *An Analysis of the Mineral Waters of Saratoga and Ballston* (Albany: E. and E. Hosford, 1817). A reprint of a 1793 treatise, Valentine Seaman, *A Dissertation on the Mineral Waters of Saratoga* (New York: Collins and Perkins, 1809), was probably out of print in 1817.
31. The *Chancellor Livingston* was 154 feet long, 32 feet beam, drew 7'3" water, with a 75 horsepower engine, two funnels, and a 17 foot paddle wheel. It made the trip from New York to Albany in 18 hours, traveling 12 miles an hour with the tide and six miles an hour against it; it slept 135 people. (David Lear Buckman, *Old Steamboat Days on the Hudson River* [New York: Grafton Press, 1903], 19–20)
32. Benjamin Myers (1778–1835), a maternal uncle, who lived in New York City. (Stern, *op. cit.*, 267)
33. Now Schuylerville; Saratoga was the post office name from 1804 to 1820. (Kay and Smith, 290)
34. Now Ballston Spa, its post office name was Ballston Springs from 1797 to 1828. (Kay and Smith, 286)
35. In double-entry bookkeeping, "Cr" is the creditor, the giver of money or value.
36. John Moore, *Mordaunt: Being Sketches of Life, Character and Manners in Various Countries* (1800); William Godwin, *Fleetwood* (1805); and Thomas Moore, *Lalla Rookh* (1817).
37. Gerardus Van Schoonhoven was proprietor of Congress Hall by 1815; he was chairman of the school board for School No.1 in 1819 but apparently did not remain long in the village. (Sylvester, 179) He is often referred to as "Guert," a nickname for Gerardus.
38. James Kirke Paulding, *Letters from the South, Written During an Excursion in the Summer of 1816* (1817).
39. William Paulding and James Kirke Paulding, *Salmagundi* (1807).
40. Ten Springs, also called Taylor's Springs after John and Ziba Taylor who settled near them in 1794, are first mentioned by James Skelton Gilliam in 1816.
41. The President Spring was known by 1784; it was later called the Star Spring. (Sylvester, 162; Swanner, 85)
42. Seekonk is a town in Bristol County, Massachusetts, near Providence, R.I.
43. The First Presbyterian Church, organized 15 January 1816. The much older Baptist Church was, at this time, still at its original site a little east of the present Geyser Spring. (Sylvester, 171)
44. Now Hudson Falls, its post office was called Sandy Hill from 1797 to 1910. (Kay and Smith, 356–357)
45. The Pavilion, on the present site of City Hall, was newly completed.
46. There were no fewer than seven Clemmons/Clements/Clement households in Saratoga Springs town in 1820.
47. These amounts were equivalent in buying power to $150 and $75 in 2000.
48. John Livingston owned the land south of West Congress Street, as shown by a map drawn by James Scott in 1822. Cold Spring Street, mentioned here, is not shown. (Saratoga County Clerk, Map Book R-1, plate 8A)
49. Langworthy (1766–1827) was not only a clock and watchmaker, but also a goldsmith, a jeweler and a Baptist minister. (William F. and Orthello S. Langworthy, *The Langworthy Family* [Rutland: Tuttle, 1940], 221–222)
50. Risley Taylor died 21 December 1830 aged 31 and was buried in the Putnam

Cemetery. He was probably a son of Doanda Risley Putnam's sister, Polly Risley Taylor. (Cornelius E. Durkee, *Some of Ye Epitaphs in Saratoga County, N.Y.* [1876], 7: 23)

51. This was the United States Hotel, built by Elias Benedict and opened in late May or early June of 1824. (*Saratoga Sentinel*, 8 June 1824)
52. This is probably the spring later known as Washington Spring, between the Drink Hall and St. Peter's Church. (Sylvester, 163; Swanner, 87)
53. Vaux Hall was a pleasure garden in London, opened in 1661.
54. This amount was equivalent in buying power to $150 in 2000.
55. The "Saratoga Reading-Room and Circulating Library" was operated by Gideon M. Davison, who advertised: "This establishment is now open for the reception of company. In the Reading-Room, besides a great variety of papers from different parts of the Union and the Canadas, are deposited elegant Maps of Europe, Asia, Africa, and America, and of the State of New-York . . . In the Library, are a variety of Theological, Historical, Biographical, and Practical Works, interspersed with a good collection of Travels, Voyages, Novels, and Miscellanies, mostly of modern date. . . . A Catalogue of the Books, together with the terms of subscription to the Library and Reading-Room, will be published the present week." In 1829 it was located at 417 Broadway, and a week's use of both the library and the reading room was one dollar; by that year the reading room included over 100 daily, semi-weekly and weekly newspapers along with maps and a mineral collection. (*Saratoga Sentinel*, 4 August 1819; *Catalogue of the Saratoga Circulating Library Kept by Gideon M. Davison* [1829])
56. Ungrammatical French; Coventry probably intended *Je veille l'homme grand*, I watch over the big man.
57. The reference is to Union Hall.
58. Dr. John H. Steel (1780–1838) read medicine with Dr. Daniel Bull of Saratoga, and built a practice based on the use of mineral waters; he published his analysis of the waters in 1817. (Sylvester, 201–202)
59. *The Battle of Waterloo* (New York: John Evans, 1819).
60. Martin Van Buren (1782–1862), president 1837–41, creator of the Democratic Republican Party, the prototype for state political machines, and opponent of DeWitt Clinton.
61. Churchill C. Cambreling (1786–1862), a native of Washington, N.C., came to New York City in 1802 and became associated with John Jacob Astor. Cambreling served in Congress from 1821 to 1839, and was the leader of the House of Representatives during Jackson's and Van Buren's administrations. He was an incorporator of the Saratoga and Schenectady Railroad. A delightful picture of him is contained in a description of decorating the Congress Hall ballroom for an 1819 ball: "To complete the scene, Mr. Cambrelaing, a man of sense, volunteering the part of a giddy trifler, parading the room as overseer to the laborers, with a sunflower as large as a pewter plate stuck in his button-hole, and the whole tree on which it grew waving in his hand as a badge of authority." (Harriet Otis, journal, in Caroline G.C. Curtis, ed., *The Cary Letters* [Cambridge, Mass.: Riverside Press, 1891], 279)
62. Winfield Scott (1786–1866), the hero of Chippewa in 1814.
63. The Columbian Spring was discovered in 1803 by Gideon Putnam about 100 feet southwest of the Congress Spring and was tubed in 1806. It was purchased by John Clarke in 1826 from the heirs of Robert C. Livingston, who had received lot 12 by division in 1792. (Swanner, 58–59; *Saratoga Sentinel*, 11 July 1826)
64. The Atheneum has not been positively identified. The reference may be to the cir-

culating library and reading room. The Saratoga Atheneum, forerunner of the Saratoga Springs Public Library (1950), was not organized until 1884.

65. *Saratoga Sentinel*, 29 June 1830.
66. "The Borough" acquired the Mechanicville post office in 1815 and was increasingly known by the latter name. (Kay and Smith, 288)
67. Dunning Street, now usually called Malta; it had a post office from 1815 to 1826, changed to Malta in the latter year. (Kay and Smith, 287–288)

68. Montgomery Hall was on the west side of Broadway across from the present head of Spring Street. It was razed in 1855. (*Saratoga Whig*, 19 May 1840, 12 October 1855)
69. The Pine Grove was on the site of the City Center. (Sylvester, 137)
70. A Dutch or Jersey wagon was similar to a "Pleasure Wagon." They usually had raved sides, sometimes a simple folding top made of coated canvas, and were painted any of the colors found in houses of the period (yellow ochre, green, etc.) There were simple bench seats or seats mounted on wooden cantilevered supports, the body had a slightly bowed bed, and they were pulled by a single horse. (Merri Ferrell, The Museums at Stony Brook, oral communication)
71. That is, woven straw: a straw bonnet.
72. The "American Automaton Chessplayer" was advertised in the *Saratoga Sentinel* on 31 July 1827, with an admission price of fifty cents (the equivalent of about $8.50 in 2000 dollars). It is believed to have been a clever hoax.
73. Caldwell was the post office name of Lake George from 1816 to 1871. (Kay and Smith, 350)
74. Bakers Falls is in the Hudson River between Kingsbury and Moreau, and tumbles 76 feet in the distance of 1,000 feet.
75. The *Saratoga Sentinel* of 26 May 1829 reported: "Among the improvements which have taken place in this village since the last year, is the lining of most of the side walks with maples and elms from our forests. These are generally of a good size, and will, in a short time, render the walks delightfully cool and refreshing, and give to the village an elegant rural appearance."
76. A famous English spa town in North Yorkshire, Harrowgate had 88 sulphur, saline and chalybeate springs.
77. Washington Spring was an iron spring in the Recreative Garden; when the Clarendon Hotel was built it became a feature of its grounds. An advertisement in the *Saratoga Whig*, 27 June 1841, announced: "Washington Grove, or Recreative Garden. Five splendid Ten-pin Alleys. Private alleys exclusively for ladies. Flying Horses, &c. A beautiful *Trout* pond full of Trout. A few doors south of Union Hall and adjoining Washington Bath House." The site is now occupied by Saratoga Central Catholic High School.
78. The cross street is, of course, East Congress Street, while Main Street and North Street are apparently references to Broadway and Circular Street.
79. Red Spring, 115 feet north of the High Rock and discovered soon after it, was used to treat skin diseases and provided the water for the first bathhouse in Saratoga Springs in 1783. (Swanner, 82–83)
80. Caughnawaga, post office name from 1806 to 1836, is now Fonda. (Kay and Smith, 179)
81. In addition to the heavily-patronized Albany, Ballston and Saratoga Mail Stage, stages ran from Saratoga Springs to Whitehall where they connected with the Lake Champlain steamboats; to Boston via Manchester, Vermont; and to Utica via Johnstown. (*Saratoga Sentinel*, 25 May 1824, 27 December 1825, 21 February 1826, 3 April 1827) By the decade following there was a direct stage to Caldwell [now Lake George].

82. I have been unable to identify Rev. John Freeman. No deed for the sale to Beekman Huling is on record.
83. In 2003 standing on the northeast corner of Church Street and Woodlawn Avenue.
84. Ellis' Spring, a chalybeate spring issuing from a side hill into a branch of the Kayaderosseras in a deep valley, was near the present Geyser Spring. (Swanner, 61)
85. These amounts were equivalent in buying power to $20, $25, and $30 in 2000.
86. Work on the railroad began in mid September 1831; on 10 July 1832 the *Saratoga Sentinel* reported that "carriages passed over the whole line last week, except a short carrying place at the village of Ballston Spa." A trip from Albany was projected to take three and a half hours by the new railroad, and "a trip from New-York to the Springs is merely a pastime of about 15 or 16 hours, without fatigue or perplexity." The connection at Ballston Spa was completed, and continuous service was begun on 10 April 1833. (*Saratoga Sentinel,* 10 July 1832, 9,16,23 April 1833)
87. The year of Irving's visit was one of a bad cholera outbreak. For a discussion, see William L. Stone, *Reminiscences of Saratoga and Ballston* (New York: Virtue and Yorston, 1875), 173–177.
88. Diego Portales Palaznelos (1783–1837) was the principal influence in establishing a stable government in Chile, where he was a cabinet minister from 1830 until his assassination.
89. This is probably the Luke Moore, aged 55, who was living in Stillwater town in 1850.
90. In the first English edition, a footnote cites the source of this quotation as William Cox, *Crayon Sketches; By an Amateur,* 2 vols. (New York: Conner and Cooke, 1833), 1:65.
91. Nullification was the formal suspension by a state, within its territory, of a federal law. Since Southern states profited little from tariff protection, a South Carolina convention of November 1832 declared the tariff acts of 1828 and 1832 null and void. In February 1833, Congress passed the Force Bill giving the president power to collect customs in South Carolina.
92. Another name for Stamford, Delaware County.
93. Another name for North Blenheim, Schoharie County.
94. The shop's location has not been established, but its proprietor was probably Isaac Spaulding, cabinetmaker, who was a 40-year-old widower at the time of the 1850 census of Saratoga Springs.
95. This is incorrect. Gideon Putnam's grandfather was a cousin of Gen. Israel Putnam. (Eben Putnam, *A History of the Putnam Family in England and America* [Salem, Mass.: The Salem Press, 1891], 87–126)
96. Sir Walter Scott, *Ivanhoe* (1791).
97. The reference is to *Isaiah* 35:6.
98. Apparently a reference to a "large addition planned" for the Pavilion. (*Saratoga Sentinel,* 11 February 1834) The hotel burned 14 October 1843. (Durkee, 10)
99. A story reprinted from a Charleston paper explained that the panorama was "discovered" by a London artist named Barker about 40 years earlier, and was introduced to Paris by Robert Fulton about 1800. It placed the spectactor in the center of the scene; "much satisfactory information, as well as pleasure, can be derived from an exhibit of this kind." In 1835 a panorama of Geneva was exhibited in the Panorama Building (also called the Rotunda) in the rear of the Pavilion. (*Saratoga Sentinel,* 25 August 1835, 8 September 1835)
100. A reference to Union Hall; see Buckingham, *infra.*
101. Organized 4 October 1830, Bethesda Episcopal Church was first housed in a

chapel provided by Dr. John Clarke on the northeast corner of East Congress and Putnam streets. (Sylvester, 172)

102. A reference, apparently, to Judge Henry Walton.
103. Located on Broadway about where the "new" Adelphi Hotel was built in 1876–77.
104. Charles A. Davis (1795–1867), a merchant, published "Major Jack Downing's Letters" containing a detailed interview with Andrew Jackson on his plan to overthrow the United States Bank. First published in the New York *Commercial Advertiser*, they were issued in book form, *Letters of J. Downing* (New York: Harper, 1834).

105. This passage demonstrates that Martineau had read Dwight's *Things As They Are* (1834), with its memoir by Abigail (Alsop) Dwight, quoted *supra*.
106. In 1832, John Clarke built a water tower about 50 feet high in Congress Park; water was pumped to a reservoir at the top. It was largely replaced by a reservoir out Church Street in 1847, but probably remained in place until the 1875 redesign of the park. (Sylvester, 191)
107. This is the first-known reference to the Circular Railroad. It is unlikely it was constructed earlier than the 1832 completion of the Saratoga and Schenectady Railroad and it may have been new at the time of Martineau's visit.
108. Dr. John Clarke first leased Congress Spring from the Livingston family, purchasing it in 1826. As its proprietor he made improvements in 1826, 1829, and 1830. (*Saratoga Sentinel*, 30 May 1826, 11 July 1826, 23 June 1829, 29 June 1830)
109. The reference is to Sir Walter Scott, *The Lady of the Lake: A Poem* (1810).
110. Georges Cuvier (1769-1832), a French comparative anatomist, who is considered the father of paleontology and functional anatomy.
111. Lord Byron's poem, *Mazeppa* (1819).
112. Veazie was a Troy coachmaker by 1815, Eaton by 1820; Eaton and Gilbert formed a partnership in 1831. Sources say they began building passenger cars in 1841 but this document indicates they started much earlier. (Arthur J. Weise, *Troy's One Hundred Years* [Troy: William H. Young, 1891], 168–169)
113. Benjamin Alston (1833–1900), one of the five children of Robert Alston who survived to adulthood. Five died young, apparently including "Rob," mentioned in the letter. (Joseph A. Groves, *The Alstons and Allstons of North and South Carolina* [Atlanta: Franklin Printing, 1901], 18, 64)
114. LeGrand Cannon of Troy sold the south part lot 52 between Broadway and Long Alley on 30 August 1838 to Milo Linus North for $1,650. This is the present site of 467 Broadway. (Saratoga County Deeds, GG:234)
115. Gideon M. Davison (1791–1869) came to Saratoga in 1817–18 from Rutland, where he had founded the *Rutland Herald*. In April 1818, he commenced Saratoga Springs' first newspaper, the *Saratoga Sentinel*. (Sylvester, 197–198)
116. Apparently this was the first season of photography in Saratoga Springs. The first advertisement appeared in the *Saratoga Whig*, 18 May 1841: "Miniature Portraits. Messrs. SHAW & CO., take this method of announcing to the inhabitants of Saratoga Springs, that they will, in a few days, open rooms for the accommodation of those who may wish Portraits by the celebrated DAGUERROTYPE process. They will be taken in the most elegant style. Further particulars in a further notice."
117. Footnote in manuscript: "Fort Edward Center, Washington Co."
118. The second building of the Presbyterian Church (1842–57) was located on the corner of Broadway and Caroline Street. (Sylvester, 171)
119. A large reservoir was built in Greenfield and the water was conducted through iron pipes lined with cement; it was replaced in 1871 by the Loughberry system. (Sylvester, 191) The reservoir was probably north of Route 9N west of Locust Grove Road.

120. The Iodine Spring (also called the President and the Star) was north of High Rock Spring. (Sylvester, 162; Swanner, 85)
121. Footnote in manuscript: "at $110 p. an. a reduced rate as it is late. not the office"
122. This, and the following paragraph, illustrate Saratogians' strategies to generate income from their houses during the tourist season. Apparently the Norths twice rented their house but retained a bedroom and perhaps a sitting room; in the first case they arranged to take meals in the hotel across the street, in the second with their tenant
123. This property has not been identified in the deeds but, on 5 June 1832, Daniel and Jane O'Brien sold part of Lot 67 on Congress Street to the Saratoga and Schenectady Railroad for $135. (Saratoga County Deeds X:271)
124. The Rensselaer and Saratoga Railroad was incorporated 14 April 1832 and began service in 1835. (Sylvester, 129)
125. Cephas Parker and William Perry were both listed in the 1850 census of Saratoga Springs as merchants.
126. This sentence is internal evidence that an amanuensis was the actual writer of the book. No African American, uneducated or educated, would have thought or written in these terms.
127. Loco Focos were the members of a radical urban wing of the Democratic-Republican party, which emerged in New York State in opposition to Jackson's banking policies; they fought financial interests aided by regular Democrats that sought bank and corporate charters in the legislature.
128. James Gordon Bennett (1795–1872), a Scot who immigrated in 1820, started the *New York Herald* in 1835 as a penny paper for the working and middle classes of New York City; by the late 1830s it and the *Sun* (1833) were the largest-circulation dailies in the United States.
129. Henry Clay (1797–1852), stateman, congressman, and opponent of Jackson; the reception given him in Saratoga County was described by the *Saratoga Whig* on 13 August 1839.
130. Emerson's Tavern was at Emerson's Corners, now called Gurn Spring, just west of Exit 16; it was operated by Lyndes Emerson, a town officer of Wilton. (Sylvester, 464)
131. Frank Johnson, an African American bandleader, was a perennial at the spa. (Gretchen Sullivan Sorin and Jane Rehl, *Honorable Work: African Americans in the Resort Community of Saratoga Springs 1870–1970* [Saratoga Springs: Historical Society, 1992], 4)
132. John W. Taylor (1784–1854) of Charlton, a graduate of Union College 1803, became an assemblyman in 1811, served as congressman from 1812 to 1832, twice Speaker of the House, and was finally a state senator from 1840 to 1842. (*Biographical Directory of the U.S. Congress 1774–1989* [Washington: GPO, 1989], 1917)
133. "Descant" is probably the word intended.
134. William Henry Harrison (1773–1841), Whig president elected in 1840, died on 4 April 1841.
135. Flying horses were advertised as being in operation in the Pine Grove, north of the Pavilion, "for a few weeks" in 1832. (*Saratoga Sentinel*, 29 May 1832)
136. Beekman's Woods were presumably on the premises of J.K. Beekman, west of Ballston Avenue and south of West Circular Street. ("Map of the Village of Saratoga Springs," 1842, ms. in private collection)
137. Richard G. Parker's *Aids to English Composition* was a textbook used in girls' academies.

138. William Miller (1782–1849), lay Baptist preacher from Low Hampton, Washington County, who, in 1831, began to predict the end of the world would come in 1843; the founder of the Adventist churches.
139. Though discovered in 1816, the Pavilion Spring was not successfully tubed until 1839, when Daniel McLaren accomplished it. (Sylvester, 163; Swanner, 80)
140. The *Saratoga Whig* reported the cabin's erection in its issues of 7 and 14 April 1840; it was later sold. (*Saratoga Whig*, 30 March 1841)
141. Horace Greeley (1811–1872) founded the literary weekly, *The New Yorker* (1834) and in 1840 launched the *Log Cabin* which strongly endorsed the Whig ticket of Harrison and Tyler; Park Benjamin (1809–1864) began the enormously successful semi-literary weekly, *The New World*, in June 1840; he was also a purveyor of popular fiction.
142. The American Institute took place at Niblo's Garden in New York City and exhibited the "fruits of genius and industry . . . from the field, the garden, and the workshop." (Cyrus Mason, *The Oration on the Thirteenth Anniversary of the American Institute* [New York: Hopkins and Jennings, 1840], 5)
143. Liverwort is a common name for several plants believed to have beneficial effects on the liver, and a balsam is an aromatic vegetable juice. Dr. Taylor advertised his Balsam of Liverwort for sale through Beekman Huling in Saratoga Springs, recommending it for consumption and liver complaint. (*Saratoga Whig*, 15 December 1840, 4)
144. Note that Christmas was then a community holiday, rather than the almost-exclusively family holiday it is today.
145. It's notable that Morleigh made a passing reference to a Quebeçois neighborhood, apparently atop the escarpment just west of the High Rock. The Quebeçois are not thought particularly to have formed an ethnic community in Saratoga Springs, although much later they did organize a short-lived French speaking Catholic parish; but the state census of 1855 reveals that there were 145 Canadian-born residents in the village, more than double the number of any other foreign-born group.
146. Felo de se is a legal term for suicide, originating in seventeenth century Anglo Latin. Here it is incorporated into a play on the word "sea," for *lac* is the French word for a lake.
147. In 2000 dollars, this sum had the purchasing power of $3,150. Unfortunately, the Hutchinsons wrote with sarcasm; they were not making much money at all. (John J. McCusker, *How Much Is That in Real Money? A Historical Commodity Price Index for Use as a Deflator of Money Values in the Economy of the United States* [Worcester, Mass.: American Antiquarian Society, 2001])
148. The Congress Spring House, a small hotel in operation by 1828, was about where 267 Broadway is in 2004. It was conducted on religious and temperance principles, and was sold in 1852 to Dr. Norman Bedortha for use as a Water Cure. (*Saratoga Sentinel*, 5 August 1828; *Saratoga Whig*, 26 March 1852)
149. Commemorating a 1757 event, "The Battle of Prague" was a sonata for piano forte or harpsichord composed in 1795 by Frantisek Kotzwara; it was probably the most popular battle piece in nineteenth-century America.
150. See discussion of the Dutch or Jersey waggon, *supra*.
151. The earliest known reference to bowling alleys is in Elihu Hoyt's 1827 journal; a bowling alley and bar near the depot were advertised "to be let" in the *Saratoga Whig*, 2 April 1839.
152. The Saratoga and Schenectady Plank Road Company was organized 22 December 1848 and followed the approximate route of Ballston Avenue, so marked on the

1852 John Bevan map. A brief enthusiasm, plank roads were constructed of heavy planks on stringers.

153. Abraham Richards, aged 76, died 2 July 1849. (Federal Census, 1850, Saratoga Springs, mortality schedule)
154. James M. Marvin (1809–1901), proprietor of the United States Hotel.
155. The New York State Fair was held on East Congress Street [now Union Avenue]near Nelson Avenue in 1847, and a small race course was laid out, on which both running and harness races were held. (Durkee, 12)
156. The hydrants were connected with the Greenfield water system (*supra*).
157. Properly, the Columbian Hotel, built 1809 and enlarged 1819 at the southeast corner of Broadway and Lake Avenue. (Sylvester, 167–168)
158. The *Saratoga Whig* of 26 April 1842 announced the opening of the Saratoga Academy in Covent Garden, a pleasure resort located on the site of the present Algonquin Building.
159. In 1839 the Roman Catholics purchased a lot on Broadway at William Street, on which stood the Lyceum, which was then converted into a church. It was replaced with the present building, the Church of St. Peter, in 1853. (Sylvester, 175; Durkee, 81)
160. Judge Thomas J. Marvin (1803–1852) was a brother of James M. Marvin, proprietor of the United States Hotel. (Sylvester, 192)
161. A private bank, the village's first, was organized in 1847, and became the Bank of Saratoga Springs in 1854. (Sylvester, 188)
162. This amount was equivalent in buying power to $26,000 in 2000.
163. Greenridge Cemetery, a classic "rural cemetery" of its era, was consecrated on 13 June 1844. (Sylvester, 190; Durkee, 10)
164. This may be the *R.B. Coleman*, built and launched in 1845. (Durkee, 11) Another visitor, in 1847, wrote "A steamer plies on this lake for the amusement of visitors; but, something having gone wrong in its machinery, we had to return to Saratoga disappointed." (Robert Playfair, *Recollections of a Visit to the United States and British Provinces of North America, in the Years 1847, 1848, and 1849* [Edinburgh: Thomas Constable and Co., 1856], 46) A small steamer can be seen in a stereoscope view of Saratoga Lake. (Joki, 141)
165. The William L.F. Warren residence at 473 Broadway.
166. In 1855, the town of Saratoga Springs produced an inconsequential eight gallons of "maple molasses" (syrup) and 20 pounds of maple sugar, while Lucy's hometown of Milford made 57 gallons of molasses but 3,325 pounds of sugar. In Otsego County as a whole, 4,399 gallons and 193,206 pounds were made. (*Census of the State of New York for the Year 1855* [Albany: Charles Van Benthuysen, 1857], 290, 300)
167. Miss Bond probably intended to write *"à la bonne franquette,"* meaning an informal meal of ingredients on hand.
168. On the village map published early in 1852 by John Bevan, the Indian Encampment is shown at the southwest corner of Broadway and Ballston Avenue. It is first mentioned by Robert Playfair who visited in 1847. (Playfair, *op. cit.*, 44–48)
169. This passage is a strong suggestion of the presence of Black tourists in Saratoga Springs.
170. The machine described, commonly called a "horse power," was a treadmill.
171. Eleanor Shackelford, her daughter, later the founder of St. Faith's School, Saratoga Springs.
172. Van Amburgh & Co's Mammoth Menagerie and Grand Moral Exhibition an-

nounced in an advertisement in the *Saratogian*, 30 May 1861, that it would appear in Saratoga Springs on 3 June under a "New Six Centre-Pole Canvas." Admission was 25 cents, children under nine years of age, 15 cents: about $11.50 and $7.00 in 2000 dollars.

173. George R. Putnam (b 1827), her brother. (Putnam, *op. cit.*, 2: 58–59)
174. The Clarendon Hotel, on Broadway south of Congress Street, was built in 1860 by Mrs. Mary L. Jones. (Sylvester, 168)

175. Lorin Bradley Putnam (1827–1895), her cousin. (Putnam, *loc. cit.*)
176. For his biography, see "The Bedortha Obsequies," *Saratogian*, 15 February 1883, 3. The *Saratoga Whig*, 26 March 1852, reported that he had purchased the Congress Spring House for use as a water cure. There were two other noted practitioners: Dr. Sylvester S. Strong arrived the same year, and Dr. Robert Hamilton came to the village in 1854.
177. In fact, there was: the Commercial Hotel, remodeled from the original Presbyterian Church building, stood near the depot at the corner of Church and Matilda [now Woodlawn Avenue] streets.
178. That is, Dr. Bedortha's Water Cure. It relocated in the Continental Hotel. (*Saratogian*, 14 July 1864)
179. The Empire Spring, on High Rock Avenue near the foot of Circular Street, was discovered about 1793 and originally known as the Walton Spring; it was tubed in 1846. (Sylvester, 160; Swanner, 62)
180. The reference is to the Scottish poem *Ossian*: "I have seen the walls of Balclutha, but they are desolate."
181. Gaetan Vestris (1729–1808), Italian, the greatest dancer of his day.
182. The United State Hotel burned to the ground on 18 June 1865. (Durkee, 19)
183. An annual race meeting was begun in 1863. (Edward Hotaling, *They're Off: Horse Racing at Saratoga* [Syracuse: Syracuse University Press, 1995], 41–50)
184. The Putnam Spring, off Phila Street, was discovered by Lewis Putnam in 1835; it was chalybeate. (Swanner, 81)
185. The United States Hotel burned on 18 June 1865; Congress Hall burned on 30 May 1866. (Durkee, 19–20)
186. John Morrissey (1831–1878), a Democratic congressman from 1869 to 1871, fought only three prize ring contests. He was an infamous gambler, and built the Casino in 1870–71.
187. John Carmel Heenan (1833–1873) fought Morrissey in 1858 for the American championship at Long Point, Ontario.
188. The Everett House at 432 Broadway was built in 1843, and was substantially enlarged in 1866. In 2004 it is known as the Inn at Saratoga.
189. "Saratoga potatoes," now called potato chips, were invented in Saratoga Springs in the 1850s, probably by George Crum or his sister, Catherine Wicks, at a restaurant operated by Cary B. Moon. (William S. Fox and Mae G. Banner. "Social and Economic Contexts of Folklore Variants: The Case of Potato Chip Legends," *Western Folklore* 42 [May 1983]: 111–126) Moon's obituary calls him the "originator of Moon's fried potatoes, which have come into general use." (*Ballston Journal*, 19 January 1895) See also Sylvester, 214.
190. Begun as a remembrance for the Civil War dead, Decoration Day, now called Memorial Day, was first observed nationally in 1868 and in Saratoga Springs at the same time. (*Saratogian*, 4 June 1868, 2 June 1870)
191. The reference is to the African Methodist Episcopal Church, organized 1863, on Willow Walk (now High Rock Avenue); Rev. J.C. Gilbert was its pastor for five years, leaving at the end of the summer. (Sylvester, 178)

192. Charles S. Lattimore (b 1837), a coachman living at South Street [Lincoln Avenue] corner of Stratton Street, was a member of Saratoga Springs' most established middle-class black family.
193. Luzerne, Warren County, was a lake resort about 21 miles north of Saratoga Springs on the Adirondack Railroad; service had begun in 1865, making such excursions possible. (Jim Shaughnessy, *Delaware and Hudson* [Berkeley: Howell-North Books, 1965], 118)
194. The Continental Hotel, Washington Street, corner of East Beekman Street.
195. The rider cannot be identified, but the horse was R.W. Walden's chestnut horse, Metairie. (Sanders D. Bruce, *American Turf Register* [New York: Turf, Field and Farm, 1871], 59)
196. Although Oberlin College educated African Americans in this era, college records show no Sophia Hunter as a student. (Letter, Anne G. Pearson, Oberlin College, to Field Horne, 17 October 1986)
197. Rev. Henry Highland Garnet (1815–1882) was one of the nation's most prominent African American abolitionists.
198. "J.M. French's Grand Oriental Circus & Egyptian Caravan" presented two shows "on the Congress Street Lot, Above Regent St." (*Saratogian*, 25 August 1870)
199. Apparently a quote from an unidentified book, it means "What would one do with a house, only to dream?"
200. Built 1870–71 as "Morrissey's Club House." (Kettlewell, 41–43)
201. Moon's Lake House, opened by Cary B. Moon (1813–1895) in 1853 when he gave up proprietorship of Montgomery Hall on Broadway, Saratoga Springs. (Sylvester, 214)
202. From the description, this was Congress Hall.
203. The reference is to the novelist James Fenimore Cooper (1789–1851).
204. This amount was equivalent in buying power to $36.65 in 2000.
205. There were actually five, counting the six-year-old rebuilt Congress Hall (1868–1913). The others were the Grand Central (1872–1874), Columbian (1872–1965), United States (1874–1946), and Grand Union (1874–1953).
206. The United States Hotel burned 18 June 1865. (Durkee, 19)
207. The reference is apparently to a dance hall in Paris; see Winslow Homer, "A Parisian Ball – Dancing at the Mabille, Paris," *Harper's Weekly*, 23 November 1867.
208. Alexander Turney Stewart, a New York City department store magnate, bought the Grand Union Hotel in the spring of 1872. (*Saratogian*, 18 April 1872)
209. James M. Marvin (1809–1901) was associated with the United States Hotel beginning in 1830. ("Fifty Years in Saratoga," *Saratogian*, 6 October 1881; Sylvester, 196–197).
210. William D. Field (1823–1883). (*Boyd's Saratoga Springs Directory for 1874* [Saratoga Springs: Andrew Boyd, 1874], 97; Frederick C. Pierce, *The Field Genealogy* [Chicago: Hammond Press, 1901], 1: 514)
211. The regattas, intercollegiate rowing events, took place in 1871, 1873 and 1874.
212. No such law is known, according to Dr. Martha Stonequist, city historian.
213. This seems to be a reference to Snake Hill, which might appear as an island from a distance.
214. It was published (actually by E.J. Hale) in the year of the Hungarian's visit. Its resort town setting is never identified but, in it, one character writes to another, "Go where the eggs and the morals are both unexceptional."
215. A news story about the same event a decade later is "The Garden Party," *Saratoga Evening Journal*, 28 August 1886.
216. The reference is to the portrait of Jonathan Bittell, "The Blue Boy," by Sir Peter Lely (1618–1680).

217. M. de Molinari was probably conflating his Saratoga Springs guide with *Hunter's Panoramic Guide from Niagara Falls to Montreal* (Montréal: Hunter and Bishop, 1860), which did not cover Saratoga.
218. "Gamache's Wedding" was a ballet based on the tale of Don Quixote, first produced at the Paris Opéra in 1801. "Le Petit Manteau Bleu" (literally, little blue coat) is a reference to the eighteenth-century philanthropist Edme Champion, who distributed food wearing one; the phrase passed into the French language to represent any benevolent man. The meaning of the quotation is a lavish feast in comparison to a soup kitchen.
219. In 1880, of eight tobacconists, three were apparently Jewish: Isidore Brand, Benjamin J. Goldsmith, and Abram Lichtenstein. (*Boyd's Saratoga Springs Directory for 1880–81* [Saratoga Springs: S. Fred Boyd, 1880], 182)
220. Dr. J. Parker Pray, a New York City chiropodist, kept an office at 370 Broadway "during the season." (*Huling's Saratoga Springs Directory for 1884–5* (Saratoga Springs: Huling and Co., 1884), 207.
221. This amount was equivalent in buying power to $93 in 2000.
222. Ira David Sankey (1840–1908), singing evangelist and gospel songwriter, associated with Dwight Lyman Moody from 1870 onward.
223. Elmwood Hall, at 48 Front Street, was directly across the street from the Vermont House. It was open all year with an in-season rate of $1.50–$2.00 per day. (*Kirwin's Saratoga Springs Directory, 1886* [Saratoga Springs: W.H. Kirwin, 1886], 134)
224. Yet Sing's laundry was at 26 Phila Street; Dong Sing worked there as well. (*Ibid.*, 222) As a "Chinese laundry," it was listed in directories from 1884 to 1888.
225. A town in Windsor County, Vt., on the White River. Vermonters visiting Saratoga Springs were naturally attracted to a hotel named the Vermont House.
226. The Congress Spring pavilion was rebuilt in the Stick Style in 1876. (Joki, 68)
227. A Rothschild did visit in 1860: Salomon de Rothschild (b 1835). See his *A Casual View of America: The Home Letters . . . 1859–61* (Palo Alto: Stanford, 1961), 66–67.
228. This amount was equivalent in buying power to $74 in 2000.
229. Now known as Canfield Casino.
230. Hanover (1884–99), chestnut colt, won the Belmont in 1887, recorded 20 wins in 27 starts, and was America's greatest money winner.
231. Such an event is illustrated by a print reproduced from an unidentified issue of *Leslie's Weekly* in George Waller, *Saratoga: Saga of an Impious Era* (Englewood Cliffs, N.J.: Prentice Hall, 1966), 252
232. Built 1871 and now called City Hall. (Kettlewell, 43-44)
233. Woodlawn Park actually consisted of 1,080 acres, of which 600 were in the main tract. (S.J. Mott, *Outline Map of Woodlawn Park* [1916])
234. Denton's Vly was one of the ponds in Woodlawn Park. "Vly," from the Dutch "valley" meaning lowland or meadow, is a term used in the Saratoga region to designate a small, shallow pond.
235. The present site of Birch Run condominiums.
236. These amounts were equivalent in buying power to $105 and $95 in 2000.
237. John Crary ran a saloon at 2 High Street in 1895; presumably his wife kept the store as Sullivan suggests. (*Directory of Saratoga Springs 1895* [Saratoga Springs: Saratogian, 1895], 65, 161)
238. Gottfried Walbaum (1845–1933) was a majority owner of the Hudson County Jockey Club (Guttenberg, N.J.), which bought the track at the end of the 1891 season. He built the grandstand, clubhouse and betting ring, most of which are in use

today, opening them 25 July 1892. (Andrew Radloff, "The Unruly Reign of Gottfried Walbaum," *National Museum of Racing and Hall of Fame Quarterly*, vol. 5, no. 3, pp. 6-8; vol. 5, no. 4, pp. 6-7)

239. Yaddo, a mansion of 55 rooms, was built in 1891 by Spencer and Katrina Trask. It is today a retreat for artists. (Kettlewell, 88–90)
240. This amount was equivalent in buying power to $167 in 2000
241. George Ryall, a farmer, lived at 7 High Street. (*Directory of Saratoga Springs 1895* [Saratoga Springs: Saratogian, 1895], 65, 319)
242. Headed by William Collins Whitney, the syndicate ordered track renovations to be executed in 1901–02; for $12,000, Miles D. Bradley was to move the grandstand, clubhouse, betting ring, field stand, eight stables and a house, to be complete by 1 June 1902. (Agreement, Miles D. Bradley with The Saratoga Association, 11 October 1901, National Museum of Racing) The track, too, was reoriented; see "The Improved Saratoga Track for 1902 Meeting," map, National Museum of Racing.

Glossary

à la belle étoile in the open, literally under the stars
Adams Ale water
advert to remark
anathematized to utter anathemas, to curse

annealed toughened or tempered after fusion
antipodes places on the surface of the earth directly opposite to each other
apogee the highest point, climax, culmination
asparagus *asparagus officinalis,* its greenery used as a decoration
axed colloquial form of asked
barouche a four-wheeled carriage with a half-head behind, which can be raised or let down at pleasure, having a seat in front for the driver, and seats inside for two couples to sit facing each other
bate to give food or drink to a horse, especially while on a journey
bedizened dressed up with vulgar finery
bent mental inclination or tendency
bilious affected by, or arising from, too great a secretion of bile
blackleg a turf swindler, or one in other species of gambling
blancheuse laundress
blanc-mange sweet almond-flavored milk pudding thickened with gelatine and usually moulded
blind any thing or action intended to conceal one's real design
boroughmongers those who trade in parliamentary seats for boroughs
Boston the American Waltz, introduced at Boston in 1834, a slower and smoother waltz than the Viennese
calcareous containing lime or limestone
calliope an instrument consisting of a series of steam-whistles tuned to musical notes, played by a keyboard like that of an organ
chair a light vehicle drawn by one horse, also called a chaise
chalybeate impregnated or flavored with iron
chignon a large coil or hump of hair, usually folded around a pad, worn by women at the nape of the neck
chloroform a liquid, the vapor of which produces insensibility, hence it is much used as an anaesthetic; discovered in 1831 and 1832
climacteric a critical stage in human life, here used figuratively
coach lace a tightly woven material, 1–3" wide, used in carriages to cover seams on the face of the seat, the swings, and the inside of door upholstery, and as edging
cobbler a drink made of wine, sugar, lemon, and pounded ice, and imbibed through a straw or other tube
comme il faut as it should be
consommé printanier à la royal springtime broth, Royal Style
cotillion a dance for four or eight persons; a quadrille
couleur de rose rose-colored
coup de cil a glancing look; literally, strike of an eyelash
coup de main a sudden or vigorous attack for the purpose of instantaneously capturing a position
cream ice cream
Crœsus the last King of Lydia (d. 546 BC), by extension a very wealthy man

curricles a light, two-wheeled carriage, usually drawn by two horses abreast
dashers a dashing person, showing liveliness in dress, manners, etc.
demi-monde the class of women of doubtful reputation and social standing, upon the outskirts of "society"
demireps a woman whose reputation is only half reputable
déshabillé the state of being partly undressed, or dressed in a negligent or casual style
desideratum something for which a longing or desire is felt
dished to defeat completely
dispraise to do the opposite of praise
dromios having the form of a crustacean, closely allied to a true crab
dummy a moveable frame with which dishes are passed from one room or story of a house to another; a dumbwaiter
dyspeptic suffering from dyspepsia, difficulty or derangement of digestion, usually involving weakness, loss of appetite and depression of spirits
empressement animated display of cordiality
encomium a formal or high-flown expression of praise
ennuyant boring
en retraite retired
en suite forming a "suite" or set
enunciator a self-acting telegraphic signal
equipages carriages and horses, with the attendant servants
excrescence a natural outgrowth or appendage
eyetooth skinners persons characterized by quickness or sharpness of understanding
faro a gambling game using cards, in which the players bet on the order that certain cards will appear when taken singly from the top of the pack
fathom a measure equal to six feet
fille de chambre chambermaid
fresco a kind of painting executed in water color on a wall or ceiling, etc., of which the mortar or plaster is not quite dry so that the colors sink in and become more durable
gig a light two-wheeled, one-horse carriage
gin sling an American cold drink composed of gin, etc., flavored and sweetened with powdered white sugar, into which are stuck leaves of fresh gathered mint
glaube salts sulphate of sodium, named for Johann Rudolf Glauber (1604–1668), who first made it artificially in 1656
grasshopper springs springs that fix under the shaft of a one-horse chaise to the axletree
gravel aggregations of urinary crystals that can be recognized as such by the naked eye
Hygeia health personified; a system of sanitation or medical practice
ignoble vulgus (Latin) unknown multitude
induct to lead or conduct
journal the part of a shaft or axle that rests upon the bearing
kangaroo this word is probably being used figuratively to mean people who hop while dancing
keeping wedding rural folk custom of entertaining following a wedding
king's evil scrofula, so called because it was formerly thought to be cured by the touch of a king
laissez-aller absence of restraint; unrestrained ease or freedom

lambrequin a cornice with a valance of pendent labels or pointed pieces, placed over a door or window; a short curtain suspended for ornament from a mantel-shelf
laving to wash against
liberty pole a tall mast or staff with a Phrygian cap or other symbol of liberty at the top
lion one who is strong, courageous, or fiercely brave
maitre d'hotel a steward or butler
medicable possessing medicinal properties
muscular Christianity the practice and opinion of those Christians who believe that it is a part of religious duty to maintain a vigorous condition of the body, and who therefore approve of athletic sports and exercises as conducive to good health, good morals and right feelings in religious matters
natrium sodium
négligé informal or unceremonious attire as worn by women when not in complete toilette
old stagers veterans, old hands
pannier a basket of considerable size for carrying provision; a frame of whalebone, wire or other material, used to distend the skirt of a woman's dress at the hips
partie quarée quartet
patois a dialect spoken by the common people in a particular district
pellucid translucent, transparent; clear
petrifaction conversion to stone or a stony substance
phalanstery in Charles Fourier's scheme for the reorganization of society, a building or set of buildings occupied by a phalanx (a socialistic community)
piscatorial of or pertaining to fishers or fishing
plume à la main pen-in-hand
pocket a small bag that might be attached to the clothing in which to carry objects
porringer a small basin of metal, earthenware or wood from which broth or porridge is eaten
porter a kind of beer of a dark brown color and taste, brewed from malt partly charred or browned by drying at a high temperature
porter's knot a shoulder pad, kept in position by a loop round the forehead, and used for carrying heavy loads (British English)
pour manger for eating
probity moral excellence, integrity, rectitude, uprightness
quenelles dumplings made of flour and egg, flavored with meat or fish
qui vive on one's guard
rampart a mound of earth raised for the defense of a place, here used figuratively
redowa a slow waltz, of Bohemian origin, resembling the mazurka
repine to feel or manifest discontent or dissatisfaction; to fret, murmur or complain
restringent having the tendency to restrain the action of the bowels
rised (her) the word has not been located in a dictionary, but from context it has the meaning of (mis)treatment
rod a measure of length equal to 16.5 feet
rude health robust or vigorous health
sable a small carnivorous quadruped, nearly allied to the marten, native to arctic and subarctic regions of Europe and Asia, not black but brown
sans feu ni lieu literally "without fire or place," utterly homeless

schottische a dance of foreign origin resembling the polka, first introduced in England in 1848
scorbutic of or pertaining to scurvy
sententiously tersely and pithily
shoddy-contractor shoddy being a cloth comprised of wool made by tearing to refuse old wool rags; the term refers to those who made fortunes by means of army contracts at time of Civil War; literally, *nouveau-riche*
slaked lime to become hydrated or slacked, to cause lime to disintegrate by the action of water or moisture
solar lamp an argand lamp having a cylindrical wick that allows a current of air to pass both inner and outer surfaces of the flue, thus securing more perfect combustion and brighter light; invented *circa* 1782
St Anthony's Fire a disease, caused by the fungus ergot, with action similar to lysergic acid, provoking hallucinations, disorientation, muscle cramps, convulsions, miscarriage and gangrene
stooling an old country game somewhat resembling cricket
stoop an uncovered platform before a house, raised, and approached by means of a series of steps; from the Dutch, *stoep*
strathspey a lively dance or reel for two dancers; the music or tune (usually in common time) to accompany it
studio man in the 19th century, "studio" was used for many kinds of business locations; see John T. Dumpelmann, "Studio," *American Speech* II (1926), 158
surtout coat a man's greatcoat or overcoat
table d'hôte the hotel's set menu; the opposite of *à la carte*; literally, the host's table
tantivy to ride full tilt; to hurry away
tippers those who render themselves unsteady, make themselves drunk or intoxicated
toddy a beverage composed of whiskey or other spiritous liquor with hot water and sugar
tonic strengthening, invigorating, bracing effect on systems or organs
toute de suite immediately
tout ensemble all together
tres jolie fille very pretty daughter
trundle to cause to roll along upon a surface
vandyked cut or shaped at the edge into deep indentations; zigzagged
verdurous clothed in the fresh green of vegetation
vie en plein air life in the open air
vinaigrettes a holder for a flower or fragrance, attached to the clothing
vociferation an act or instance of loud speaking or shouting; an outcry
voila tout there! everyone . . .
waist a bodice, blouse (American English)
watchpocket a small pocket in a garment for carrying a watch
wheels Catherine wheels, a type of firework
whist a game of cards played by four persons
whistle something as transient as a whistle

Bibliography

Finding Aids

Arksey, Nancy Pries and Marcia Reed. *American Diaries: An Annotated Bibliography of Published American Diaries and Journals* (Detroit: Gale Research, 1983)

Goodfriend, Joyce D. *The Published Diaries and Letters of American Women: An Annotated Bibliography* (Boston: G.K. Hall, 1987)

Havlice, Patricia Pate. *And So to Bed: A Bibliography of Diaries Published in English* (Metuchen, N.J.: Scarecrow Press, 1987)

Manzer, Bruce M. *Saratoga County, N.Y. From the Earliest Times to 2000: An Exhaustive Bibliography and Union Catalog*, 3rd ed. (Manama, Bahrain: The Author, 2003)

Matthews, William. *American Diaries: An Annotated Bibliography of American Diaries Written Prior to the Year 1861* (Berkeley: University of California Press, 1985)

————. *American Diaries in Manuscript, 1580–1954: A Descriptive Bibliography* (Athens, Ga.: University of Georgia Press, 1974)

Similar Anthologies

Bassett, T.D. Seymour. *Outsiders Inside Vermont: Three Centuries of Visitors' Viewpoints on the Green Mountain State* (Canaan, N.H.: Phoenix Publishing, 1967)

Haydon, Roger. *Upstate Travels: British Views of Nineteenth-Century New York* (Syracuse: Syracuse University Press, 1982)

Kammen, Carol. *What They Wrote: 19th Century Documents from Tompkins County, N.Y.* (Ithaca: Department of Manuscripts and Archives, Cornell University Libraries, 1978)

Naylor, Natalie A., ed. *Journeys on Old Long Island: Travelers' Accounts, Contemporary Descriptions, and Residents' Reminiscences 1744–1903* (Interlaken, N.Y.: Empire State Books, 2002)

Still, Bayrd. *Mirror for Gotham: New York as Seen by Contemporaries from Dutch Days to the Present* (New York: New York University Press, 1956)

Van Zandt, Roland. *Chronicles of the Hudson: Three Centuries of Travel and Adventure* (Hensonville, N.Y.: Black Dome Press, 1992)

Website

American Notes: Travels in America, 1750–1920, http://memory.loc.gov/ammem/lhtnhtml/lhtnhome.html

Index

The documents are indexed under authors' names with page numbers in boldface. In addition, the heading "visitors' writings" indexes them by place of origin. Page numbers in italics denote illustrations. Passing mention of non-residents and of places outside Saratoga County are not indexed.